Contents

KU-609-429

MORE READING POWER

Reading for Pleasure • Comprehension Skills
Thinking Skills • Reading Faster

Beatrice S. Mikulecky / Linda Jeffries

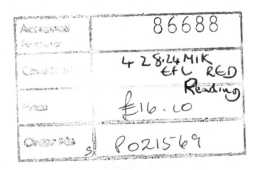

Longman

A Publication of the World Language Division

Executive Editor: Elinor Chamas
Developmental Editor: Kathy Sands Boehmer
Permissions/Photo Research: Anita Palmer
Manufacturing/Production: James W. Gibbons
Interior Design and Production: Michelle Taverniti
Cover Design: Marshall Henrichs

Acknowledgments

We'd like to express our thanks to the many people who provided feedback about *More Reading Power*: Suzanne M. Koons and Betsy Kyle from Bentley College, Jane Stevenson of Modena, Italy and Valerie Ashenfelter who piloted and reviewed the manuscript and a special thank you to Masako Kirihara of ECC Foreign Language Institute of Osaka, Japan, for her many valuable comments.

We'd also like to thank the students in the Bridge Program at Bentley College who worked on all of the units in the book and made many helpful suggestions for its improvement.

BSM and LJ

ISBN 0-201-60970-3
12 13 14 15 CRS 05040302

How to use More Reading Power

This book is different from other reading books. *More Reading Power* is divided into **four parts**. You should work on exercises in all four parts simultaneously when you use the book. This gives you practice in four different kinds of reading skills.

Part One. Reading for Pleasure. The more you read, the better you will read. In Part One, you will choose books to read and you will learn how to keep a record of your reading. You will also talk about your books with your classmates and your teacher.

Part Two. Reading Comprehension Skills. Reading is a very complex task involving many different skills. In this part, you will learn to use some essential reading skills.

Part Three. Thinking in English. Reading is not just understanding the words or the grammar. It is not just translating. Reading is thinking. In order to read well in English, you must think in English. The exercises in Part Three will give you practice in following ideas in English.

Part Four. Reading Faster. There are many advantages to reading faster. Your comprehension will improve, you will save time on reading assignments, and your reading will become more enjoyable. In this part of the book, you will develop the skill of reading faster with good comprehension.

Why is reading important?

Reading is one important way to improve your general language skills in English. How does reading help you?

- Reading helps you learn to think in English.
- Reading can enlarge your English vocabulary.
- Reading can help you improve your writing.
- Reading may be a good way to practice your English if you live in a non-English-speaking country.
- Reading can help you prepare for study in an English-speaking country.
- Reading is a good way to find out about new ideas, facts, and experiences.

Thinking about your reading habits

Reading can help much more if you can read well. That means being able to read many different materials and being able to understand them.

How well you read depends a lot on your reading habits. Find out about your reading habits by using the two questionnaires below. Answer all of the questions according to your own experience.

➤ **Fill in Questionnaire 1 about your reading habits in your first language (your native language). Then go on to Questionnaire 2 about your reading habits in English. (If your native language is English, skip Questionnaire 1. Go directly to Questionnaire 2.)**

questionnaire 1

Reading in Your Native Language

Native language: _____

➤ **For each statement, circle Y (Yes) or N (No).**

1. I always read every word of a passage.	Y	N
2. Reading aloud helps me improve my reading.	Y	N
3. I say the words aloud when I read.	Y	N
4. I use different reading methods in my native language and in English.	Y	N
5. When I read my native language, I understand more when I read slowly.	Y	N
6. If I don't know the meaning of a word, I always look it up in the dictionary.	Y	N
7. The best way to improve my reading in my native language is by learning as much grammar as possible.	Y	N
8. The best way to improve my reading in my native language is by learning as much new vocabulary as possible.	Y	N
9. When I am reading in my native language, I need to know every word in order to understand.	Y	N
10. To read well in my native language, I must be able to pronounce every word.	Y	N
11. I can't understand a paragraph if it has several new words in it.	Y	N
12. I use the same reading methods for all kinds of texts (books, newspapers, etc.).	Y	N

questionaire 2

Reading in English

➤ *For each statement, circle Y (Yes) or N (No).*

1. I always read every word of a passage.   Y   N

2. Reading aloud helps me improve my reading.   Y   N

3. I say the words aloud when I read.   Y   N

4. I use different reading methods in my native language and in English.   Y   N

5. When I read in English, I understand more when I read slowly.   Y   N

6. If I don't know the meaning of a word in English, I always look it up
   in the dictionary.   Y   N

7. The best way to improve my reading in English is by learning as much
   grammar as possible.   Y   N

8. The best way to improve my reading in English is by learning as much new
   vocabulary as possible.   Y   N

9. When I am reading material in English, I need to know every word in
   order to understand.   Y   N

10. To read well in English, I must be able to pronounce every word.   Y   N

11. I can't understand a paragraph if it has several new words in it.   Y   N

12. I use the same reading methods for all kinds of texts (books,
    newspapers, etc.).   Y   N

- *Compare your answers to the two questionnaires. Are your answers the same for both?*

- *Compare your answers with another student. Do you agree? Look at questions which you answered similarly and questions you answered differently.*

➤ **Check your answers.**

You should have circled **N** for every question in both questionnaires! If you marked some answers "Yes," then you may need to learn more about reading. *More Reading Power* will help you change your reading habits and your ideas about reading.

Part One

Reading for Pleasure

Why read for pleasure?

The best way to improve your reading is by reading. Reading, like sports or music, requires lots of practice. The best readers are people who *love to read* and who *read a lot.*

The easiest way to learn to love to read, if you don't already, is by *reading for pleasure.*

Reading for pleasure is different from the reading you do for study. When you read for pleasure, *you* choose the book that you read. You can read mysteries, romance novels, science fiction, biographies, or whatever you want. It is not *what* you read, but your *enjoyment* that matters.

When you read for pleasure, you will not be tested about what you have read. You will not have to remember every detail. All you have to do is *enjoy the book!*

questionaire

➤ 1. For the following statements, give a number from 1 to 10.

(1 = totally disagree; 10 = totally agree)

_____ a. I enjoy reading for pleasure.

_____ b. My parents enjoy reading for pleasure.

_____ c. Most of my friends read for pleasure.

_____ d. I read only books assigned by a teacher.

_____ e. I have no time to read for pleasure.

2. Do you have a favorite book? Write the title of the book and its author here:

_____

What did you like about this book?_____

_____

Would you recommend it to a friend?_____

Why? _____

3. Circle the types of books you generally enjoy reading for pleasure:

a. novels   b. adventures

c. romances   d. mysteries

e. spy thrillers   f. nonfiction (factual books)

g. other (give examples) _____

4. In what language do you usually read for pleasure? _____

5. Do you read for pleasure in English?

If so, what book(s) have you read? Title:_____

Discuss your answers with some classmates. Have you read any of the books they recommend?

What are the advantages of reading for pleasure?

Many educators have done research about pleasure reading. They have found that it can help you to be more successful in many ways. Regular reading for pleasure can:

- improve vocabulary.

- increase reading speed.

- improve reading comprehension.

- help improve writing.

- give you a chance to gain more knowledge.

- provide examples of the many different ways people speak and write in English.

Guidelines for Choosing a Pleasure Reading Book

1. Choose a book which interests you. Ask your teacher, your friends, your family, and your classmates for suggestions. But choose the book that is best for you, not for them!

2. Preview a book to help you decide if you want to read it. Paperback book covers provide plenty of information for that. Pictures often give some idea what the book is about. On the back cover there is usually some information about the book's contents. By reading the first few pages, you can tell if a book is easy or difficult for you.

3. Choose a book which is not too easy or too difficult. If your book is too easy to read, you may become bored. If it is too difficult, you are likely to become discouraged. A book is too difficult if there are more than five unknown key words on a single page. (A key word is a word which you must know in order to follow the author's general meaning.)

4. Choose a book that is printed clearly. Make sure the print is not too small. The size and clarity of the print will make a difference. You can read longer if the print does not make your eyes tired.

5. Remember, you are reading for pleasure. You don't need to memorize what you read when you read for pleasure! The important thing is to follow the story or the ideas presented by the author.

6. Some popular books have been made into movies. Avoid reading a book if you have already seen the movie. You may get bored if you already know what happens in the story. But *do* see a film version *after* you have read a book. It's often interesting to see how a film director has brought a book to life. You may enjoy comparing the director's ideas with your own.

7. Do not choose a book that you have already read in a different language. The fact that you are already familiar with it may make it less interesting. Also, do not choose a book that has been translated from another language. A translation is not always natural English, which can make it more difficult to read.

Hints for success in reading for pleasure

- Set a specific goal in your pleasure reading. Decide on a certain number of books to read during a semester. Fill in the reading goal below.

- Make pleasure reading a part of your daily routine. Plan to read a certain number of pages or for a certain amount of time every day.

- Read for at least 30 minutes at one time so that you can become involved in your book. This is especially important when you start a new book. It may take a little time before you begin to enjoy it.

- Choose a paperback book (paperbacks are small and lightweight), and carry it with you wherever you go. Read it whenever you have some free time. This is a good way to escape boredom when you are waiting in line or riding a bus or subway.

- Keep a journal. When you finish several chapters, write down your thoughts about the book and about what you expect to happen next.

- Talk to your friends about your book.

- Keep a record of the books you read in the chart on the next page.

- After you finish a book, fill in a book response sheet. (See page 10.)

- Your teacher may ask you to meet for a book conference when you have finished a book. This is not a test about the book. In fact, your teacher may not have read your book and may not know anything about it. This is your chance to talk and to share your feelings about the book.

My Goal for Pleasure Reading

Your name_____

Today's Date _____

I plan to read _____ books in the next _____ months.

Record of Books Read

1. Title _____

   Author _____

   Date begun _____ Date finished _____

2. Title _____

   Author _____

   Date begun _____ Date finished _____

3. Title _____

   Author _____

   Date begun _____ Date finished _____

4. Title _____

   Author _____

   Date begun _____ Date finished _____

5. Title _____

   Author _____

   Date begun _____ Date finished _____

6. Title _____

   Author _____

   Date begun _____ Date finished _____

7. Title _____

   Author _____

   Date begun _____ Date finished _____

8. Title _____

   Author _____

   Date begun _____ Date finished _____

9. Title _____

   Author _____

   Date begun _____ Date finished _____

Book Response Sheet

Title of Book: _____

Author: _____

Publisher: _____

Date Published: _____ Number of Pages: _____

Type of Book: _____Fiction _____Nonfiction:

What did you like best about this book?

What did you like least about this book?

Your language: _____ Your country: _____

Level of difficulty for you: _____Easy _____OK _____Difficult

Suggested books

The books listed here have been read and enjoyed by other students. These titles are found in many libraries and book stores. Note that these are suggested titles. You may, of course, choose a title not on the list. What matters most is to read a book that interests *you*.

Almost all of these titles are fiction (not true stories). Fiction gives many examples of the use of English in daily life.

You may also choose a non-fiction book (biography, history, etc.) if you prefer. However, it should not be too technical or include difficult vocabulary words.

Book List

A star (*) after an author's name is a signal that this author has written other books that you might enjoy.

Level One. These books are not difficult to read. If you have not read many books in English, you may want to begin with a selection from this level.

Avi	*Sometimes I Think I Hear My Name*
Jay Bennett *	*Deathman, Do Not Follow Me*
Judy Blume *	*Forever*
John Christopher	*The White Mountains*
James L. Collier and Christopher Collier	*My Brother Sam Is Dead*
Robert Cormier *	*The Chocolate War*
Lois Duncan *	*Killing Mr. Griffin*
Rosa Guy	*Friends*
S. E. Hinton *	*That Was Then, This Is Now*
M. E. Kerr *	*Dinky Hocker Shoots Smack*
Norma Klein *	*Sunshine*
Joanna Lee	*I Want to Keep My Baby*
Richard Peck	*Are You In the House Alone?*
Anne Snyder	*My Name is Davy—I'm an Alcoholic*
John Steinbeck	*The Pearl*
E. B. White	*Charlotte's Web*
Laura Ingalls Wilder *	*Little House on the Prairie*
Paul Zindel *	*The Pigman*

Level Two. The books in this section are a little more difficult.

Louisa May Alcott *	*Little Women*
Jean Auel	*The Clan of the Cave Bear*
Sheila Burnford	*The Incredible Journey*
Mary Higgins Clark *	*Where Are the Children?*
Robin Cook *	*Coma*
Esther Forbes	*Johnny Tremain*
Ernest J. Gaines	*The Autobiography of Miss Jane Pitman*
William Gibson	*The Miracle Worker (a play)*
Bette Green	*The Summer of My German Soldier*
Jean George	*My Side of the Mountain*
Nat Hentoff *	*Jazz Country*
John Hersey *	*Hiroshima*
James Hilton	*Good-bye, Mr. Chips*
Jean and James Houston	*Farewell to Manzanar*
Lee Iacocca	*Iacocca*
Daniel Keyes	*Flowers for Algernon*
Jerzy Kosinski	*Being There*
Madeleine L'Engle *	*A Wrinkle In Time*

Jack London *	*The Call of the Wild*
Lucy Maud Montgomery	*Anne of Green Gables*
Farley Mowatt	*The Dog Who Wouldn't Be*
George Orwell *	*Animal Farm*
Ayn Rand	*Anthem*
Marjorie Kinman Rawlings	*The Yearling*
Johanna Reiss	*The Upstairs Room*
W. H. D. Rouse	*Gods, Heroes, and Men of Ancient Rome*
Elizabeth G. Speare	*The Witch of Blackbird Pond*
Danielle Steele *	*The Promise*
John Steinbeck *	*The Red Pony*
Carrie Ten Boom	*The Hiding Place*
Anne Tyler *	*Dinner At the Homesick Restaurant*
Elie Weisel *	*Night*

Level Three. Books on this list are quite difficult.

Maya Angelou	*I Know Why the Caged Bird Sings*
James Baldwin	*If Beale Street Could Talk*
Willa Cather	*My Antonia*
Michael Chrichton	*Jurassic Park*
Agatha Christie *	*The Secret of Chimneys*
Gail Godwin *	*Father Melancholy's Daughter*
William Golding	*Lord of the Flies*
Sue Grafton *	*C is for Corpse*
John Grisham *	*The Firm*
Alex Haley	*Malcolm X*
Ernest Hemingway *	*For Whom the Bell Tolls*
Farley Mowatt *	*A Whale for the Killing*
Sara Paretsky *	*Blood Shot*
Mary Renault *	*The Bull from the Sea*
Sidney Sheldon *	*The Sands of Time*
Marjorie Shostak	*Nisa: The Life and Words of a !Kung Woman*
Mary Stewart *	*This Rough Magic*
Amy Tan *	*The Kitchen God's Wife*
Alice Walker	*The Color Purple*

Part Two

Reading Comprehension Skills

Introduction

Comprehension is part of life. Every waking minute, your brain is busy making sense of your world. It could be compared, in fact, to a very complicated computer. Messages are constantly coming in about what you see, hear, smell, touch, or taste. Your brain receives these messages, interprets them, sorts them, and saves them.

When new information arrives, your brain looks for some connection to information already there. If it finds a connection, the new information becomes part of a network and is saved in your long-term memory. When it does not find a connection, the new information is quickly forgotten and lost.

The same process happens when you are reading. As you read, your brain tells your eyes what to look for in order to make connections. Sometimes the connection seems to happen by itself—especially when the information is important or interesting to you. But at other times, it is not so simple. The text may seem a mass of information with no meaning that will stick.

However, you can learn how to make sense of what you read and remember it. In this part of the book, you will practice some important reading comprehension skills. You will learn to think in new ways about what you are reading. And you may find that your reading comprehension in your native language will improve.

Scanning

What is scanning?

Scanning is very high-speed reading. When you scan, you have a question in mind. You do not read every word, only the words that answer your question. Practice in scanning will help you learn to skip over unimportant words so that you can read faster.

In this unit, you'll practice scanning many different kinds of materials. You should work as quickly as possible on all the exercises. Remember that scanning is a high-speed skill.

➤ *Look at the list of art exhibits below.*

Will you be able to see the exhibition of Leonardo da Vinci's drawings in March?

Crèche
through January 10

The Grand Tour: European and American Views of Italy
through January 17

Joel Sternfeld: Photographs of the Roman Campagagna
through January 17

***Late 20th Century Prints**
through January 31

On Kawara: Date Paintings in 89 Cities
through February 7

Leonardo da Vinci: The Anatomy of Man
Drawings from the Collection of Her Majesty Queen Elizabeth II
through February 21

Master European Paintings from the National Gallery of Ireland: Mantegna to Goya
January 13–March 28

Building a Collection: The Department of Contemporary Art, Part I
January 28–July 3

***Photography: Close-Up/Still Life**
February 10–May 23

*Closed Thursday and Friday evenings

MUSEUM OF FINE ARTS • 465 Huntington Avenue • Boston, Massachusetts 02115

Did you read the whole list of exhibitions to find out? No! You knew what to look for. You scanned the list to find the information that you needed.

Scanning in everyday life

Scanning is a skill that you often use in daily life. For example, you might scan the list of names in a telephone directory in order to find a phone number.

What else might you scan?

exercise 1

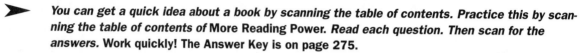

You can get a quick idea about a book by scanning the table of contents. Practice this by scanning the table of contents of More Reading Power. Read each question. Then scan for the answers. Work quickly! The Answer Key is on page 275.

1. How many parts are there in *More Reading Power*?

2. In which part will you find information about reading faster?

3. How many units are found in Part Two?

4. Which reading skill is found in Unit 6?

5. On what page can you find the unit on Topics?

6. In which part will you find information about pleasure reading?

7. Where is the unit on Hawaii?

8. How many exercises are there in the unit on Thinking Skills?

exercise 2

In this exercise, you will scan a newspaper ad for new cars. Read each question. Then scan the advertisement to locate the correct answer. Work quickly!

1. What is the cheapest car in this ad? 3

2. Which cars have air conditioning? 8, 3, 5

3. How many Crown Victorias are available? 50

4. Does the Escort Wagon have power windows? NO

5. Can college graduates get a rebate for all the cars in this ad?

6. For which car can you get a "Daniel discount?"

7. Which car has the least discount? 6

8. Which car has an original list price of $13,499? 5

9. How many cars have cassette players? 1

10. In what town is Daniel Ford located? Branford

Check your answers with another student.

Would you buy one of these cars or vans? Why or why not?

1996 TAURUS GL SEDANS & WAGONS
SAVE $4500 OFF ORIGINAL LIST
Before Discount (Includes Rebate)

Sedan Ex #F204
- 204A Pkg • Air Bag
- Air Cond.
- Rear Window Def.
- Cruise
- Power Seats
- Power Windows
- Cassette

Original List	$19,199
Discount	−$3100
Cash Back	−$1000
Grad Rebate	−$400

YOU PAY **$14,699**

50 AVAIL AT THIS DISCOUNT

1996 EXPLORERS 4X4
(4 DR.) XLTs & EDDIE BAUER
SAVE $3200 OFF ORIGINAL LIST
Before Discount (Includes Rebate)

EXAMPLE: No. F23F7
- Cloth Captain Chairs
- Power Windows
- Power Door Locks
- Cruise Control
- Air Cond.
- Auto Trans.

Original List (Before Discount)	$23,983
Discount	−$2800
Recent College Grad Rebate	−$400

YOU PAY **$20,763**

73 AVAIL. AT THIS DISCOUNT

1996 ESCORT WAGONS
$3500 OFF ORIGINAL LIST
Before Discount (Includes Rebate)

Example No. F2415
- Air Conditioning
- Power Steering
- Rear Wiper
- Rear Defroster
- Luggage Rack
- Electronic Mirrors
- Conv. Group
- Clearcoat Paint
- Stereo Radio

ORIGINAL LIST	$12,499
DISCOUNT	−$2700
CASH BACK	−$400
Recent College Grad Rebate	−$400

YOU PAY **$8999**

OVER 150 ESCORT WAGONS AVAIL.

1996 CROWN VICTORIAS

Ex: #F2875
- Air Bag
- Air Cond.
- Cruise Control
- P. Windows
- P. Locks
- R. Defrost
- Convenience Group
- Clearcoat Paint

New Lower Price	$18,999
Recent College GradRebate	−$400

YOU PAY **$16,599**

OVER 50 CROWN VICTORIAS IN STOCK!

1996 TEMPOS
$3800 OFF ORIGINAL LIST
Before Discount (Includes Rebate)

EXAMPLE: NO. F2008
- Air Conditioning
- Tilt Wheel
- Floor Mats
- Pwr. Door Locks
- AM/FM Cassette
- Clearcoat Paint
- Polycast Wheels
- Light Group

Orig. List (Before Discount)	$13,499
CASH BACK	−$700
DISCOUNT	−$2700
College Grad rebate	−$400

YOU PAY **$9699**

100 AVAILABLE AT THIS DISCOUNT

1996 F150 SUPER CABS

EXAMPLE: #F1913
- AUTOMATIC TRANSMISSION
- REAR BENCH SEAT
- XL TRIM
- STEP & TOW BUMPER

SALE PRICE COMMERCIAL ACCT.	$14,295
REBATE	−$500

YOU PAY **$13,795**

25 AVAILABLE AT THIS DISCOUNT

1996 RANGER XLT SUPER CABS
SAVE $3000 Off Original List
Before Discount (Includes Rebate)

EXAMPLE: #F2784
- AM/FM Cassette
- Cust. Alum. Wheels
- Sliding Rear Window
- Cargo Cover
- XLT Trim

Orig. List	$13,766
Cash Back	−$400
Recent College Grad Rebate	−$400
Discount	−$200

YOU PAY **$10,766**

10 AVAILABLE AT THIS DISCOUNT

1996 TAURUS SHOS
SAVE $7000 OFF ORIGINAL LIST
(Includes Rebate)

Ex: #F1322
- Auto Air Cond.
- Power Antenna
- Air Bag
- Hi Level Audio System
- Cloth/Leather Interior

Orig. List	$25,354
Daniel Discount	−$5600
Cash Back	−$1000
Grad Rebate	−$400

YOU PAY **$18,354**

40 AVAILABLE AT THIS DISCOUNT

DANIEL FORD
540 Southern Ave • Branford 555-0070

exercise 3

In this exercise, you will scan supermarket ads. Read each question. Then scan the advertisement to locate the correct answer. Work quickly!

A. Scan only ad number 1 to answer these questions:

1. How many different beverages are advertised?
2. What is the price of a 9" Pie?
3. How many ounces (oz.) of vegetables can you buy for .79?
4. How many Eggo Waffles are in a package (pkg.)?
5. What is the name of the company which sells frozen carrots?
6. Which juice is 100% natural?
7. How many pieces of pizza can you buy for $2.39?
8. Which pizza is cheaper?
9. What is the weight of the frozen bread dough?
10. Is pink lemonade on sale?

Ad 1

TIMESAVING FROZEN FOODS

Minute Maid OJ
Calcium Fortified, Country Style or Regular. 12 Oz Can. Or Reduced Acid 10 Oz Can. Frozen
.99

Seneca Juice
100% Natural Grape, Granny Smith Apple or Apple. 12 Oz. Can. Frozen
1.29

Lemonade
Shop & Go. Regular or Pink. 12 Oz Can. Frozen
2 for $1

Large Crispy Bagels
Shop & Go. Assorted Varieties 15.6 Oz Pkg. of 5. Frozen.
.69

Eggo Waffles
Homestyle or Buttermilk 11 Oz Pkg. of 8 Frozen .
1.29

Cool Whip
Lite, Extra Creamy or Regular 8 Oz Container. Frozen
.99

9" Homestyle Pie
Sara Lee. Assorted Varieties 37 Oz Pkg. Frozen
1.99

White Bread Dough
Shop & Go. 5 lb Pkg of 5. Frozen .
1.89

Birds Eye Deluxe
Microwaveable Vegetables. Baby Whole Carrots, Broccoli Florets, Sugar Snap Peas, Tendersweet Corn, Baby Broccoli Spears, Whole Green Beans or Tiny Tender Peas. 8 Oz Pkg. Frozen.
.79

Shop & Go Carrots
Whole Baby 16 Oz or Crinkle Cut 20 Oz Bag. Frozen
.89

Ellio's Pizza
6 Slice Double Cheese 19 Oz Pkg. Frozen
2.39

Cheese Ravioli
Shop & Go. 16 Oz Pkg. of 36 Frozen
1.39

Weaver Chicken
Fried Crispy Dutch Frye 28 Oz Pkg. or Batter Dipped or Dutch Frye Breasts. 22 Oz Pkg. Frozen
3.49

Totino's Pizza
Party. Assorted Varieties 9.8 Oz Pkg. Frozen
1.39

Fish Sticks
Van de Kamp's Value Pack 26.4 Oz Pkg. of 44. Frozen
3.49

B. Scan both ads to answer these questions:

1. Which ad has a lower price for orange juice (OJ)?

2. Do both ads include chicken?

3. Which ad has a lower price for Totino's Pizza?

4. Which is cheaper, Ellio's or Tony's pizza?

5. How many different kinds of bagel bites can you buy?

6. Do both ads include fish?

7. How many different brands of pizza are found in ad number 2?

8. Is Cool Whip less expensive in ad 1 or ad 2?

9. What is the name of the company that makes garlic bread?

10. Which ad offers more different kinds of foods?

Check your answers with another student.

If you were shopping and you had only $7.50 to spend, which items would you buy?

Ad 2

TIMESAVING FROZEN FOODS

Tropicana OJ
100% Pure. Regular or
Homestyle. 12 Oz Can. Frozen
.99

Cheese Ravioli
Shop & Go. 16 Oz Pkg. of 36
Frozen .
1.39

Cool Whip
Birds Eye. Lite, Extra Creamy
or Regular. 12 Oz Container. Frozen
1.29

Celeste Zesty Pizza
Four Cheese Italian Bread
9.25 Oz Pkg. Frozen
1.59

Tony's Pizza
Italian Pastry. Pepperoni
Extra Cheese or Supreme.
15.3 Oz Pkg. Frozen
2 for $4

Cheese Pizza
Tree Tavern. 16 Oz Pkg. Frozen
1.99

Totino's Pizza
Party. Assorted Varieties
9.8 Oz Pkg. Frozen
1.29

Pizza Shells
Calise. 27 Oz Pkg. of 3. Frozen
1.99

Jeno's Pizza Rolls
Assorted Varieties. 6 Oz Pkg.
Frozen
1.39

Garlic Bread
Cole's. Butter Flavored
16 Oz Pkg. Frozen
1.59

Cheese Pizza
Shop & Go. 9 Slice
24 Oz Pkg. Frozen
2.19

Tina's Burritos
Assorted Varieties. 5 Oz Pkg.
Frozen
3 for $1

Bagel Bites
Double Cheese or Cheese
& Pepperoni. 7 Oz Pkg. of 9. Frozen
1.99

Banquet Chicken
Fried. Country or Regular
25 Oz Pkg. Frozen
2.99

Ravioli Kitchen
Cheese Ravioli 22 Oz Pkg. of 48
Frozen
2 for $3

Van de Damp's Fish
Value Pack. Bread Sticks
26.4 Oz Pkg. or Batter Portions 25 Oz Pkg.
Frozen
3.49

Scanning tables

exercise 4

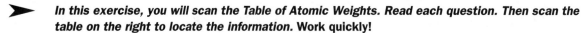

> *In this exercise, you will scan the Table of Atomic Weights. Read each question. Then scan the table on the right to locate the information. Work quickly!*

1. What are the four kinds of information given in this table?

2. What is the symbol for Iron?

3. What is the atomic number for Tin?

4. Which has a higher atomic weight, Zinc or Lead?

5. What is the atomic weight of Hydrogen?

6. Which has a higher atomic number, Phosphorus or Chlorine?

7. What is the symbol for Silicon?

8. Which has a higher atomic weight, Gold or Platinum?

9. Which element has the highest atomic weight?

10. Find an element which was probably named for a scientist.

Check your answers with another student.

> *Write three more questions about this table. Working with your partner, ask questions of each other. Work as fast as you can.*

1.

2.

3.

Table of Atomic Weights*

Element	Symbol	Atomic number	Atomic weight	Element	Symbol	Atomic number	Atomic weight
Actinium	Ac	89	(277)	Mercury	Hg	80	200.59
Aluminum	Al	13	26.9815	Molybdenum	Mo	42	95.94
Americium	Am	95	(243)	Neodymium	Nd	60	144.24
Antimony	Sb	51	121.75	Neon	Ne	10	20.179
Argon	Ar	18	39.948	Neptunium	Np	93	237.0482
Arsenic	As	33	74.9216	Nickel	Ni	28	58.71
Astatine	At	85	(210)	Niobium	Nb	41	92.9064
Barium	Ba	56	137.34	Nitrogen	N	7	14.0067
Berkelium	Bk	97	(249)	Nobelium	No	102	(254)
Beryllium	Be	4	9.01218	Osmium	Os	76	190.2
Bismuth	Bi	83	208.9806	Oxygen	O	8	15.9994
Boron	B	5	10.81	Palladium	Pd	46	106.4
Bromine	Br	35	79.904	Phosphorous	P	15	30.9738
Cadmium	Cd	48	112.40	Platinum	Pt	78	195.09
Calcium	Ca	20	40.08	Plutonium	Pu	94	(242)
Californium	Cf	98	(251)	Polonium	Po	84	(210)
Carbon	C	6	12.011	Potassium	K	19	39.102
Cerium	Ce	58	140.12	Praseodymium	Pr	59	140.9077
Cesium	Cs	55	132.9055	Promethium	Pm	61	(145)
Chlorine	Cl	17	35.453	Protactinium	Pa	91	231.0359
Chromium	Cr	24	51.996	Radium	Ra	88	226.0254
Cobalt	Co	27	58.9332	Radon	Rn	86	(222)
Copper	Cu	29	63.546	Rhenium	Re	75	186.2
Curium	Cm	96	(247)	Rhodium	Rh	45	102.9055
Dysprosium	Dy	66	162.50	Rubidium	Rb	37	85.4678
Einsteinium	Es	99	(254)	Ruthenium	Ru	44	101.07
Erbium	Er	68	167.26	Samarium	Sm	62	150.4
Europium	Eu	63	151.96	Scandium	Sc	21	44.9559
Fermium	Fm	100	(253)	Selenium	Se	34	78.96
Fluorine	F	9	8.9984	Silicon	Si	14	28.086
Francium	Fr	87	(223)	Silver	Ag	47	107.868
Gadolinium	Gd	64	157.25	Sodium	Na	11	22.9898
Gallium	Ga	31	69.72	Strontium	Sr	38	87.62
Germanium	Ge	32	72.59	Sulfur	S	16	32.06
Gold	Au	79	196.9665	Tantalum	Ta	73	180.9479
Hafnium	Hf	72	178.49	Technetium	Tc	43	98.9062
Helium	He	2	4.00260	Tellurium	Te	52	127.60
Holmium	Ho	67	164.9303	Terbium	Tb	65	158.9254
Hydrogen	H	1	1.0080	Thallium	Tl	81	204.37
Indium	In	49	114.82	Thorium	Th	90	232.0381
Iodine	I	53	126.9045	Thulium	Tm	69	168.9342
Iridium	Ir	77	192.22	Tin	Sn	50	118.69
Iron	Fe	26	55.847	Titanium	Ti	22	47.90
Krypton	Kr	36	83.80	Tungsten	W	74	183.85
Lanthanum	La	57	128.9055	Uranium	U	92	238.029
Lawrencium	Lr	103	(257)	Vanadium	V	23	50.9414
Lead	Pb	82	207.2	Xenon	Xe	54	131.30
Lithium	Li	3	6.941	Ytterbium	Yb	70	173.04
Lutetium	Lu	71	174.97	Yttrium	Y	39	88.9059
Magnesium	Mg	12	24.305	Zinc	Zn	30	65.37
Manganese	Mn	25	54.9380	Zirconium	Zr	40	91.22
Mendelevium	Md	101	(256)				

*Based on atomic weight of carbon-12 = 12.0000. Numbers in parentheses are mass numbers of most stable isotopes.

Scanning newspaper listings

exercise 5
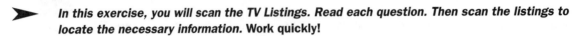

➤ In this exercise, you will scan the TV Listings. Read each question. Then scan the listings to locate the necessary information. Work quickly!

1. Which channel shows a movie starring Clint Eastwood?

2. What hours are included in the listing?

3. What movie listed is given four stars?

4. What time can we watch a baseball game?

5. How many news programs are shown at 11:00 p.m.?

6. What is the title of the movie to be shown on TNT at 8:00?

7. What is the title of the oldest movie to be shown?

8. How many channels have numbers? Names?

9. Which channels show more movies, the numbered or the named?

10. Which channel has Spanish language programs?

Check your answers with another student.

➤ Write three more questions about this TV Listing. Ask your partner to scan for the answers. Work as fast as you can.

1.

2.

3.

WEDNESDAY TV

	6:00	6:30	7:00	7:30	8:00	8:30	9:00	9:30	10:00	10:30	11:00
2	MacNeil/Lehrer		Are You Served?	Wednesday Group	National Geographic		Empire of the Air: The Men Who Made Radio ★★★ (1992)				Are You Served?
4	News		NBC News	Olympic Summer Games: Track & Field, Volleyball, Wrestling							
5	News		ABC News	Chronicle	The Wonder Years	The Wonder Years	Doogie Howser	Doogie Howser	Civil Wars (R)		News
6	News	CBS News	A Current Affair	Inside Edition	To Be Announced	Davis Rules	Raven		48 Hours (R)		News
7	News	CBS News	Wheel of Fortune	Jeopardy!	To Be Announced	Davis Rules	Raven		48 Hours (R)		News
9	News	ABC News	Entertainment	Hard Copy	The Wonder Years	The Wonder Years	Doogie Howser	Doogie Howser	Civil Wars (R)		News
10	News	NBC News	Entertainment	Olympic Summer Games: Track & Field, Volleyball, Wrestling							
11	MacNeil/Lehrer		Business Report	Carmen Sandiego	Evening at Pops		Keeping America No. I: Business		Columbus & The Age of Discovery		News
12	News	ABC News	Wheel of Fortune	Jeopardy!	The Wonder Years	The Wonder Years	Doogie Howser	Doogie Howser	Civil Wars (R)		News
27	Ocurrio Asi	Noticiero	Marielena		Mundo de Fieras		Bandido ★★★ (1956, Spanish) Robert Mitchum, Ursula Thiess				Carma con Percel
38	Hogan Family	Family Ties	Cheers	M*A*S*H	Inside the Third Reich (Part 2) (1982) Rutger Hauer, Derek Jacobi				Odd Couple	Hogan's	M*A*S*H Heroes
44	Sesame Street	Nightly Business	MacNeil/Lehrer		Championship Ballroom Dancing 1992			Lighthouses	States of Mind (Part 7 of 7)		Nightly Business
50	Simon & Simon		Star Trek		Copacabana ★ (Color, 1947) Groucho Marx, Carmen Miranda				All in the Family	All in the Family	Twilight Zone
56	Growing Pains	Who's the Boss?	Full House	Night Court	Running on Empty ★★★ (1988, Drama) Christine Lahti, River Phoenix				News		Arsenio Hall
58	Inner City Beat		Feature Story	Feature Story	One Norway Street		Childhood: A Journey		Rodina: "Russian Homeland"		50 Years Ago

	6:00	6:30	7:00	7:30	8:00	8:30	9:00	9:30	10:00	10:30	11:00
BRAVO	Off the Air				Duchess of Duke Street		La Gazza Ladra				
CNN	The World Today		Moneyline	Crossfire	Primenews		Larry King Live		World News		Sports Tonight
ESPN	Inside the PGA	Up Close	Sports Center	Baseball						Baseball Tonight	Sports Center
FAMILY	Batman	New Zorro	The Waltons: "The Long Night"		Big Brother Jake	Maniac Mansion	Scarecrow & Mrs. King		The 700 Club		Batman
HBO	← (4:30) Stanley/Iris	Lisa ★★ (1990, Suspense) Cheryl Ladd, D.W. Moffett			Another 48 Hrs. ★★ (1990, Action), Eddie Murphy, Nick Nolte				Tales from Crypt	Dream On	One Night Stand
LIFE	Supermarket	Shop/Drop	China Beach		L.A. Law: "On the Toad Again"		The Attic: The Hiding of Anne Frank ★★★ (1988) Mary Steenburgen				thirtysomething
MC	← (5) People Across the Lake		Pascali's Island ★★ (1988, Drama) Ben Kingsley, Charles Dance				Narrow Margin ★★★ (1990, Crime Drama) Gene Hackman, Anne Archer				Trust ★★ (1990)
NESN	Sportfishing	Fishing the West	Triathlon	Baseball: Toronto Blue Jays at Boston Red Sox						Baseball Action	High Five
NICK	What Would	Wild Kids	Looney Tunes	Rocky/Bullwinkle	F Troop	Superman	Get Smart	Dick Van Dyke	Dragnet	Alfred Hitchcock	Lucy Show
SHOW	The Gods Must Be Crazy II ★★★ (1989) Nixau, Lena Farugia				Shocker ★ (1989) Michael Murphy, Peter Berg			Comedy Club	Raging Bull ★★★ (1980, Drama) Robert DiNiro, Cathy Moriarty		
SPORT	Horse Racing	Horse Racing	Forever Baseball	Talking Sports	NBA Basketball: Celtics Encore: New York Knicks at Boston Celtics				Team Tennis: Los Angeles Strings at Newport Beach Dukes		
TBS	I Love Lucy	Andy Grffith	Beverly Hillbillies	Sanford & Son	A Fistful of Dollars ★★★ (1964) Clint Eastwood Marianne Koch				Big Jake ★★ (1971, Western) John Wayne Richard Boone		
TNT	Gilligan's Island	Bugs Bunny			True Confessions ★★★ (1981) Robert DiNiro Robert Duvall				In Cold Blood (10:15) ★★★★ (1967) Robert Blake, Scott Wilson		
USA	Cartoon Express		MacGyver: "Second Chance":		Murder, She Wrote		Lies of the Twins ★★ (1991, Suspense) Isabella Rossellini, Aidan Quinn				
WPIX	Charles in Charge	Happy Days	Star Trek: The Next Generation		Body Heat ★★★ (1981, Crime Drama) William Hurt, Kathleen Turner				News		Cheers
WWOR	Cosby	Who's the Boss?	Gimme a Break	Temperatures	Incredible Hulk		Quincy, M.E.		News		

exercise 6

➤ *In this exercise, you'll scan a "Best-Sellers" list from a newspaper. Read each question and then scan the lists to locate the answer. Work quickly!*

1. Which authors have two fiction books on this list?

2. What is the title of the book about World War II?

3. Who wrote a book with a plot set in Chicago?

4. How long has *Jurassic Park* been on the list?

5. What is the title of the book by Sidney Sheldon?

6. Who wrote the book about the Princess of Wales?

7. What is the price of *A Year in Provence*?

8. What is *The Prize* about?

9. Who wrote a book about living a successful life?

10. What company published the book about Malcolm X?

Check your answers with another student.

➤ *Write three more questions about the paperback best-sellers list. Ask your partner to scan for the answers. Work as fast as you can.*

1.

2.

3.

Is there a book listed which interests you? Which one?

Why does this book interest you?

January 31, 1994

Paperback Best Sellers

Fiction
Weeks on List

1 **ALL AROUND THE TOWN,** by Mary Higgins Clark   2
(Pocket,$6.50.) A college student is accused of
murdering her professor.

2 **RISING SUN,** by Michael Crichton. (Ballantine, $5.99.) 6
An investigation following the death of a woman stirs
up Japanese-American rivalry.

3 **THE ROAD TO OMAHA,** by Robert Ludlum. (Bantam 2
$6.99.) A lawyer and a retired general want to help an
Indian tribe take over the state of Nebraska.

4 **THE FIRM,** by John Grisham. (Island/Dell, $5.99.) 53
The secret, and possibly illicit dealings of a law firm
create a dilemma for a young lawyer.

5 **MCNALLY'S SECRET,** by Lawrence Sanders. 5
(Berkley, $5.99.) In his search for some valuable
stolen stamps, a detective brings scandal to light.

6 **JURASSIC PARK,** by Michael Crichton. (Ballantine, 28
$5.99.) A biotechnician uses genetic cloning to make
dinosaurs live again in a theme park.

7 **A TIME TO KILL,** by John Grisham. (Island/Dell, 42
$5.99.) A trial sets off racial tensions.

8 **BLINDSIGHT,** by Robin Cook. (Berkley, $5.99.) 1
The strange deaths of some New York yuppies are
investigated by a woman physician.

9 **BEYOND EDEN,** by Catherine Coulter. (Onyx, $5.99) 3
A private detective helps a young woman to escape
threats from her past.

10 **THE LINE OF FIRE,** by W.E.B. Griffin. (Jove, $5.99) 2
The latest volume from the World War II series "The
Corps" is the story of attempts to rescue two marines
on a South Pacific island.

11 **A THOUSAND ACRES,** by Jane Smiley. (Fawcett, 19
$12.) The life and fortunes of a family on a farm.

12 **THE DOOMSDAY CONSPIRACY,** by Sidney 11
Sheldon. (Warner, $5.99) A mysterious balloon incident
is investigated by an American.

13 **COMPELLING EVIDENCE,** by Steve Martini. (Jove, 5
$5.99.) When charged with the murder of her husband,
a woman is defended by her ex-lover.

14 **GUARDIAN ANGEL,** by Sara Paretsky. (Dell, $5.99) 1
Detective V.I. Warshawski investigates a strange scandal
case in Chicago.

15 **A RIVER RUNS THROUGH IT,** by Norman 14
Maclean. (Pocket, M $4.99) Three stories that take
place in the great outdoors of Montana.

Nonfiction
Weeks on List

1 **THE AUTOBIOGRAPHY OF MALCOLM X,** with 14
the assistance of Alex Haley. (Ballantine, $5.99) A new
edition of the life story of the black leader.

2 **EARTH IN THE BALANCE,** by Al Gore. (Plume, 5
$13) An assessment by the Vice President of the environ-
mental situation on earth and what needs to be done.

3 **THE ROAD LESS TRAVELED,** by Scott Peck, 482
(Touchstone /S&S, $10.95) A psychiatrist writes to
give spiritual and psychological inspiration.

4 **YOU JUST DON'T UNDERSTAND,** by Deborah 89
Tannen. (Ballantine, $10.) Problems of communication
between the sexes and how to resolve them.

5 **REVOLUTION FROM WITHIN,** by Gloria Steinem. 3
(Little Brown, $11.95) A leading feminist reflects on
women's struggle for self-esteem.

6 **DIANA: Her True Story,** by Andrew Morton. 10
(Pocket, $5.99) The life story of the Princess of Wales.

7 **BACKLASH,** by Susan Faludi. (Anchor/Doubleday, 16
$12.50) A journalist writes about the battles of the
media and politicians against women's rights

8 **THE PRIZE,** by Daniel Yergin. (Touchstone/S&S, $16.) 1
How world history since the 19th century has been
influenced by the need for oil.

9 **A YEAR IN PROVENCE,** by Peter Mayle (Vintage, 75
$10.) A British writer describes his experiences in
southern France

10 **MOLLY IVINS CAN'T SAY THAT, CAN SHE?** 13
by Molly Ivins, (Vintage, $11.) An essayist analyzes
recent cultural and political events.

Advice, How-to and Miscellaneous

1 **THE T-FACTOR FAT GRAM COUNTER,** by 119
Jamie Pope-Cordle and Martin Katahn. (Norton,$2.50)
How to cut down on the fat content of one's diet.

2 **LIFE'S LITTLE INSTRUCTION BOOK,** by 77
H. Jackson Brown, Jr. (Rutledge Hill, $5.95.) Tips for
how to fulfill yourself in life.

3 **THE SEVEN HABITS OF HIGHLY EFFECTIVE** 102
PEOPLE, by Stephen R. Covey. (Fireside/S&S, $9.95)
How to achieve success: the principles and the practice.

4 **THE WORLD ALMANAC AND BOOK OF** 8
FACTS 1993. (World Almanac/Pharos, $7.95) The
latest edition of a classic.

5 **RAND MCNALLY ROAD ATLAS.** (Rand McNally. 1
$7.95) The 1993 edition of road maps for the United
States, Canada and Mexico.

Scanning magazine articles

exercise 7

➤ *You will be visiting Boston with some friends in the autumn. They would like to spend a day in the country. You see this article about picking apples and decide you want to know more about it. Scan the article for the answers to the questions below.*

1. Where does this article recommend picking apples?

2. Who picks the apples?

3. What kind of apples are the very first to ripen?

4. Do you need to bring bags for the apples?

5. How much time does it take to pick apples?

6. What else can you do at an orchard besides pick apples?

7. How many apples should you pick?

8. What should you do with the apples when you get home?

9. What can you do if you pick too many apples?

10. How can you find out where to go apple-picking in Massachusetts?

Picking Apples—A New England Tradition
By Gennadi Preston

Throughout New England, people know that fall has arrived when the McIntosh apples begin to turn red in the orchards in early September. After the "mac" come the Cortlands, the Empires, the McCoons and, finally, the Red and Golden Delicious. All through September and October, the aroma of ripe apples fills the air on sunny days—an invitation to come picking.

A day of apple picking is, in fact, a popular way to spend a fall day in New England. From Connecticut to Maine, it is generally possible to find an orchard within an hour's drive and the trip is well worth the time. Not only will it provide you with plenty of the freshest apples to be found, but it also will give you a chance to take in some sunshine and autumn scenery and get some exercise. And the picking is usually best done by adults. Children should not climb up into trees and risk hurting themselves and damaging the trees—younger members of the family can

have fun just romping around the orchard.

The picking may not take long —two hours at most—but many of the orchard owners now offer other kinds of entertainment. At some orchards, you can go for pony rides or ride on a hay-filled wagon. You may be able to watch a horse-show or visit the cows or sheep in the pasture. Or you may decide to take a hike and have a picnic along a country lane. Some orchards have set up refreshment stands in their barns where you can taste local products, such as apple cider and homemade baked goods.

A few hints:

I. Call before you go. Check the local newspaper for the names and locations of orchards which offer pick-your-own apples. Then phone to find out their hours, since they may vary from one orchard to another.

You should also ask about the rules regarding

too many of the delicious looking fruit, and then find that the apples go bad before you can eat them. Since the apple season lasts for almost two months, you can always return for another load of apples later.

5. Keep what you pick! Once you take an apple off the tree, you must keep it. It's not fair to the orchard owner to leave apples on the ground where they will quickly spoil.

6. Store your apples properly. Put your apples in the refrigerator as soon as you get home. Studies by the Vermont Department of Agriculture have shown that apples last seven times longer when kept under refrigeration.

If you do pick too many apples to eat in a week or two, you could try freezing them to use later in pies and cakes. Simply peel, core and slice them, and then put them in airtight plastic bags. They may be kept in the freezer for up to a year.

Write to the Department of Agriculture in the state that interests you and ask them to send a list of orchards that offer pick-your-own.

For Further Information

Write to one of these departments of Agriculture to obtain a list of orchards in each New England state.

- Connecticut Dept. of Agriculture, State Office Building, Hartford, CT 06106

- Maine Dept. of Agriculture, State House Station 28, Augusta, ME 04333

- Massachusetts Dept. of Agriculture, 100 Cambridge Street, 21st Floor, Boston, MA 02202

- New Hampshire Dept. of Agriculture, Division of Agricultural Development, 10 Ferry Street, Concord, NH 03302

- Rhode Island Dept. of Environmental Management, Division of Agriculture, 22 Hayes Street, Providence, RI 02908

- Vermont Dept. of Agriculture, 120 State Street, Montpelier, VT 05620

bags and containers. Most orchards provide bags, but a few do not and some will allow only certain types of containers.

2. Check in when you arrive. Before you start picking, you should check with the orchard owner about which varieties are ripe in that period, and which parts of the orchard are open for picking. Respect the owner's privacy and do not go where you are not allowed!

3. Pick carefully. When you pick the apples, treat them gently. Some orchard owners advise pickers to treat the apples as though they were eggs. If they bruise, they will spoil more quickly. The technique for picking is simple: hold the apple firmly but not too tightly and twist it off the branch, taking care to leave the stem attached, since removal of the stem will also cause rot.

4. Don't waste apples. Be careful to pick only the apples you need. You may be tempted to pick

Scanning newspaper articles

exercise 8

➤ **You are doing a report on ethnic diversity, and you find this newspaper article. Scan the article for the answers to the questions below. Work quickly!**

1. In what year were the population statistics calculated?

2. Who was the governor of Hawaii at the time of this article?

3. How did D.H. Hwang describe Hawaii at the time of this article?

4. What is the name of the professor who studies Hawaiian society?

5. Which group in Hawaii is the largest?

6. What is the combined total of mixed and pure Hawaiians?

7. How many Chinese residents are listed?

8. What is the percentage of Samoans?

9. How many Caucasians live in Hawaii?

10. Does any ethnic group have a majority?

➤ **Check your answers with another student. Write three more questions about the population of Hawaii. Ask your partner to scan for the answers. Work as fast as you can.**

1.

2.

3.

Would this information be useful for a report on ethnic diversity? Why or why not?

Hawaii's ethnic rainbow: shining colors, side by side

by Susan Yim
Advertiser Managing Editor/Features & Design

America is going through an identity crisis. Nationally, early in the 21st century, the white population is expected to go from majority to less than 50 percent. Ethnic groups—especially Hispanic and Asian—are increasing due to immigration, and already there's more interracial marriage, especially in such trend-setting states as California and New York.

Sociologists and others ponder: How will all these people with different roots get along?

Time magazine celebrated the Fourth of July last year with a cover story about the nation's ethnic diversity and asked the questions "Who Are We?" and "What Do We Have in Common?"

To someone in Hawaii, all this concern about ethnic diversity seems like so much fuss. For most of this century, Hawaii has been a mulitcultural society, a community of different ethnic groups where no one group is the majority.

Back in 1961, sociologist Lawrence Fuchs came to Hawaii and wrote "Hawaii Pono," a very good book about the islands' march toward statehood. In it, he concluded:

"This is the promise of Hawaii, a promise for the entire nation, and indeed, the world, that peoples of different races and creeds can live together, enriching each other, in harmony and democracy."

But not many people beyond Hawaii's shores have paid much attention to what's going on socially here.

So when New York-based playwright David Henry Hwang spoke at the University of Hawaii last summer about Hawaii being a model multicultural community for the rest of the country, it raised the obvious question:

What could others learn?

The Hawaii model

Gov. John Waihee likes to call Hawaii "a marketplace bazaar." He's made several speeches recently about the Hawaii model to Mainland audiences.

"In Hawaii, you have something a little different, in which people are encouraged to be proud of their heritage," says Waihee. "There's a pride in that kind of a society that allows you to pick and choose and enjoy the cultural contributions and uniqueness of different groups."

Hawaii's population		

Here are the latest population statistics by ethnic group for Hawaii. Total population in 1988 was 942,564 excluding military and dependents.

	Population	Percent
Japanese	222,697	23.9%
Mixed (Part Hawaiian)	202,134	21.4%
Caucasian	191,553	20.3%
Filipino	118,694	12.6%
Mixed (Non-Hawaiian)	112,411	11.9%
Chinese	47,787	5.1%
Other unmixed	12,579	1.3%
Korean	10,720	1.1%
Pure Hawaiian	9,344	1%
Samoan	5,106	.5%
Puerto Rican	3,336	.3%
Black	3,203	.3%

Source: State Department of Health, Hawaii Health Surveillance Program for 1988. Because of rounding, percentages may not total 100.

"In a way, we've tried to call that culture which allows everybody to kind of exchange, go in and out of, enjoy various things...in its best sense, local culture," he says. "What glues it all together is the native Hawaiian culture."

UH professor and political analyst Dan Boylan is an even bigger cheerleader for Hawaii's multicultural model, pointing out multicultural societies in Southeast Asia and the Pacific where ethnic groups don't get along.

"We are the nation's experiment in multiculturalism. I don't think anybody's paid attention to that at all," Boylan says.

We get along because no one group has enough people to be in the majority and to dominate, Boylan adds, and that extends into politics.

"Our political model is no one constitutes that 50.1 percent that's necessary to oppress anyone else," he explains. "Whoever has wanted to govern in this state has had to form a coalition across ethnic lines. (Unlike the Mainland,) politicians have to appeal to different ethnic groups to win elections.

> ## *Life is not easy for any of us. But, what of that? We must have perseverance and above all confidence in ourselves.*

Scanning encyclopedia entries

exercise 9

➤ *You are writing a report about Marie Curie for your history class. You look in the encyclopedia for some basic information. Scan the encyclopedia entry below to find the answers to the questions below.* **Work quickly!**

   1. When was Marie born?

   2. What is her middle name?

   3. Where was she born?

   4. Where was she educated?

   5. What was her husband's name?

   6. What was her specialty in scientific work?

   7. How many years did the Curies work on their radium study?

   8. When did they receive the Nobel Prize?

   9. Which American president helped her with her work?

  10. What is the name of her most famous book?

➤ *Check your answers with another student. Write three more questions about Marie Curie. Ask your partner to scan for the answers. Work as fast as you can.*

   1.

   2.

   3.

> **We must believe we are gifted for something and that this thing, at whatever cost, must be attained.** —*Marie Curie*

CURIE [kü´ri´], the name of a distinguished French family whose most prominent members have been scientists.

Marie Sklodowska Curie (1867-1934) was born in Warsaw, Poland, Nov. 7, 1867. She received her early education and scientific training from her father and for several years taught in a Warsaw high school. In 1891 she moved to Paris, where she studied physics at the Sorbonne, receiving her degree in 1893. Two years later she

MARIE CURIE

married the French chemist Pierre Curie. After A.H. Becquerel's investigation of the radioactive properties of uranium, she commenced her researches in radioactivity, and in 1898 the discovery of polonium and radium in pitchblende was announced, her husband having joined in the research. It took them four more years of work to isolate radium in its pure form; during this time they made numerous discoveries regarding the properties of the new element. While they were conducting their researches, the Curies suffered from financial hardship, and Marie Curie was obliged to teach physics in a school for girls. In 1903 the Curies were awarded, with Henri Becquerel, the Nobel Prize for physics. The process for obtaining radium they freely gave to the world without any thought to their own gain.

Marie Curie became chief of the laboratory in her husband's department at the Sorbonne in 1903 and upon his death in 1907 succeeded him there as a professor of physics. She was awarded a second Nobel Prize, for chemistry, in 1911 for her work on radium and its compounds, and in 1914 she was placed in charge of the radioactivity laboratory of the new Institute of Radium in Paris. Here she was later joined in her work by her daughter Irene, who married Mme. Curie's assistant Joliot. During World War I she organized radiological service for hospitals. In 1921 she visited the United States, and in 1929 President Herbert Hoover presented her with a check for $50,000 which had been raised by subscription and which was intended for the purchase of a gram of radium for a laboratory in Warsaw that she had helped to establish. In addition to the classic *Traité de radioactivité* (1910), she published numerous papers on radium. Mme. Curie died at Saint-Cellemoz, Haute-Savoie, July 4, 1934.

CALEB W. DAVIS

Pierre Curie (1859-1906), French physicist, was born in Paris on May 15, 1859, and was educated at the Sorbonne. He became professor of general physics at the École de Physique et de Chimie in 1895 and professor of general physics at the Sorbonne in 1904. Much of his early work was concerned with the subject of magnetism in crystals. With his brother Paul-Jean Curie he investigated piezoelectricity in crystals in 1880. His discovery of a relation for electrical susceptibility is known as "Curie's law," while "Curie's point" is that critical point of temperature at which ferromagnetism suddenly disappears. He was run over and killed by a dray, in Paris, on Apr. 19, 1906.

exercise 10

➤ *You have an assignment to do an oral report on a recent development in technology. Scan this passage from an encyclopedia to answer the questions below.* **Work quickly!**

1. Whose idea was the satellite in the first place?

2. What was the name of the first communications satellite?

3. Who was president of the United States when the first communications satellite sent a Christmas message?

4. Which countries cooperated to develop Echo 2?

5. Which satellite was the first to send television broadcasts?

6. About how far above the earth were the experimental satellites?

7. How many kinds of commercial satellites are mentioned in the text?

8. When was the first commercial satellite placed in operation?

9. Which satellite first carried both telephone calls and color television between North America and Europe?

10. What is the name of the newest satellite mentioned in the article?

➤ *Check the accuracy of your answers with another student. Then write three more questions about communications satellites. Ask your partner to scan for the answers.* **Work as fast as you can.**

1.

2.

3.

Is the information in the article useful?

Would it help you to make a good oral report?

Why or why not?

What additional information would you like to have?

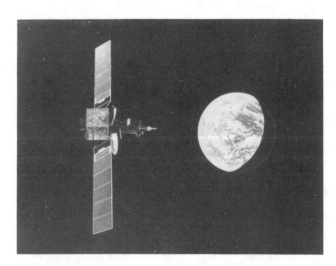

Intelsat 5

SATELLITES

The higher powered satellite amplifiers of the 1980's made possible TV transmission into antennas small enough to be mounted on the roof of a private home or on the side of a building. With such an antenna, ghosting of the picture due to reflections from buildings or hills no longer occurs. Also, the bandwidth per channel, wider than that used for conventional TV broadcasting, makes for pictures of better quality and higher definition.

In addition to countries using their own satellites for domestic service (Australia, Canada, Indonesia, Mexico, the United States, and the Soviet Union), about two dozen countries lease satellite transponders from Intelsat for domestic communication services.

HISTORY

The idea of a satellite system for communications was first suggested in 1945 by Arthur C. Clarke, an English engineer and writer. About 1954, John R. Pierce, an American engineer, made a thorough study of all types of satellite systems for communications. His work ultimately led to the active-repeater satellite program.

Experimental Satellites. The first communications satellite, called Score, was launched on Dec. 18, 1958. Score, which consisted of two radio receivers, two transmitters, and two tape recorders, transmitted to the world the prerecorded Christmas message of President Dwight D. Eisenhower. On Aug. 12, 1960, a passive communications satellite, Echo 1, was orbited to conduct communications experiments. A ten-story-high balloon, Echo 1 was used to bounce radio and television signals between the United States, England, and France. Echo 2, part of a cooperative program of experiments between the United States, England, and the Soviet Union, was launched on Jan. 26, 1964.

The first electronic active-repeater satellite, Courier 1B, was launched on Oct. 4, 1960. It was also the first satellite to use solar cells rather than chemical batteries for power, and it transmitted for 17 days.

After a hiatus of almost two years, the Telstar, Relay, and Syncom projects provided a series of spectacular successes that proved the feasibility of satellites for commercial communications. Telstar 1 was orbited on July 10, 1962, and Telstar 2 on May 7, 1963. Telstar 1 was the first communications satellite to relay experimental television broadcasts. Relay 1, launched on Dec. 13, 1962, and Relay 2, launched on Jan. 21, 1964, were similar to the Telstars.

Syncom 1, the first synchronous satellite, was successfully launched on Feb. 14, 1963, but an electronics failure prevented it from being used. Syncom 2, launched on July 26, 1963, was used to test the synchronous satellite concept thoroughly, and Syncom 3, launched on Aug. 19, 1964, was used to relay telecasts

of the 1964 Olympic Games, held in Japan, to the United States and Europe.

The low-orbiting satellites (up to 6,000 miles; 9.600 km) such as Score, Echo, Courier, Telstar, and Relay provided many useful experiments. But the evolving technology made synchronous satellites the choice for commercial uses.

Commercial Satellites. The history of the Intelsat system comprises several successive generations of satellites.

Intelsat 1. Early Bird (Intelsat 1), the world's first commercial communications satellite, was launched from Cape Canaveral, Fla., on Apr. 6, 1965, and was placed in commercial operation over the Atlantic Ocean on June 28, 1965. Early Bird had a capacity of 240 simultaneous telephone calls, or one color television channel, between points in North America and Europe. Early Bird introduced live commercial television across oceans.

Intelsat 2. Three satellites of the Intelsat 2 series were successfully launched and placed in commercial service during 1967. One was placed over the Atlantic Ocean augmenting Early Bird, and two were placed over the Pacific Ocean. These satellites had the same capacity as Early Bird and each covered one third of the globe. They introduced multipoint communications capability—that is, each satellite could link earth stations in all countries within its area of coverage. These satellites extended satellite coverage to two thirds of the world.

Intelsat 3. A third generation of Intelsat satellites was placed in commercial operation over the Atlantic, Pacific, and Indian Oceans between January and July 1969 to establish the initial global system. These satellites had a capacity of 1,200 simultaneous telephone calls or 4 television channels, or combinations thereof.

Intelsat 4. An even further advanced fourth generation of satellites was launched beginning in January 1971, and by July 1972 an improved global system of Intelsat 4 satellites was operating over the Atlantic, Pacific, and Indian Oceans. This series, larger and heavier than the Intelsat 3 series, had a capacity of 4,000 simultaneous telephone calls plus two television channels per satellite. The Intelsat 4A version of the series was first launched in 1975 and, by using a number of satellite amplifiers, provided 6,000 telephone circuits plus two television channels per satellite.

Intelsat 5. Intelsat 5, first launched in 1980, had a capacity of 12,000 simultaneous telephone circuits plus two television channels. This series uses a flywheel driven by an electric motor, rather than a spinning satellite, to maintain stability. The Intelsat 5A, an expanded version of the Intelsat 5, provides 14,000 telephone circuits and two television channels.

JOSEPH V. CHARYK

Previewing and Predicting

What is previewing? What is predicting?

There are two skills that are essential for a good reader: Previewing and Predicting. When you gather information about a book by examining its cover, you are *previewing*. The aim of previewing is to help you to *predict* or make some "educated guesses" about what is in the book. You should develop the habit of applying these skills whenever you read.

Previewing and predicting before you read can make a big difference. You can get some ideas about what you will read. That way you will begin to process the information far more quickly. You will also be able to follow the writer's ideas better. Though it takes a few minutes to preview and predict, those few minutes are well invested. You will find that later you save reading time and gain comprehension.

➤ *You can tell a lot about a book from its cover! Examine the book cover on the next page. Then fill in the following information.*

1. Title

2. Author

3. Fiction or nonfiction?

4. What do you predict that this book is about?

5. List some of the adjectives which are found in the reviews on the back cover of the book.

6. Find any additional information about the author and write it here.

7. Would you like to read this book? Why?

MALCOLM X

If there was any one man who articulated the anger, the struggle, and the beliefs of American Blacks in the sixties, that man was Malcolm X. His Autobiography is now an established classic of modern America, a book that expresses like none other the crucial truth about our violent times.

"A great book. Its dead level honesty, its passion, its exalted purpose will make it stand as a monument to the most painful truth."

Truman Nelson, THE NATION

"Extraordinary. A brilliant, painful, important book."

THE NEW YORK TIMES

"This book will have a permanent place in the literature of the Afro-American struggle."

I.F. STONE

This book is the result of a unique collaboration between Malcolm X and Alex Haley, whose own search for his African past, inspired by his encounter with Malcolm X, led him to write the celebrated bestseller Roots.

THE AUTOBIOGRAPHY OF
MALCOLM X
ALEX HALEY
"ROOTS"

Ballantine/
Autobiography/
36068
(Canada $7.95)
U.S $5.95

exercise 1

➤ *Find a book that you have not read. For example, you could exchange pleasure reading books with another student. Use the previewing and predicting list below to find out all you can about the book. Then tell another student about it.*

Title:

Author:

Type of book: _____ Fiction   _____ Nonfiction

What is it about?

Date of publication:

Number of pages:

Quality of print: _____ Easy to see   _____ Difficult

Front and back cover information:

Based on your preview, what can you predict about this book?

Would you like to read it? Why?

exercise 2

➤ *You are staying at a friend's house for a few days. You have forgotten to bring something to read, so your friend offers you three books. Read the information from the book covers given below and make some predictions about each book. Decide which one you would like to read. Time limit: 60 seconds.*

Book 1

***Things Fall Apart* by Chinua Achebe.** This book was first published in England in 1958. It is the author's first and most famous novel. A classic of modern African writing, it is the story of a man whose life is dominated by fear and anger. It is a powerful and moving story that has been compared with Greek tragedy. The writer's style is uniquely and richly African. Subtly and ironically, Achebe shows his awareness of the human qualities common to people everywhere.

Things Fall Apart is also a social document. It shows traditional life among the Ibo people in a Nigerian village. The novel documents life before Christianity, and demonstrates how the coming of white people led to the end of the old tribal ways.

Book 2

***This Rough Magic* by Mary Stewart.** This novel was on *The New York Times* best-seller list for eight months, and the reviewer wrote that the tale is "a magical concoction...warm and sunny for all its violence."

Stewart's book tells the story of a beguiling young actress, Lucy Waring, who visits Corfu for a holiday. With no warning, she stumbles into strange violence and is threatened with terror and death.

Other reviewers call this book "romantic, suspenseful, delightful...rating A" and "a polished and lively novel...luscious from start to finish."

Book 3

***Black Cherry Blues* by James Lee Burke.** Winner of the Edgar Award for best novel, this 1989 detective story is "full of low-lifes and rich crooks. Burke shows that 'serious' literary craftsmanship is compatible with the hard-boiled genre" of the crime novel.

Burke's story leads his hero from Louisiana to Montana as he strives to escape a phony murder charge, protect his little girl, and find a professional killer. Reviewers call this novel "a fine book, tough and vital."

Which book would you choose?

Why?

Tell another student about your choice. Did you choose the same book?

exercise 3

Often an author includes photographs or illustrations with a text. Since they are usually closely connected to the author's ideas, it is important to preview these, too. Make predictions about what might be in the article based on the photograph below.

➤ **Study the photograph. Write your predictions about the article. Be specific.**

Predictions:

Compare your predictions with another student. Then read the article on the next page. Did you make accurate predictions?

Western University Graduates Encouraged to Support Education

PRESTON, CALIF.—MAY 20— After a rock band version of "Pomp and Circumstance," the California State Treasurer, Katherine Greene, spoke to graduating law students about their future role in supporting education. "This state has been generous to you. Remember that, and be generous in return," she said.

"This is a time when many are talking about budget imperatives and education is being sacrificed for short-term budget goals. You should be the first to refuse this kind of sacrifice. The future of California —and the nation—lies in education: in the universities, the high schools and even in the most remote small-town elementary schools. The present budget cuts to education are scandalous. You are the ones who must fight this shortsightedness. Make a personal commitment to education, whether it's with your money, your time, your energy, or your vote."

Ms. Greene, a graduate of Columbia University Law School in 1984, spoke with fervor to the 250 members of the graduating class of Sherman School of Law. She told these future lawyers that they must "go to battle" and "take a stand" for their beliefs. "You must not think that career advancement precludes any efforts to improve the world you live in," she said.

The ceremony at Sherman Hall was just one of more than 30 ceremonies to mark Western University's 75th commencement. A total of 5,560 degrees, including 3,700 bachelors degrees, were conferred on Saturday.

The theme of remembering one's origins was echoed in another part of the campus at a special graduation ceremony for 204 Hispanic students from all departments. The ceremony was half in Spanish and half in English, and the celebratory nature of the occasion was marked by a performance of dancers in Aztec costumes. The stage was decorated with a red and white banner reading "Viva Caesar Chavez."

The life and work of Mr. Chavez, the late union organizer, was recalled by Maria Aruyo, master of ceremonies and professor of comparative literature in the ethnic studies department. "He would have been proud of one of our students here today, who picked lettuce for 15 years and is now receiving his degree in civil engineering," she said. "This is the kind of person we should all be proud of, the kind of person we need for our future."

At this same ceremony, Carla Cruz, a graduating psychology major, spoke on behalf of the students, saying that in her years at Western University, she had experienced a significant change in the political atmosphere and in the attitudes of her fellow students and her self. While she initially referred to herself as a Hispanic student, that term had changed to Mexicana and then to Latina as her sense of identity changed and expanded.

But she added, "many of us have been forced by the realities of higher tuition fees and shrinking scholarships to abandon our dream of education.'

Among the other speakers at Western's graduation ceremonies were Sam Strickart of the rock group Stricken, who spoke to graduates of the College of Letters and Science, the author Jane Stevenson, who spoke to mass communication graduates, and the San Francisco environmentalist, John Broome, who spoke to biology graduates.

exercise 4

➤ *Before you read an assigned textbook, preview to find out what you will find in it.*

A. Fill in the information about More Reading Power.

Title: *More Reading Power*

Author(s): _____

Date of publication: _____ Number of pages: _____

Is there a Preface or Introduction? _____

Number of parts: _____

Check to see if the textbook has these features:

_____ table of contents

_____ index

_____ glossary

_____ bibliography (references)

_____ end-of-chapter questions

_____ illustrations, charts, graphs

B. Now fill in this information about a textbook from another class.

Title: (Name of your textbook) _____

Author(s): _____

Date of publication: _____ Number of pages: _____

For what course is the textbook used? _____

Is there a Preface or Introduction? _____

Number of parts: _____ Number of chapters _____

Check to see if the textbook has these features:

_____ table of contents

_____ index

_____ glossary

_____ bibliography (references)

_____ end-of-chapter questions

_____ illustrations, charts, graphs

_____ other helpful features:

➤ *Discuss what you have learned with another student.*

How are the textbooks alike? How are they different?

Guidelines for Previewing and Predicting about Longer Passages

1. Read the title—What is the passage about? Do you know anything about this subject?

2. Decide what kind of text it is—is it an essay, an argument, a story, an explanation? Does it seem difficult?

3. Look at the way the text is organized—is it divided into parts? Are there sub-titles? If so, what do they tell you about the way the subject is presented?

4. Read very quickly the first line of each paragraph or sub-division—can you tell what the passage is about? Do you already know something about it?

5. Notice names, numbers, dates, and words that are repeated—do you recognize any of them?

6. Read quickly the last few sentences in the final paragraph—what is the author's final point? Is it a conclusion or a summary?

exercise 5

➤ *Preview the following story. Read only the underlined parts. Time limit: 30 seconds.*

Carmelita's Amazing Rescue

At the Santos family's apartment in Sao Paulo, the doorbell is constantly ringing. All the friends and neighbors are there to hear what happened to two-year-old Carmelita. Her mother has tears in her eyes, but they are tears of relief, of thankfulness. Her Carmelita is smiling shyly, safe in her father's lap.

The story could easily have had ended very differently, not so happily. It all started this morning just before noon. Mrs. Santos was returning from the supermarket with her daughter and a friend, their neighbor. They stopped on the stairway of their building at their fifth floor apartment. The neighbor opened her door first, and little Carmelita ran past her. She knew the apartment well, since she had visited it many times. The friend put down her keys and shopping bags, and turned back a moment to Mrs. Santos. At that moment, there was a sudden gust of wind and the door to the apartment slammed shut. Carmelita was inside, alone.

The friend remembered then that she had left her kitchen window open. She and Mrs. Santos rushed to the Santos' apartment and telephoned the police. But there was no time to get help in opening the neighboring apartment. They could see that Carmelita was already leaning out of the kitchen window. She had climbed

onto a chair, and soon she was climbing out onto the window sill. Mrs. Santos called to Carmelita to go back inside. But the little girl did not understand the danger and did not want to go back. She only waved to her mother.

Then she lost her balance and her feet slipped off the window sill. She managed to hold on for a while with her hands, but she began to be afraid. Her mother screamed for help, and now Carmelita was crying desperately. And then she could hold on no longer.

But several people had run out into the street on hearing all the screaming. They saw the child hanging onto the window sill and got ready to catch her. Down she fell, five long stories—and landed safe and sound in the arms of three strong men. They were Luis, Augusto, and Alfonso Nunes, father and sons. When they heard the screams, they were in their auto repair shop across the street.

"I never thought we'd do it," said Alfonso afterwards. But I kept thinking, if we don't catch her, she'll die and it'll be on my conscience all my life."

All the neighbors want to shake hands with the three heroes. Carmelita's parents cannot believe how close they came to losing their daughter. And how lucky they are to have her still.

➤ *Now turn the page and answer the questions.*

> *Answer the questions. Remember, do not look back!*

1. Where do you think this passage originally appeared?

2. Where does this take place?

3. Who is Carmelita?

4. What happened to her?

5. Who is Alfonso and what did he do?

Compare your answers with another student. Then go back and read the whole passage.

exercise 6

> *Preview this article. When you have finished previewing, go on to answer the questions. Time limit: 30 seconds.*

Long Live Women!

Both men and women are living longer these days in the industrialized countries. However, women, on the average, live longer. In general, they can expect to live six or seven years more than men. The reasons for this are both biological and cultural.

One important biological factor that helps women live longer is the difference in hormones between men and women. Hormones are chemicals which are produced by the body to control various body functions. Between the ages of about 12 and 50, women produce hormones that are involved in fertility. These hormones also have a positive effect on the heart and the blood flow. In fact, women are less likely to have high blood pressure or to die from heart attacks.

The female hormones also protect the body in another way. They help the body to defend itself against some kinds of infections. This means that women generally get sick less often and less seriously than men. The common cold is a good example: women, on average, get fewer colds than men.

Women are also helped by their female genes. Scientists are still not exactly sure how genes influence aging, but they believe that they do. Some think that a woman's body cells have a tendency to age more slowly than a man's. Others think that a man's body cells have a tendency to age more quickly. Recent research seems to support both of these possibilities.

The cultural context can also influence life expectancy for men and women. (Life expectancy is the expected length of a person's life.) For example, women generally smoke cigarettes less than men. They also drink less alcohol on average. Both cigarettes and alcohol have been proven to cause many health problems and to shorten lives.

Another factor that has influenced the lives of women is the lack of stress. Stress is well known to shorten lives. Until recently, women who worked were usually in less responsible, less stressful positions. At home, housework tends to keep women in better physical condition than men. This generally better physical condition is yet another factor in women's longer lives.

These cultural factors have played an important part for the women who are now getting old. But the social habits of women are changing. Young women are smoking and drinking more than women used to. More women are working now and holding more responsible positions. These changes may mean that the cultural context will no longer help women live healthier lives. However, the other, biological factors in life expectancy remain unchanged. Women probably will therefore continue to live longer than men.

➤ *Answer the questions. Remember, do not look back!*

1. What is this article about?

2. What are some biological reasons for women's long lives, according to this article?

3. What are some of the other reasons mentioned?

4. Does the author think the situation is likely to change? Why?

5. Is the information in this article new to you?

Compare your answers with another student. Then go back and read the whole passage.

exercise 7

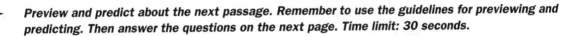

➤ *Preview and predict about the next passage. Remember to use the guidelines for previewing and predicting. Then answer the questions on the next page. Time limit: 30 seconds.*

A Free Woman

Twenty-five years ago, the worst they could say was "nice girls don't smoke" or "it'll stunt your growth."

Even years later when the Surgeon General's report showed the connection between smoking and lung cancer and other diseases, the facts were only about men. But now we know that women who smoke are dying of lung cancer and other diseases at twice the rate of women who don't. Women who smoke are sick more often than women who don't. Women who smoke heavily have three times as much bronchitis or emphysema and 50 percent more peptic ulcers. Smoking even affects pregnancy. so you don't have to wait until you're old to feel the effects of smoking. If you're pregnant and you smoke, it can harm the health of your baby.

What happens when you smoke a cigarette?

In just three seconds a cigarette makes your heart beat faster and shoots your blood pressure up. It replaces oxygen in your blood with carbon monoxide and leaves cancer-causing chemicals to spread through your body. As the cigarettes add up, the damage adds up. It's the total amount of smoking that causes the trouble. The younger you start smoking, the greater your danger will be. For instance, if you're fifteen, you will have smoked many more cigarettes by the time you're thirty than someone who started at twenty.

And people who start young tend to become heavy smokers. Heavy smokers run a greater risk. Again, the more cigarettes you smoke, the faster they add up.

You're still young. The younger you are, the easier it is to quit. It takes years to develop a real cigarette habit. So even if you think you're hooked, chances are you're not. If you quit now, you will never be sorry. Your body will repair itself. Food will taste better. Everything will smell better (including your hair and your clothes). And don't let anyone tell you stories about gaining weight. Haven't you ever seen a fat smoker? If you have the willpower to quit smoking, you have the willpower not to overeat. If is as simple as that. You know what you've got to look forward to. You can grow into a truly free woman, or you can ruin yourself for life.

The only one who can make the choice is you.

➤ *Do not lool back at the passage.*

Recalling Facts

1. The connection between smoking and cancer was made by

   a. the A.M.A.   b. government doctors.   c. the Surgeon General.

2. Smoking can increase a person's chances of developing

   a. liver disease.   b. ulcers.   c. colds.

3. Smoking makes the heart beat faster after a lapse of

   a. three seconds.   b. ten seconds.   c. twenty seconds.

4. According to the article, smoking

   a. causes dizziness.   b. kills red blood cells.   c. raises blood pressure.

5. The author points out that giving up smoking requires

   a. courage.   b. patience.   c. willpower.

Understanding Ideas

6. This article is mostly about

   a. giving up smoking.
   b. attitudes toward smoking.
   c. the connection between growing and smoking.

7. The author implies that a person who gives up smoking

   a. gains weight.
   b. enjoys food more.
   c. sleeps more soundly.

8. The reader can infer that

   a. smoking can cause the common cold.
   b. the odor of smoke clings to cloth.
   c. cigarettes are more popular than cigars and pipes.

9. Giving up smoking is easiest for someone who is

   a. twenty years old.
   b. forty years old.
   c. sixty years old.

10. The reader can conclude that

   a. cigarette sales have declined in the past few years.
   b. illnesses and smoking are often related.
   c. cancer kills more people than any other disease.

➤ *Check your answers in the Answer Key on page 276. How many questions were you able to answer correctly? Discuss this exercise with another student. Why could you answer so many questions correctly after just previewing and predicting?*

exercise 8

➤ **Preview and predict about the next passage. Then answer the questions on the next page. Time limit: 30 seconds.**

Poles Apart

Many are surprised to learn that Antarctica is nearly twice the size of the United States. The name Antarctica was coined to mean "opposite to the Arctic." It is just that in many ways. Antarctica is a high, ice-covered landmass. In the Arctic the landmasses are grouped around the ice-covered Arctic Ocean.

Largely because of this difference, the climate of the two areas is very different. Antarctica is the coldest area in the world. On the average it is about 30 degrees colder than the Arctic. At the South Pole, nearly 10,000 feet high, monthly mean temperatures run well below zero. Only in coastal regions do temperatures sometimes rise about freezing in the summer (December to March). In contrast, near the North Pole monthly mean temperatures often rise above freezing.

At both poles, daily temperatures may drop far below the monthly mean. At the American South Pole Station, winter temperatures sometimes fall below -100 degrees Fahrenheit. Elsewhere, on higher parts of the south polar plateau, even lower temperatures are recorded. A temperature of -127 degrees Fahrenheit was measured in August 1960. It is the world's record low temperature.

Partly because of this climatic difference, the land animals and plants of the two regions are very different. On the continent of Antarctica, there are very few plants. In the Arctic there are many plants. In some of the few ice-free areas of Antarctica, mosses, lichens, and algae are found. Penguins populate Antarctic coastlines but do not exist in the Arctic. The land animals of the Arctic are foxes, bears, reindeer, and lemmings. These animals are unknown in the Antarctic. Old rock layers show that this "oppositeness" between north and south extends far back into the early chapters of earth history.

Ice is the great feature of Antarctica. More than 4.5 million square miles of ice sheet cover the area. Great rivers of ice, called glaciers, push down the mountains. Antarctica is the storehouse of about 85 percent of the total world supply of ice.

The icecap is very thick, averaging nearly 8,000 feet. At one spot, scientists have found the distance from the surface to the rock underneath the ice to be more than 13,000 feet.

If this great volume of ice were to melt, the volume of the world oceans would increase, and sea level would rise. Extreme atmospheric changes would have to take place for this to happen.

➤ *Do not lool back at the passage.*

Recalling Facts

1. The coldest area in the world is

   a. the Arctic.   b. Antarctica.   c. Siberia.

2. The world's record low temperature was recorded in

   a. 1950.   b. 1960.   c. 1970.

3. How much of the world's ice is located in Antarctica?

   a. 15 percent.   b. 55 percent.   c. 85 percent.

4. Compared to the United States, Antarctica is

   a. the same size.   b. twice the size.   c. four times the size.

5. Some areas of Antarctica are

   a. ice free.   b. very humid.   c. quite mild.

Understanding the Passage

6. One type of animal found in the Arctic is the

   a. fox.
   b. wolf.
   c. opossum.

7. The author develops his point through

   a. comparison and contrast.
   b. theories and proof.
   c. characters and actions.

8. The author implies that if Antarctica's ice melted,

   a. coastal areas of the world would be flooded.
   b. ocean currents would shift direction.
   c. climate would change drastically everywhere.

9. The name Antarctica, meaning "opposite to the Arctic," was based on

   a. insufficient exploration.
   b. inaccurate information.
   c. adequate knowledge.

10. We may conclude that

    a. life at the North Pole is more tolerable than at the South Pole.
    b. the Arctic is a solid land mass.
    c. penguins could not live at the North Pole.

➤ *Check your answers in the Answer Key on page 276. How many questions were you able to answer correctly?*

Vocabulary Knowledge for Effective Reading

Guessing unknown vocabulary

What do you usually do when you come to a word you do not know in your reading? Do you

a. look it up in the dictionary?

b. ask your teacher?

c. ask another student or a friend?

d. try to guess what it means?

If you answered *a*, *b*, or *c*, then you are not reading as effectively and efficiently as you could be. In fact, the best strategy for dealing with an unknown word is to try to guess what it means. This strategy

- is fast because you don't interrupt your reading.

- helps your comprehension because you stay focused on the general sense of what you are reading.

- helps build vocabulary because you are more likely to remember the words.

- allows you to enjoy your reading more because you don't have to stop often.

Guessing meaning from context in sentences

When you try to guess the meaning of an unknown word, you use the text surrounding the word—the context. One sentence may be enough to give you the meaning, or you may need to use a longer passage.

Example: Do you know what "misogynist" means? If not, try to make a guess:

A misogynist is _____

Now read these sentences. Try again to guess what *misogynist* means.

a. She realized that her boss was a misogynist soon after she started working for him.

b. It is difficult for a woman to work for a misogynist. She is never sure of the reasons for his criticism.

c. She knew that no woman would ever get a top-level job in a company owned by a misogynist.

We know from sentence *a* that a misogynist is a man. From sentence *b* we learn that a misogynist criticizes women's work. Then from *c* we understand that a misogynist has negative feelings about women.

These exercises will help you develop the skill of guessing vocabulary in context if you:

• Do not use a dictionary!

• Do not talk about the vocabulary with other students until you have tried to make a guess on your own and everyone else has finished.

• Do not try to translate the unknown words into your own language. Instead, you should try to describe them or give words with similar meanings in English!

exercise 1

➤ *In each of the following items, there is a word you may not know. Guess the meaning of the word from the context of the sentences. Then compare your work with another student.*

1. What does "ravenous" mean?

_____

Could I have a piece of bread? I missed breakfast and I'm simply ravenous.

The poor horse was ravenous and it ate the leaves and bark off the trees.

2. What does "flippers" mean?

_____

We were all surprised to see how fast Johnny was swimming. Then we saw that he was wearing flippers.

With my flippers on my feet, I felt like a fish. I had never swum so fast and so far!

3. What does "wink" mean?

_____

George winked to me from across the room. It was a signal not to say anything about what we had seen.

I've only known one cat that could wink and that was Tinker. She really could close just one of her eyes and she did it often.

4. What does "sallow" mean?

_____

The poor child had sallow skin and very thin, bony arms and legs.

You could tell from his sallow complexion that he had lived in an unhealthy climate for many years.

5. What does "dike" mean?

_____

After so much rain, the river flowed over the dike and into the fields.

People in this area began building dikes many centuries ago. It was the only way to keep the sea out of their villages.

6. What does "gaudy" mean?

_____

She was wearing such gaudy clothes that it was easy to find her in the crowd.

My mother always said that old ladies shouldn't wear bright colors. She thought that they would look gaudy and foolish.

exercise 2

> In each of the following items there is a word you may not know. Guess the meaning of the word from the context of the sentences. Then compare your work with another student.

1. What does "pitch" mean?

_____

The singer was so terribly off pitch that it hurt my ears to listen.

The ambulance siren was at such a high pitch that we all jumped.

2. What does "shred" mean?

_____

He read the letter carefully and then tore it to shreds.

Sammy was a real mess when he came home: his clothes were in shreds and he was covered with mud.

3. What does "mold" mean?

_____

The liquid plastic was poured into a mold and left there until it was hard.

The dentist first makes a mold of his patient's teeth. From that he makes a model of the teeth to decide how to correct any problems.

4. What does "eaves" mean?

_____

Some birds had built a nest high up on the eaves of our house.

Houses in the mountains have wide eaves so the snow will not pile up against the windows.

5. What does "pressing" mean?

_____

Mr. Brewster had some very pressing business, so he had to leave before the meeting was over.

The state of the environment is one of the most pressing problems of our time.

6. What does "porch" mean?

_____

On nice days, old Mrs. Willows always sat out on her porch and watched the people pass by.

From the second floor porch, there was a wonderful view of the ocean.

exercise 3

 In each of the following items, there is a word you may not know. Guess the meaning of the word from the context of the sentences. Then compare your work with another student.

1. What does "stoop" mean?

_____

The old man walked slowly along, all stooped over and leaning on a stick.

When I stooped down to get a better look, I realized that it was a dead rabbit. It must have been hit by a car.

2. What does "squall" mean?

_____

The squall arrived so suddenly that we all got wet when we ran home from the beach.

When they saw the squall coming, the sailors took down the sail and headed for the port.

3. What does "gush" mean?

_____

When the fountain was turned on, the water gushed up several feet into the air.

The blood gushed out of his wound until the doctor put on a tight bandage.

4. What does "rugged" mean?

_____

Susan and her husband led a rugged life in the Alaskan mountains, with no electricity and no running water.

The young man's face was rugged, but his smile was friendly and the children soon forgot their fears.

5. What does "imp" mean?

_____

What an imp he was! Little Tommy was always getting into trouble, but making us laugh about it.

With her pointed little chin, bright eyes and impish expression, we didn't know whether to believe the child.

6. What does "soggy" mean?

_____

The study window had been left open during the storm, and my papers were a soggy mess.

We gathered up the soggy towels and bathing suits and hung them all in the sun to dry.

Using grammar to guess word meaning

Another way context can help you guess meaning is by giving you information about the grammar. When you find a word you do not know, look at the grammatical structure of the sentence. It will tell you about the function of the word—as a noun, verb, pronoun, adjective, or adverb, etc. Then you have a much narrower range of choices for guessing the meaning.

In each of the following sentences, there is one word that you probably do not know. Look at the grammatical structure of the sentence and decide whether the word is a noun, verb, adjective, or adverb. Then guess the meaning. Compare your answers with another student.

Example: The news that John was resigning from his job surprised us all. We simply couldn't <u>fathom</u> why he wanted to leave now that the company was finally doing so well.

What is the grammatical function of <u>fathom</u> in this sentence?

If you wrote "verb," you were correct. Only a verb makes sense here after "couldn't."

Now can you guess what <u>fathom</u> means?

If you answered "understand" or something similar, you were correct.

exercise 4

> *In each of the following sentences, there is one word you probably do not know. Look at the grammatical structure of the sentence and decide what the grammatical function of the word is. Then try to guess the meaning. Compare your work with another student.*

1. The only person in the room was a <u>doddering</u> old man who didn't seem to understand our question.

   Grammatical function of <u>doddering</u>:

   Approximate meaning:

2. "What's all that <u>ruckus</u>?" Dad called to us. "If you can't be quiet you'll all go to bed with no supper!"

   Grammatical function of <u>ruckus</u>:

   Approximate meaning:

3. His breath <u>reeked</u> of whiskey, and from the way he walked, we guessed he had been drinking for some time.

   Grammatical function of <u>reeked</u>:

   Approximate meaning:

4. When the robber pulled out his gun, everyone in the bank ran <u>helter skelter</u> for cover.

   Grammatical function of <u>helter skelter</u>:

   Approximate meaning:

5. We'll have to <u>buckle down</u> if we want to get this finished by the end of the month.

   Grammatical function of <u>buckle down</u>:

   Approximate meaning:

6. Even a simple procedure like applying for a license could lead you into a never-ending bureaucratic <u>morass</u>.

   Grammatical function of <u>morass</u>:

   Approximate meaning:

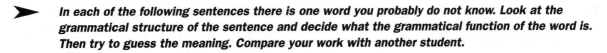

exercise 5

➤ *In each of the following sentences there is one word you probably do not know. Look at the grammatical structure of the sentence and decide what the grammatical function of the word is. Then try to guess the meaning. Compare your work with another student.*

1. Her father looked <u>askance</u> at the idea of a civil marriage in the city hall. He wanted his daughter to be married in a religious ceremony.

   Grammatical function of <u>askance</u>:

   Approximate meaning:

2. Due to the <u>unflagging</u> efforts of the rescue team, the children were found after a few hours.

   Grammatical function of <u>unflagging</u>:

   Approximate meaning:

3. The unhappy girl continued to <u>carp</u> at her mother, blaming her mother for all her problems.

   Grammatical function of <u>carp</u>:

   Approximate meaning:

4. After the war, Gunther went back to his hometown to look at the pile of <u>rubble</u> where his house had been.

   Grammatical function of <u>rubble</u>:

   Approximate meaning:

5. The strange bulge under Timmy's blanket frightened him for a moment until he realized it was his teddy bear.

   Grammatical function of <u>bulge</u>:

   Approximate meaning:

6. "What a <u>slipshod</u> job this is!" Mr. Jenkins shouted. "Go back and do it again more carefully."

   Grammatical function of <u>slipshod</u>:

   Approximate meaning:

exercise 6

➤ *In the paragraphs below, one word has been replaced with a nonsense word. Working with another student, try to guess what that nonsense word means. If you do not know the exact meaning in English, try to describe it. Read the whole paragraph first.*

1. What do you think "zip" means?

_____

The zips always run along the same routes in Istanbul. They usually stop only at the main bus stops. But if you ask the driver, you can get off anywhere. These zips are faster and more comfortable than the buses. At the same time, they are also much cheaper than normal taxis. The cost of a trip is divided among the passengers, usually four or five people. For these reasons, zips are a very popular way of getting around the city.

2. What do you think "zap" means?

_____

Everyone who visits Russia should first get a zap. If you come by train you must already have a zap. You will not be allowed to enter at all without one. Travelers without zaps will be sent back where they came from. Zaps are given on the spot if you arrive by plane or by car. However, you may have to wait a long time for one. This can be avoided by getting a zap before you leave.

3. What do you think "zep" means?

_____

Various kinds of zeps are available in Oslo. Some are for only an hour, some for a day, some for three days. The three-day zep is useful for the tourist who wants to visit different parts of the city. It allows you unlimited travel for three days on the local trains and buses. Zeps—and information about the buses and trains—are available at all tourist offices.

4. What do you think "zop" means?

_____

In Paris it is wise to get yourself a zop as soon as possible. It is very easy to get lost if you leave the main streets. You can buy zops in the train station, but they are not complete. Better zops can be found in the bookstores. These have more details and they show all the named streets.

5. What do you think "zup" means?

_____

Trains connect the larger cities in Tunisia, but there are not many smaller train lines. To travel between the smaller cities and towns, most people take buses or zups. These zups are often cheaper than the buses or trains. They leave as soon as they have five people who want to go to the same place. That might be a distant city, or a town nearby. The destination of the zup is written on a sign on the roof of the vehicle.

exercise 7

➤ *In the paragraphs below, one word has been replaced with a nonsense word. Working with another student, try to guess what that nonsense word means. If you do not know the exact meaning in English, try to describe it. Read the whole paragraph first.*

1. What do you think "zip" means?

_____

   Nobody wants a zip near their home. First of all, the usually do not smell very pleasant. If the wind is from the right direction, you may get that smell at home. Zips attract lots of insects, such as flies and mosquitoes. Animals such as rats and mice often come to live in the neighborhood too. A nearby zip may also mean you will have noisy trucks on your street all day. And finally, the most serious problem with zips is that they may pollute the drinking water. This does not always happen. But sometimes, the garbage has dangerous chemicals in it. Then when it rains, the chemicals enter the water underground and make it unsafe to drink.

2. What do you think "zap" means?

_____

   When people think about sources of water pollution, they do not usually think of zaps. However, as the demand grows for fish to eat, the number of zaps is increasing. In some areas, they are beginning to create environmental problems. In fact, when fish are in their natural environment, they do not pollute. But in zaps, the situation is not natural. There are usually lots of fish in very little water. This means that the water must be changed very often. And each time it is changed, the dirty water must be thrown away. It is usually poured directly from the zaps into a river or the ocean. The chemical balance of the river or coastline is changed by this dirty water. And the plants and animals living there may suffer.

3. What do you think "zep" means?

_____

   In the United States and in many European countries, there is a serious problem. What should be done with the garbage? There is no more room for garbage dumps. It is not possible to burn garbage, because that pollutes the air. So the governments are looking for ways to reduce the amount of garbage that is produced. One way to do this is to zep as much as possible. Not all kinds of garbage can be zepped, of course. The easiest things to zep are probably glass and paper. However, one can also zep many kinds of metal and plastic. Many cities now require people to zep these materials. The people must put them separately from the regular garbage. Then special trucks take them away and bring them to private companies. These companies will buy them and use them again.

exercise 8

 In the paragraphs below, one word has been replaced with a nonsense word. Working with another student, try to guess what that nonsense word means. If you do not know the exact meaning in English, try to describe it. Read the whole paragraph first.

1. What do you think "zip" means?

   _____

   Experiments have shown that some animals have an extraordinary sense of direction. The zip is a good example of this. In 1957, some scientists took eighteen zips from their home on the island of Midway in the Pacific Ocean. These zips were sent by airplane to some distant places, such as Japan, the Philippines, and the Hawaiian Islands. Then they were set free. Scientists already knew that zips could fly for great distances because of their huge wings. But no one thought that the zips would be able to find their way home. After all, Midway is just a very little island in the middle of a very large ocean. However, fourteen of the zips did get to Midway. They got there very quickly, too. One flew from the Philippines—4,120 km.—in only 32 days!

2. What do you think "zap" means?

   _____

   Another animal with a very good sense of direction is the Monarch butterfly. The Monarch is a beautiful orange-colored butterfly. It is one of the larger kinds of butterflies, but is still only an insect. All Monarchs spend the winter in a certain area of central Mexico. In the early spring, they begin to zap north. The butterflies that leave Mexico will die on their way. However, their children or grandchildren will zap all the way to northern United States or Canada. Then, in the fall, these new butterflies start zapping south. They have never been to Mexico, but they manage to find the place their parents left. They will even go to live in the same trees. Scientists believe that genetic programming makes this possible, but they do not know how.

3. What do you think "zep" means?

   _____

   Genetic programming is also probably the answer to the mystery of the salmon. These fish are born in zeps far from the ocean. When they are big enough, they travel all the way down the zep. Then they swim out into the deep ocean water, sometimes for thousands of miles. One salmon from Washington State in the United States was caught half-way to Japan. But no matter how far away they are, the fish start home in the spring. Somehow they know where home is. Along all the many miles of coast, each salmon finds the mouth of its own zep. Then it swims all the way up to the very same spot where it was born.

Recognizing words that connect ideas

Do you ever find that you are understanding words but not understanding the writer's ideas? Sometimes this happens when you do not pay attention to the words which connect the ideas. These words are often short, but important. Three useful kinds of words to notice are pronouns, synonyms, and summary words.

Pronouns

Writers use pronouns because repeating the same word or name many times is boring and clumsy. Pronouns can be singular or plural. This means they can replace a single name/idea or a group of names/ideas. Here is a list of some commonly used pronouns:

he, she, it, we, you, they	myself, yourself, herself
me, him, her, us, them	this, these, those
my, your, her, his, our, their	

exercise 9

 In each paragraph, the pronouns are underlined. Write the referent for each pronoun below. Compare your work with another student.

Example: Modern technology has dramatically changed the way we view the world. With air travel, satellite communications, and computers, <u>it</u> seems a much smaller place these days.

What is <u>it</u>?

"The world" is the referent for "it."

The Problem of Old Computers

1.   When a computer stops working or is replaced, one of three things can happen to <u>it</u> (1). <u>It</u> (2) might be fixed up and given to someone else who can use <u>it</u> (3). Or perhaps <u>it</u> (4) could be taken apart and the various parts could be recycled. The greatest possibility is that <u>it</u> (4) might be sent to the dump. There, <u>it</u> (5) would join countless other computers in filling up the limited dumping space.

Write the referent for:

it

2.   In the United States, about 10 million computers are thrown away every year! Because most unwanted computers are sent to a dump, <u>they</u> (1) have caused a problem. The computer industry and the government are working on ways to solve <u>it</u> (2). <u>They</u> (3) have concluded that there must be changes in the way computers are built. <u>They</u> (4) must be made in ways that will allow their parts to be recycled. These parts include the electronic parts, the glass screen of the monitor, and parts of the printer.

Write the referent for:

1. they	3. They
2. it	4. They

3. A new company has started to recycle computer parts. When old computers and computer parts are received at the company, they (1) are carefully broken down into parts. These (2) include circuit boards, bits of aluminum, gold, and electronic chips. Sometimes it takes an hour to break an old personal computer down into its parts. Eventually, they (3) are all carefully sorted and stored. Then the company sells them (4) to the many customers it has found for used parts.

Write the referent for:

1. they   3. they

2. These   4. them

exercise 10

 In each paragraph, the pronouns are underlined. Write the referent for each pronoun on the lines below. Compare your work with another student.

Pedicabs

1. A pedicab is a small cab which is pulled by a bicycle. This human-powered transportation has been popular in Asian countries for many years. Two years ago, a local businessman decided to introduce it (1) in Denver, Colorado. So far, he (2) has four of them (3) on the road. He explained that they (4) do not take the place of taxis, because people use them (5) for short rides. The passengers are often people who don't want to walk because they (6) are dressed in evening clothes.

Write the referent for:

1. it   4. they

2. he   5. them

3. them   6. they

2. The drivers of pedicabs are usually students with strong legs and friendly personalities. They (1) pay the owner $15 to $25 to rent a pedicab for a night. He (2) expects them (3) to keep the cab in good condition. A typical driver earns about as much as he (4) would by working as a waiter. He (5) can keep all the money he (6) is paid. One pedicab driver said that he (7) feels like a businessman. He (8) can earn a good wage and he (9) is his own boss.

Write the referent for:

1. They   6. he

2. He   7. he

3. them   8. He

4. he   9. he

5. He

3.   Pedicabs could be a good addition to the total transportation system in many cities. In Denver, the owner of a pedicab company plans to invest in a total of twenty of <u>them</u> (1). <u>He</u> (2) believes that <u>they</u> (3) will be popular with baseball fans at the new baseball stadium. <u>They</u> (4) can use <u>them</u> (5) to ride to their parked cars or to nearby restaurants. Furthermore, <u>he</u> (6) thinks that pedicabs could help carry some of the crowds in Atlanta during the 1996 Olympics. And <u>he</u> (7) thinks <u>they</u> (8) would be useful in port cities where cruise ships dock. Tourists could use <u>them</u> (9) to get from the port to the city center.

Write the referent for:

1. them   6. he

2. He   7. he

3. they   8. they

4. They   9. them

5. them

Synonyms

Writers make their writing interesting and enjoyable to read by using a variety of words. They may use a few different words to name the same thing. It is important to remember that even though two different words are used, they could name the same thing.

Example: An <u>orange</u> can be a delicious snack. This <u>citrus fruit</u> is also very healthy for you because it is a good source of vitamin C.

Both <u>orange</u> and <u>citrus fruit</u> name the same thing.

exercise 11

 In the following sentences, circle the synonym for the underlined word. Sometimes the synonym will be more than a single word. Compare your work with another student.

1. During its history, <u>Estonia</u> was occupied and ruled by forces from Germany, Sweden, and other countries. Nevertheless, this small eastern-European nation still boasts a rich cultural heritage.

2. The Estonians are especially proud of their historic <u>capital city</u>. The walls and gates of old Tallinn date back to the 13th century.

3. A favorite activity of Estonians is <u>singing in groups</u>. They are very fond of giving choral concerts.

4. Every year, an all-Estonian song <u>festival</u> is held. This event is a century-old tradition much loved by everyone.

5. On the square in the center of old Tallinn stands the <u>old city hall</u>. This beautiful medieval building is used now for concerts and special events.

6. Tartu, a smaller city to the southeast of Tallinn, is the home of Estonia's oldest and largest <u>educational institution</u>. Tartu University is the only university in the world where Estonian is the language of instruction.

7. Both Tallinn and Tartu were originally built to be <u>fortresses</u>. The two strongholds were built on hills with good views of the surrounding countryside.

8. Many Estonians have country <u>homes</u> on the nearby island of Saaremaa in the Baltic Sea. They visit their simple cottages often and plant large gardens there.

9. A controversial <u>organization</u> was recently recognized by the government. Now the Society of Estonian Nudists can meet legally in their clubs—without clothes.

10. Estonians love a good cup of <u>coffee</u>. In the center of Tallinn, there are many small shops where people can enjoy their favorite beverage.

The order of synonyms

Sometimes a writer will use several synonyms to refer to the same thing. These synonyms usually follow a pattern of specific to general.

Example: In the movie, *Jurassic Park,* viewers can see a tyrannosaurus rex, velociraptors, a triceratops, and a brachiosaurus. Scientists in the film found a way to bring these long-dead <u>dinosaurs</u> to life. The <u>creatures</u> are shown with great realism. It is easy to understand why some movie-goers (especially children) were very frightened by the movie.

What does <u>dinosaurs</u> refer to?

What does <u>creatures</u> refer to?

These synonyms refer to the same thing. The synonyms were used in order, from specific to general:

Most specific: tyrannosaurus rex, velociraptors, triceratops, brachiosaurus
More general: dinosaurs
Most general: creatures

exercise 12

 Write each of these groups of words in order, from specific to general. Work with another student.

1. forests, oaks, trees, maples,

2. university, biology class, medical school, physiology department

3. State Street Bank, financial institution, loan department, bank

4. office equipment, personal computers, modern technology, disks

5. coins, currency, money, exchange

6. Hungarian, languages, Finnish, Estonian, Finno-Ugric language family

7. Haiti, Caribbean, western hemisphere, Port-au-Prince

8. Sistine Chapel, Italian Renaissance, Michelangelo, history of western art

9. baseball, skiing, sports, football, outdoor activities

10. Big Mac with fries, meal, lunch

exercise 13

 In each of these paragraphs, underline the synonyms and their referent. Write "R" above the referent. After you finish, compare your work with another student.

R

Example: The hard-working student reread <u>page 9</u>, as the teacher had suggested. The <u>page</u> was very difficult for her. In fact, the whole <u>chapter</u> was almost impossible to understand. She took a break, sighed, and went back to her <u>book</u>. She wished that the teacher would assign easier <u>reading materials</u>.

1. Lassie was a famous actor in the movies and on TV. Stories about this brown and white collie were first written in books. Millions of children have learned to love the beautiful dog. She may have been an animal, but to her fans, she was as smart as any living creature.

2. Mt. McKinley is one of the world's most beautiful sights. Many people believe that if you want to climb a real mountain, this is the one! Its summit is the tallest in North America, rising 6,197.6 meters above sea level. The snow-capped peak was first climbed in 1913.

3. Jackie went canoeing on the Saco River in Maine last weekend. Although she had never paddled such a boat before, she learned very fast. When the craft went through some rough, rocky places in the river, she kept it afloat. After an hour, Jackie brought the vessel safely to shore, proud of her new-found talent.

4. Steve has been playing the oboe for many years. He first started to learn to play this woodwind instrument when he was in college. Now he performs in the woodwind section of the Denver Symphony Orchestra. He is proud to be a part of such a great musical organization.

5. Many people enjoy the paintings of Rembrandt. Masterpieces by this Dutchman are found in many of the world's museums. Some of the master's best works can be seen in New York's famous Metropolitan Museum. There, museum visitors can fully appreciate the work of this 17th century genius.

   (There are two referents in this paragraph! Can you find them?)

Summary words

A summary word (or phrase) names a general idea that has many examples or parts. For example, in the paragraph below, what are the referents for the summary word, <u>process</u>?

> One morning, Ayako decided to make some egg salad. First, she boiled the water. Then she added a drop of vinegar and six eggs. She boiled them for ten minutes. After that, she placed the eggs in some cold water for half an hour to cool them. Then she peeled the eggs and chopped them. Finally, she added some mayonnaise and chopped celery and the salad was ready. The whole process had taken about an hour.

<u>Process</u> refers to each step Ayako took in <u>making egg salad</u>.

exercise 14

➤ *The words in each list are members of the same group or parts of the same process. Write the summary word (or phrase) for each list.*

1. _____

   baseball
   basketball
   football
   swimming
   tennis

2. _____

   Mars
   Uranus
   Jupiter
   Saturn
   Mercury

3. _____

   malaria
   tuberculosis
   scarlet fever
   diphtheria
   measles

4. _____

   television set
   VCR
   cellular phone
   personal computer
   phone answering machine

5. _____

   get a shovel
   dig a hole in the ground
   put lots of water in the hole
   unwrap the roots of the tree
   place the roots in the hole
   be sure the tree is straight
   cover the roots with lots of soil
   stamp down the soil
   add more water

6. _____

    put a slice of bread on a plate
    get a knife
    open a jar of peanut butter
    put a small amount of peanut butter on the bread
    spread it around
    open a jar of jelly
    spread a small amount of jelly over the peanut butter
    cover with another slice of bread

7. _____

    Every body continues in a state of rest or of motion at a constant speed in a straight line unless it is disturbed by a force acting on it.

    A force is required to accelerate a body. The strength of the force is directly proportional to the mass of the body.

    To every action there is an equal and opposite reaction. The action is on one body, the reaction on another.

8. _____   9. _____

    cathedral   verb
    church   noun
    temple   adjective
    mosque   pronoun
    chapel   adverb

10. _____

    put your mask around your neck
    hold your flippers in one hand
    walk into the surf until the water is about two feet deep
    sit down, facing the shore
    put your flippers on your feet
    stand up and turn around to face the sea
    place the breathing tube in your mouth
    adjust your mask
    start swimming
    be sure to keep the end of the air tube above the surface of the water

Referents in a longer essay

exercise 15

➤ *In this exercise, you will reread the passage "Poles Apart," on page 47. Read the essay all the way to the end. Go back to the beginning and number the sentences. Then fill in the table below. Write the referent for each word. Check your work with another student.*

Sentence	Word or Words	Referents
3	It	
3	that	
6	this difference	
8	it	
12	both poles	
16	It	
17	this climatic difference	
17	two regions	
23	These animals	
26	the area	
31	this great volume of ice	
32	this	

exercise 16

Read this essay all the way to the end. Then fill in the table below. Write the referent for each word. Check your work with another student.

The Effects of Dumping Hazardous Wastes
by Elizabeth A. Mikulecky

(1) In recent years, concern about the environment has been growing. (2) The public has become aware of many common, dangerous dumping practices. (3) These practices, some of which have been going on for years, have increased as the population has grown. (4) Recent publicity has drawn public attention to one form of environmental pollution—the dumping of hazardous chemical wastes.

(5) These wastes include heavy metals (such as mercury) and other by-products of technology. (6) Such chemicals cause cancer, brain damage, and high infant mortality rates.

(7) Dumping of the wastes is difficult to supervise. (8) And, in fact, even careful dumping has resulted in the destruction of whole areas.

(9) When wastes are first put into a dump, they are usually sealed in large metal drums. (10) As time passes, the metal rusts, and the waste materials begin to leak out into the surrounding soil. (11) This has two effects on the environment. (12) First, the local soil is often permanently destroyed and it must be removed. (13) It becomes additional hazardous waste to be stored somewhere else. (14) Second, the chemical waste can sink lower and lower into the soil and reach the water tables deep in the earth's surface. (15) The latter effect produces pollution of the water sources for many miles around. (16) Sometimes the wastes spread into a river bed. (17) From there, they are likely to be carried to one of the oceans, spreading the pollution around the world. (USED BY PERMISSION)

Sentence	Word or Words	Referents
3	these	
3	some of which	
5	these	
6	such chemicals	
9	they	
11	this	
12	it	
13	it	
15	the latter	
17	there	
17	they	

Topics

What is a topic?

When you read for the meaning, you should begin by looking for the *topic*. This helps you connect what you read to what you already know. In order to find the topic, ask yourself:

"What is this about? What is the general idea?"

Example a:

In the group of words below, one of the words is the topic for all the other words. Circle the topic.

Elephants   Zebras   African animals   Lions   Tigers

The topic is *African animals*. All of the other words are examples of this topic.

Example b:

In the group of words below, one of the words is the topic for all the other words. Circle the topic.

wheels   tires   brakes   steering wheel   seats   doors   car

The topic is *car*. All of the other words are parts of a car.

In these exercises, you should work with another student. By discussing your work, you will learn more from the exercises and you may change the way you think about reading.

exercise 1

➤ ***In each group of words, circle the word which is the best topic for all the other words. Work with another student. Work as fast as you can. Time limit: two minutes. The Answer Key is on page 278.***

1. flippers   face mask   wet suit   surf board
   water skis   goggles   water sports   air tank

2. referees   scoreboard   basketball game
   clock   fans   baskets   players   coaches

3. air bags   seat belts   stereo speakers   car equipment
   anti-lock brakes   spare tire   windshield wipers

4. whales   sharks   dolphins   barracudas
   sea creatures   eels   octopus   skates

5. string quartet   double bass   viola   violin   cello

6. tulips   daffodils   flowers   hyacinths   crocuses

7. pistachios   cashews   nuts   almonds   pecans   filberts

8. Maui   Kauai   Hawaiian Islands
   Oahu   Hawaii   Lanai   Molokai

9. Biochemistry   Physiology   Medical Subjects
   Neurology   Anatomy   Kinesiology

10. The Old Man and the Sea   Reading for Pleasure   The Pearl
    The Chocolate War   The Incredible Journey   Night

exercise 2

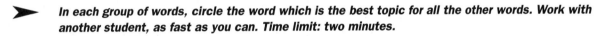

➤ *In each group of words, circle the word which is the best topic for all the other words. Work with another student, as fast as you can. Time limit: two minutes.*

1. encyclopedia   index   dictionary   reference book
   atlas   bibliography   telephone directory

2. Hausa   Yoruba   African languages   Somali
   Amharic   Swazi   Sotho   Wolof

3. Chicago   Cleveland   Chicopee   Carlsbad
   Cities   Cranston   Chippewa   Clinton

4. tent   water bottle   camping   sleeping bag
   mosquito repellent   matches   lantern

5. run   scamper   walk   move   stroll   amble   skip

6. aspirin   tetracycline   valium   quinine
   penicillin   medicine   erythromycin   ibuprophen

7. loam   fertilizer   rake   shovel   seeds
   garden   hose   sprinkler   limestone   mulch

8. Paris   Versailles   Toulouse   France   Lyon   Bordeaux

9. fax machine   typewriter   word processor

    office   mobile telephone   photocopying machine

10. table   diners   appetizers   chair   waiter

    entrees   soups   restaurant   desserts

Stating the topic

exercise 3

➤ *In this exercise, the topic is* not *included in each group of words. Write the topic above the words. Work with another student. Time limit: three minutes.*

1. Topic:

    Clinton   Ford   Nixon   Carter   Reagan   Johnson

2. Topic:

    frame   strings   hammers   keys   cover   pins   pedals   legs   front

3. Topic:

    dulcimer   zither   guitar   banjo   ukulele

4. Topic:

    modem   monitor   keyboard   disk drive   floppy

5. Topic:

    writer   producer   director   actors   camera crew

6. Topic:

    Henry   Elizabeth   George   Victoria   Edward

7. Topic:

    manager   produce buyer   stock clerk   cashier   butcher   bagger   cleaner

8. Topic:

    German   Italian   Basque   Flemish   Dutch   Spanish

9. Topic:

    pineapple   kiwi   papaya   mango   guava

10. Topic:

    Copernicus   Brahe   Kepler   Galileo   Newton

exercise 4 _____

➤ **In this exercise, the topic is not included in each group of words. Write the topic above the words. Work with another student. Time limit: three minutes.**

1. Topic:

   mercury   tin   aluminum   copper   iron   chromium

2. Topic:

   mountains   plateaus   plains   hills   cliffs   valleys

3. Topic:

   hull   sail   mast   keel   tiller   rudder   bow   stern   boom

4. Topic:

   saw   drill   plane   chisel   clamp   hammer   screwdriver

5. Topic:

   cotton   polyester   wool   silk   linen   rayon

6. Topic:

   hair dryer   microwave oven   egg beater   iron   blender   toaster

7. Topic:

   McKinley   Aconsagua   Everest   Elbrus   Kilimanjaro

8. Topic:

   fuel pump   carburetor   cylinders   valves   pistons

9. Topic:

   North America   South America   Europe   Africa   Asia

10. Topic:

    jazz   rock and roll   folk   religious   classical   reggae   heavy metal

exercise 5

➤ *In each group of words, the topic is not included. Write a topic for each group of words. Then think of one more item which fits your topic. Write it on the lines. Work with another student. Time limit: three minutes.*

1. Topic:

   Mercury   Venus   Saturn   Jupiter   Mars   Neptune _____

2. Topic:

   butter   milk   cream   yogurt   cheese _____

3. Topic:

   planets   meteors   meteorites   asteroids _____

4. Topic:

   snowy   humid   rainy   stormy   breezy _____

5. Topic:

   Quebec   Toronto   Vancouver   Halifax _____

6. Topic:

   chestnut   maple   willow   cherry   birch _____

7. Topic:

   circle   oval   pyramid   cube   square _____

8. Topic:

   slippers   sandals   galoshes   pumps   sneakers _____

9. Topic:

   Picasso   Gauguin   Monet   Pissaro _____

10. Topic:

    steam   gasoline   oil   wind   water _____

Working with the topic

exercise 6

➤ *In this exercise, the topics are given. Write a list of things that fit the topic.*

Topic 1: Reading materials

_____

_____

_____

_____

Topic 2: Money in different countries

_____

_____

_____

_____

Topic 3: Kinds of weather

_____

_____

_____

_____

Topic 4: Public Holidays

_____

_____

_____

_____

Topic 5: Major Corporations

_____

_____

_____

_____

➤ *Compare your lists with another student. Are they the same? Why or why not?*

exercise 7

In this exercise you will learn to refine your topic so that it is neither too general nor too specific.

Example: What is the best topic for this group of words?

Agean   Black   Baltic   North   Adriatic

a. bodies of water   b. Italian seas   c. European seas

If you said *c,* European seas, you were correct. Choice *a,* "bodies of water" is too general. It includes other categories of words (rivers, lakes, etc.), which are not on the list. Choice *b, "* Italian seas" is too specific. Some of the words on the list do not fit in that category (Black, Baltic, North).

➤ *Choose the best topic for each list from the possible topics below. More than one of the topics may be possible for some lists. But one topic fits best because it is neither too general nor too specific. Work with another student, as fast as you can. Time limit: three minutes.*

1. _____

   Mississippi
   Chicago
   Rio Grande
   Missouri
   Hudson

2. _____

   Beethoven
   Mozart
   Chopin
   Stravinsky
   Debussy

3. _____

   Elton John
   The Beatles
   Fleetwood Mac
   Talking Heads
   Genesis

4. _____

   Ford
   Chevrolet
   Jeep
   Cadillac
   Chrysler

5. _____

   Mercedes
   Honda
   BMW
   Toyota
   Fiat

6. _____

   Poland
   Hungary
   Bulgaria
   Rumania
   Lithuania

7. _____

   England
   Ireland
   Scotland
   Wales
   Northern Ireland

8. _____

   sedan
   convertible
   station wagon
   van
   coupe

Choices: cars, American cars, international cars, countries, Eastern European countries, types of cars, musicians, composers, rock musicians, older rock groups, rivers, American rivers, German cars, European countries, British Isles, Great Britain.

exercise 8

➤ **In this exercise,** begin by working alone. **Write the topic for each group of words. Make sure your topic is neither too general nor too specific. Time limit: three minutes.**

1. Topic:

   glass   cup   goblet   mug   bottle   can   snifter

2. Topic:

   beautiful   gorgeous   pretty   cute   attractive   lovely

3. Topic:

   cathedral   church   temple   mosque   chapel

4. Topic:

   malaria   tuberculosis   scarlet fever   diphtheria   measles

5. Topic:

   baseball   football   tennis   basketball   squash

6. Topic:

   editorials   news stories   columns   photographs
   business reports   weather report

7. Topic:

   Borneo   Kyushu   Sicily   Iceland   Hokkaido   Victoria

8. Topic:

   tongue   sole   laces   heel   shank   toe   lining

9. Topic:

   Aleutians   Alps   Urals   Cascades   Andes

10. Topic:

    Islam   Buddhism   Catholicism   Judaism   Taoism

➤ **Now compare your work with another student. Do you agree on every topic? If not, try to convince your partner that your topic fits best.**

Go back to Exercises 3 and 4 on pages 70 and 71. Working with another student, compare the topics that you wrote. Are some of them too general or too specific? Change them, if necessary, to improve them. Now compare your work with another pair of students.

exercise 9

➤ **The words in each group can be divided into two topics. Name the two topics. Remember to write topics which are not too general or too specific. Work with another student. Time limit: four minutes.**

1. Topic a: _____ Topic b: _____

   sugar   fingernails   hair   honey

   molasses   toe nails   maple syrup   skin

2. Topic a: _____ Topic b: _____

   lettuce   turnips   peas   radishes

   spinach   beans   potatoes   carrots

3. Topic a: _____ Topic b: _____

   wheels   St. Bernard   brakes   handle bars   poodle

   seat   dachshund   cocker Spaniel   collie   frame

4. Topic a: _____ Topic b: _____

   apricot   butter   margarine   pear

   peach   plum   olive oil   apple   peanut oil

5. Topic a: _____ Topic b: _____

   ribs   stomach   vertebrae   clavicle   lungs

   liver   heart   sternum   shoulder blades   kidneys

exercise 10

➤ **Which term does not belong in the list? Working with another student, think of a topic for each group of words. Note that one of the words in each group must be crossed out because it does not fit in the topic. Time limit: four minutes.**

Example:

Topic: Animated films from Disney Studios

Beauty and the Beast   *Aladdin*   *Fantasia*   *The Lion King*

The Sound of Music   *Snow White*   *The Little Mermaid*

Item to cross out: *Sound of Music* (not an animated film)

1. Topic:

   Shakespeare   Keats   Shelley   Frost

   Chaucer   Wordsworth   Blake

   Item to cross out:

2. Topic:

boring   exciting   swimming   interesting

challenging   surprising   frightening   entertaining

Item to cross out:

3. Topic:

twist   waltz   foxtrot   samba   dogtrot

swing   rhumba   tango   lambada

Item to cross out:

4. Topic:

cows   sheep   pigs   mice   goats

geese   ducks   chickens   horses

Item to cross out:

5. Topic:

actor   plumber   chef   pilot   mechanic

nurse   physicist   psychologist   professor

Item to cross out:

6. Topic:

baritone   bass   alto   soprano

mezzo-soprano   tenor   piano

Item to cross out:

7. Topic:

pine   maple   oak   elm   hickory   willow   birch

Item to cross out:

8. Topic:

air mattress   suntan lotion   ball   towel

sunglasses   bathing suit   gloves   radio

Item to cross out:

9. Topic:

curtains   blinds   shutters   screens   drapes   shades

Item to cross out:

10. Topic:

hut   palace   apartment   teepee   kitchen

ranch   mansion   cottage

Item to cross out:

➤ *Now compare your work with another pair of students.*

Topics of Paragraphs

What is a paragraph?

➤ Here are two groups of sentences that look like paragraphs. Read both of them carefully. Are they both paragraphs?

Example a:

In the Trobriand Islands, people do not celebrate birthdays. When a boy is about 14 or 15, he moves out of his parents' house. Each canoe takes about 18 months to make. Boys and girls may live together for periods of days, weeks, or months. Most islanders have no idea when they were born or how old they are. That way, they have a chance to find out if they are the right people for each other. When it is finally finished, it is named and special ceremonies are held to give it magic powers. This is also about the age that he begins to work on his own garden.

Is this a paragraph?

Example b:

In the Trobriand Islands, the yam is both an important food plant and an important part of the culture. Every village has a "yam house" with a giant four-foot yam hanging from the ceiling. It represents wealth and well-being for the village, life and strength for the people. Villagers take great pride in their gardens, especially their yam plants. The yam harvest is one of the high points of the year and also the focus for many traditions. For example, the harvest is always carried out by women. When they are bringing the yams in from the garden all together, no man is supposed to meet them. Any man they meet will be chased, attacked, and treated as a fool.

Is this a paragraph?

What is the difference between Example a and Example b?

A *paragraph* is a group of sentences that are all about the same thing. That is, they all have the same *topic*. Example a is not a paragraph because the sentences are about several aspects of life in the Trobriand Islands. Together, the sentences make no sense.

Example b is a paragraph because all the sentences are about the same aspect of life (yams) in the Trobriand Islands.

exercise 1

> *Some of these groups of sentences are paragraphs and some are not. Read them carefully and answer the questions. The Answer Key on on page 279.*

Paragraph 1

Iceland is not a place for the ordinary tourist. The landscape, first of all, is bare and strange—though many consider it beautiful, too. Then, too, the far northern climate is not ideal for tourism. The winter weather is extremely severe and the summers are short and cool, with constant strong winds. The remote location also means that many products have to be imported and so they are expensive. However, the few tourists who do put up with these difficulties are warmly welcomed by the Icelanders.

Is this a paragraph?

If yes, what is the topic?

Paragraph 2

For fewer tourists, lower prices, and more beautiful scenery, head for the Sagres Peninsula. The regional museum has a rich collection of costumes, weapons, and handicrafts. Buses will get you to most places, but for long trips, trains are cheaper and more comfortable. The Portuguese economy has expanded very rapidly in recent years, but it still has many problems. In the 15th century, Lisbon was a worldwide center of political power, religion, and culture.

Is this a paragraph?

If yes, what is the topic?

Paragraph 3

The two peoples of Belgium—the Flemish and the Walloons—are divided by language, culture, and economics. Hotels in Brussels are expensive, so most young travelers stay in youth hostels or student hotels. In Antwerp, the home of Rubens, you can visit the house where he lived and worked. Throughout the centuries, Belgium has been the scene of many terrible battles between world powers. In many parts of the world, the Belgians are best known for their chocolate and their beer. Ships to England leave either from Oostende or from Zeebrugge.

Is this a paragraph?

If yes, what is the topic?

Paragraph 4

To an outsider, Istanbul may at first seem like a Western city. The Western dress, the many new buildings, the traffic problems all make the city seem very modern. But there is another side to this great city—its rich past as the capital of the Ottoman Empire. In the narrow back streets, the bazaars, and the mosques, this past seems very near and real. And the spectacular mosques are evidence of the city's important role in history of Islam as well.

Is this a paragraph?

If yes, what is the topic?

Recognizing the topic of a paragraph

When you read a paragraph you should always ask yourself, "What is this about?" That question will lead you to the topic of the paragraph.

Example a:

What is this paragraph about?

> People have always been interested in bees. This interest may have begun with the honey bees make. In fact, archaeologists have found evidence that people have been eating honey for many thousands of years. In the more recent past, people were interested in the way bees made honey. They admired the way bees seemed to work so hard. Some languages even developed expressions about people working like bees. In English, for example, we talk about a "busy bee." Now scientists have a new reason to be interested in bees. They have discovered that bees are able to communicate with each other. Research has revealed some surprising facts about this, but there are still many mysteries.

Make a check after the best topic. Write "too specific" or "too general" after the other topics.

a. Expressions about bees in the English language
b. The story of bees
c. People's interest in bees

Explanation: The best topic is c, *people's interest in bees*. It tells best what the paragraph is about. Choice a, *expressions about bees in the English language* is too specific. This idea is only a part of the paragraph. Choice b, *the story of bees* is too general. It includes many possible ideas that are not in the paragraph.

Example b:

What is this paragraph about?

> Communication is also possible among bees through their sense of smell. A group of bees, called a colony, uses smell to protect itself from other bees. This is possible because all the bees in a colony have a common smell. This smell acts like a chemical signal. It warns the group of bees when a bee from a different colony is near. This way, bees from outside cannot enter and disturb a hive (the bee colony's home). If an outsider does try to enter, the bees of that colony will smell it and attack it.

Make a check after the best topic. Write "too specific or "too general" after the other topics.

a. The chemical signals of bees
b. How bees live
c. How bees communicate through smell

Explanation: The best topic is c, *how bees communicate through smell*. Choice a is too specific. Choice b is too general.

exercise 2

➤ **Read each paragraph. Working with another student, decide which topic is the best. Make a check after that topic. Write "too specific" or "too general" after the other topics.**

Elephants

1.   Elephants are the largest land animals in the world. Whales are the largest sea animals. These two huge animals may, in fact, be related. Biologists now believe that the ancestors of elephants once lived in the sea. There is plenty of evidence to support this idea. For example, the shape of an elephant's head is similar to a whale's. Also, elephants are excellent swimmers. Some have chosen to swim for food to islands up to 300 miles from shore. Like the whale, the elephant, too, uses sounds to show anger or for other kinds of communication. Finally, in certain ways, female elephants behave much like female whales. When an elephant or a whale baby is born, a female friend stays nearby to help the mother.

   a. How elephants are good swimmers
   b. The largest animals in the world
   c. How elephants and whales are alike

2.   The elephant's trunk is not just a large nose or upper lip. It's an essential and unique feature that serves many purposes for this animal. For one, it is used to make many kinds of sounds. With its trunk, the elephant can communicate anger, fear, or happiness. The trunk is also used as if it were a kind of hand. At the end of the trunk are two muscles shaped like fingers. These muscles can pick up food and water and carry them to the elephant's mouth. Elephants use their trunks to take dust baths, too, throwing the dust over their backs. If an elephant's trunk is seriously injured, the elephant may die. Without its trunk, it has great difficulty getting enough to eat.

   a. The elephant's trunk
   b. The elephant's body
   c. The elephant's dust baths

3.   The intelligence of the elephant is widely known. We say, "the elephant never forgets," in honor of its excellent memory. Elephants are also surprisingly good at solving problems. An Indian farmer who kept elephants discovered this fact, to his misfortune. He had noticed that his elephants were eating his bananas at night. No fence could keep out the elephants, of course, so he decided to tie bells on them. Then he would hear them when they came to eat the bananas and he could chase them away. A few mornings later, however, the bananas were all gone, though he had heard nothing at night. When he checked the elephants he found that they had played a trick on him. They had filled the bells with mud so they would not make any noise!

   a. Facts about elephants
   b. How elephants get bananas
   c. The intelligence of elephants

exercise 3

➤ *Read each paragraph. Working with another student, decide which topic is the best. Make a check after that topic. Write "too specific" or "too general" after the other topics.*

The Construction of Houses

1.　　People usually build their houses out of the materials that are easily available to them. In some areas, most people build their homes out of wood. This is true in parts of North America and in Scandinavia. These areas have large forests, so wood is easy to get and inexpensive. In many other areas of Europe, there are few forests left. Stone and brick are cheaper, so most people build their houses of these materials. In tropical regions, houses are sometimes made from plants that grow there. For example, in parts of Africa or Asia, houses may be made out of bamboo. Finally, in the very coldest areas near the Arctic, people make their homes out of blocks of ice.

　　a. Materials used for houses
　　b. The wooden houses of Scandinavia
　　c. Houses around the world

2.　　Houses in hot countries have many features that are different from houses in cold countries. Houses in hot countries usually have thick walls and small windows to keep out the heat. In colder climates and darker regions, however, people do not have to worry about too much sun and heat. The houses therefore have larger windows to let in the sunlight. Another difference is that houses in hot climates usually have an outdoor living area—a terrace, courtyard, or porch. In colder climates, of course, people spend less time outdoors, so houses often do not have such areas.

　　a. The architecture of houses
　　b. Houses in hot and cold countries
　　c. Houses with small windows

3.　　One of the most famous houses in the United States is Monticello. It was the home of Thomas Jefferson, the third President of the United States. Located on a hill near Charlottesville, Virginia, it has a beautiful view of the surrounding countryside. The house is famous, first of all, because it belonged to a President. It is also a fine example of early 19th century American architecture. Jefferson designed it himself in a style he had admired in Italy. Many American buildings of that time, in fact, imitated European styles. But while most were just imitations, his Monticello is lovely in itself. Furthermore, the design combines a graceful style with a typical American concern for comfort and function.

　　a. The view from Monticello
　　b. American architecture
　　c. Reasons for Monticello's fame

Stating the topic of a paragraph

Example:

In most industrialized countries, family patterns have changed in recent years. Families used to be large, and most mothers stayed home to take care of the children. They were usually entirely responsible for all the housework, too. Fathers did not often see the children, except to play with them on the weekends. Now that families are smaller and many women are working, this has changed somewhat. Fathers often help with the housework. More importantly, they can be much more involved in the lives of their children. They may feed and dress their children and take them to school in the mornings.

What is this paragraph about? Think carefully and then write the topic. It should not be too specific or too general.

Topic:

Explanation: A good topic for this paragraph would be *"how family patterns have changed."* If you wrote something similar, that is okay, too. For example, *"recent changes in family patterns"* is also a good answer. *"Families"* is too general. *"How fathers care for their children"* is too specific.

exercise 4

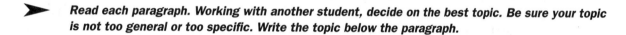

➤ **Read each paragraph. Working with another student, decide on the best topic. Be sure your topic is not too general or too specific. Write the topic below the paragraph.**

The Importance of Automobile Tires

1. If you ever get a blow-out while you are driving, you should know what to do. A blow-out is a sudden flat tire. It can be a very frightening experience, especially if you are traveling at high speed. If your car gets a blow-out, the first thing to do is to hold very tightly to the steering wheel. You can easily lose control of the car if you do not have a good hold on the steering wheel. The next step is to get off the road. You must not try to stop or turn too quickly, however. After you check the traffic, you should move over to the side of the road and slow down gradually. Then you should turn on your flashing lights so other cars will see you.

    Topic:

2. Most automobile owners check the gas and oil in their cars regularly. However, they may forget to check something else that is just as important: the tires. About 28% of automobiles in the United States have tires that are in poor condition. Some are too worn and others have too much or too little air. It is a good idea to check the amount of air in your tires every week. You should also give a quick look at your tires every time you get into your car. This way, you may avoid a flat tire or a blow-out.

    Topic:

3.   Tires are one part of the car that need a lot of attention. A quick check before you drive the car may not be enough. You should also bring your car regularly for some special measures. First, the mechanic should rotate the tires after a certain number of miles. This means removing the tires and placing them in different positions. The rear tires are usually placed in the front. The front tires are placed on opposite sides in the rear. Changing the tires like this will prevent them from becoming too worn on one side. For this same reason, the mechanic should also balance the wheels. In balancing the wheels, each wheel is taken off and adjusted to make sure it goes around evenly.

Topic:

exercise 5

 Read each paragraph. Working with another student, decide what would be the best topic. Write the topic below the paragraph.

Fatherhood in the '90s

1.   In the United States, the number of single fathers doubled between 1983 and 1993. A single father has the complete responsibility for his child or children. He may be the only parent because the mother has died. Or, more often, he may be given the full responsibility for the children by the judge in court. This may happen when there is a divorce or when unmarried parents disagree. In the past, judges almost always decided that children should stay with their mother. Now, however, it is more common for judges to decide in favor of the father. That is, a judge may decide that the mother is not able to take proper care of the children. This is the main reason why there has been such a large increase in the number of single fathers.

Topic:

2.   As more women go to work outside the home, men are doing more of the house-work and the shopping. This fact has led advertising companies to change some of their methods. Traditionally, television advertisements for household products were aimed at women and they featured women. Now some companies that sell these prod-ucts feature men in their advertisements. For example, one supermarket company has produced an advertisement showing a father shopping with his little boy. However, this is no ordinary father. The actor in this advertisement is known for his roles in films of violence. The company wants to make sure that shopping fathers don't feel any less "manly" in their new role.

Topic:

3.   Men who drink a lot of alcohol may have a higher chance of having children with physical or mental problems. Doctors have long been aware that women alcoholics may give birth to defective babies. However, scientists have recently discovered that alcoholism in men may be responsible for birth defects too. Large quantities of alcohol may affect the quality of the father's genes. This genetic change may cause a child to be born defective in some way. Scientists are not sure how this happens. But the statis-tics of the study seem to leave little doubt that it can happen.

Topic:

exercise 6

➤ **Each of these paragraphs has an extra sentence that does not belong. Read the paragraphs. Working with another student, decide on the best topic for each. Write the topic below the paragraph. Find the sentence that does not belong and cross it out.**

Basketball in the United States

1. The Los Angeles Lakers is a championship basketball team. Their home court is the Forum, a modern stadium near Hollywood, California. Among their fans are many big names in the entertainment industry, including Jack Nicholson and Johnny Carson. Most basketball teams are based in large cities. Whenever the Lakers play home games, they can be sure of a few movie stars to cheer for them. Laker fans have a lot to cheer about: their team has won four championships in recent years.

    Topic:

2. The Boston Celtics is another championship basketball team. They have won first place among American basketball teams sixteen times. Their home court for many years was the Boston Garden, an old stadium near the waterfront, but they have recently moved to a brand-new arena. Although few famous movie stars attend their games, the Celtics have many fans in Boston. Boston fans also support a baseball team, an ice hockey team, and a football team. On evenings when the Celtics are playing an important game, the theaters and clubs are half empty. All the fans are either at the game or at home watching it on television.

    Topic:

3. Basketball, like other sports, is big business in the United States. The teams are owned by people who view them as a financial investment. Each owner tries to make his team as profitable as possible. Winning is important because it will bring attention to the team. Then many companies will want to advertise their products on television during basketball games. Television advertising is now aimed at specific markets, such as ethnic groups or the elderly. When a team is profitable, the players profit as well. Some basketball players are paid more than a million dollars a year.

    Topic:

exercise 7

➤ **Each of these paragraphs has an extra sentence that does not belong. Read the paragraphs, Working with another student, decide on the best topic for each. Write the topic below the paragraph. Find the sentence that does not belong and cross it out.**

Dangers to Small Children

1. Everybody knows that cigarette smoking is harmful to one's health. However, many parents who are smokers may not be aware that it is also bad for their children. Cigarette smoke can have harmful effects not just on the smoker, but also on people who live with the smoker. Children, naturally, are more easily affected than adults. In fact, studies have shown that children of smokers get sick more often than children of

non-smokers. Many people smoke in order to feel more relaxed in social situations. One experiment, for example, studied a very common problem among small children: earaches. The statistics clearly proved that children of smokers got earaches more often than children of non-smokers. Their earaches were also more difficult to cure and tended to last longer.

Topic:

2.   In some poorer countries, over twenty percent of the children die in their first year of life. One reason for this is the lack of medical care and medicines. Many children die from diseases that could easily be prevented with the right medicines or the right care. Another cause of death among children is the food. It often is not clean or fresh and can make children very sick. Milk is a very important source of vitamins and minerals. Getting enough food is another problem. When children are weak from lack of food, they die more easily from diseases. And finally, dirty water also kills many children every year. Because of water shortages, people often are forced to drink water from dirty rivers or lakes. This water may carry serious diseases, or it may contain harmful chemicals from pollution.

Topic:

3.   Most homes are full of dangers for small children. Many of these dangers are obvious. Stairs, for example, can be dangerous, and so can the sharp corners of a table. Another well-known danger is fire and parents usually are careful about matches and candles. But other dangers may be less obvious to a parent. Many children die from poisoning in their homes. In fact, all kinds of things in the house could be poison to a child. Medicine, for example, may not be harmful for an adult, but may make a child seriously ill. The same is true of alcohol and cigarettes. Finally, soaps and chemicals used for cleaning are often extremely poisonous. Before the days of detergents, people used to make soap from animal fat. All these things should be kept far out of the reach of young children.

Topic:

Finding the topic sentence

Many paragraphs include a topic sentence that tells the topic of the paragraph. Read this paragraph and underline the topic.

The first guitarist to become known worldwide was Andres Segovia, born in 1893 in Spain. Before the 20th century, the guitar was not taken very seriously as a classical instrument. Most people thought that the guitar was suitable only for popular music or folk music. Few classical composers wrote music for the guitar, and it was never included in classical concerts. But Segovia changed all this. He believed in the guitar as a classical instrument, and he was a great musician. He used his genius to prove that the guitar could produce beautiful classical music.

The topic is stated in the topic sentence: *The first guitarist to become known worldwide was Andres Segovia, born in 1893 in Spain.* The other sentences in the paragraph explain and give details about the topic.

exercise 8

➤ *Each of the paragraphs below is missing the topic sentence. The missing sentences are all listed at the end of the exercise (with an extra sentence). Read the paragraphs. Working with another student, choose the sentence that fits each paragraph best. Put the letter for the sentence in the empty space.*

Facts about Alaska

1. _____.

   The Russians were glad to get rid of this large piece of land so far from Moscow. Many Americans, however, were not happy about buying it. The sale was arranged by William Henry Seward, the American Secretary of State. When people talked about Alaska, they called it "Seward's Folly" or "Seward's Icebox." The price for Alaska was $7,200,000—or about two cents per acre. Though this was a bargain, many thought it was money thrown away. What would America ever do with such a cold land?

2. Do you know what "white out" means, or "ice fog"? These are terms that many Alaskans know well, though other Americans may not._____
   _____. "White out," for example, happens when a very strong, cold wind blows the snow on the ground. The snow fills the air so that you lose all sense of direction. "Ice fog" occurs on very cold (–40C or F) days. When the air is this cold, it cannot absorb any moisture, so the water in the air becomes a kind of frozen fog. This fog is very dangerous to drivers or aircraft.

3. The Yukon River begins in Canada's Yukon Territory. Many other rivers flow into it as it runs from East to West across central Alaska. Some of the rivers are fed by melting glaciers. This gives the Yukon its strange whitish, or milky color. The river generally freezes in October and melts again in May. Large ice dams sometimes form and cause large-scale flooding. As the Yukon nears the Bering Sea, it breaks into many smaller rivers, forming a delta. This fact makes it impossible for large ships to travel up the river. _____.

4. The Alaskan Malamute was originally developed by the Eskimos as a sled dog.

   _____.

   It is a strong dog, related to and somewhat resembling a wolf. A thick coat of fur protects it even in the coldest weather. The Eskimos use these dogs to pull sleds for them across the Arctic snow and ice. They are intelligent dogs and quickly learn to obey the signals of the sled driver. With their strength and loyalty, they have been known to save people's lives in the Arctic. In spite of their wolf ancestry, they are also extremely gentle and friendly. Their protective nature makes them good companions for children.

Missing topic sentences:

a. That is because Alaska has very special weather that requires special expressions.

b. These days it is popular both as a sled dog and as a family pet.

c. In 1868, the United States bought Alaska from Russia.

d. The Alaskan gold rush in the 1890s nearly doubled the population of the area.

e. With a total length of 1,979 miles, the Yukon River is the fourth longest on the continent.

exercise 9

> *Read each paragraph and underline the topic sentence.* **Remember, the topic sentence is not always the first sentence in the paragraph.** *Compare your choices with another student. If your answers differ, decide whose is best and correct your work if necessary.*

Effects of Weather and Climate

1. Violent storms cause damage and deaths all over the world, but sometimes people make the consequences worse. For example, too many people living in dangerous areas can turn a storm into a disaster. In Bangladesh, the flat river valley often floods. In the past, there were few people in this area and they could escape to higher land. Now, millions of people live there and they cannot escape when there are floods. Sometimes, too, there is more damage than necessary because people do not build homes that are safe or strong enough. This was the case when a terrible storm hit southern Florida. Many people died or lost their homes because the wind blew away poorly-made buildings.

2. When summer brings very hot weather, many people suffer more than they need to. There are a number of ways to make life more comfortable in the heat. First of all, you can try to keep your home as cool as possible. It is best to close all the windows and curtains during the hottest part of the day. Then, when it is cooler in the evening, you can open them up again. It is important also to keep yourself cool by wearing loose, light clothes. Cotton is the best material for clothes in hot weather. And finally, you should try to stay calm and relaxed. You could even try a nap after lunch, like many people who live in hot climates. This way you are more rested and ready to enjoy the cool evening hours.

3. Scientists believe that the earth's climate may be warming up. This trend probably began thousands of years ago. Many areas of the earth used to be covered with ice that has now melted. However, in recent years, the warming trend has speeded up. Scientists think that part of the reason for this may be carbon dioxide pollution from industry and automobiles. The carbon dioxide mixes with other gases. This pollution covers the earth like a blanket and keeps it warmer. Another reason for the warming may be the fact that the earth is losing its forests. Forests are an important part of the earth's system for using up carbon dioxide and keeping the air temperature cool.

Main Ideas

What is a main idea?

The main idea of a paragraph is the author's idea about the topic. It is always a complete sentence that includes both the topic and the idea that the author wishes to express about the topic.

Example a:

Topic: Cats

Possible main ideas about cats:

- Cats are usually very clean animals.
- Cats have very expressive faces.
- Cats are very adaptable animals.

Write three more ideas about cats:

Compare your ideas with those of another student. You probably have some different ideas. In fact, for every topic there are many possible main ideas. The choice of a main idea depends on what the author wants to say about the topic.

Example b:

Choose one of these topics and write a main idea sentence about it.

- My favorite food
- Growing older
- Travel

Compare your main idea sentence with another student who wrote about the same topic.

Why might they be different?

Finding the main idea in the topic sentence

The topic sentence often states the author's main idea about the topic.

exercise 1

➤ *Read each paragraph and underline the topic sentence. Then compare your choice with another student. Decide whose choice is best and correct your work if necessary.*

Modern Trends in Management

1.   The "idea box" is a useful concept in management. It was first introduced in the early 20th century by Kodak in the United States and Michelin in France. The managers of these companies used idea boxes to collect suggestions from employees about improving production. Today the idea box is not used much in the United States or Europe. However, it is used a lot in Japan. Japanese managers have found it to be a very valuable resource. Employees often know more than managers about the details of production. In the long run, their suggestions can make a real difference to the company. Employees who offer useful ideas may receive extra money in their paychecks.

2.   In a recent study, researchers interviewed 1,500 business managers in the United States. They asked all kinds of questions about the managers' habits and opinions regarding their work. The researchers learned that only 33% of the managers worked 40-45 hours. The majority of them (57%) worked from 46-60 hours a week and 6% worked over 60 hours. Only 2% of the managers said they felt satisfied and had enough time to do everything. The rest of the managers felt they did not have enough time for their families or their hobbies. The study showed that American managers are generally not happy with their working schedules.

3.   At present, some managers spend much of their working time at home, especially those who work a lot on computers. They can send their work to the company by fax or by direct computer connections. There are many advantages to working at home, including more flexible hours and better productivity. "Home managers" also save time and money they would have spent on transportation. The disadvantages may be the difficulty in organizing work and the loss of direct contact with colleagues. In the future, many more managers will be able to work at home, thanks to modern technology and telecommunication.

Finding the main idea when it is not in the topic sentence

Sometimes the topic sentence does not completely state the author's idea about the topic.

Example:

> <u>In some industrialized countries, people are retiring from work at an early age.</u> This is especially true in Europe, where many workers retire at age 55. In 1970, about half the men aged 55 continued to work. Now, only about 10-30% of that age group continue to work. The reason for this trend is economic. Some European governments wanted people to retire early so that their jobs could go to younger people. But early retirement has created new economic problems. Governments are having trouble paying the pensions and health costs for all the additional retired people.

Topic: Early retirement

➤ *Underline the topic sentence. Then circle the letter in front of the best statement of the author's main idea.*

a. Early retirement starts at age 55.

b. In some industrialized countries, more people are retiring early.

c. The trend to early retirement is creating economic problems in Europe.

The best choice is *c*. Choice *a* is too specific. Choice *b* does not include an important part of the main idea—the economic problems which are the result of early retirement.

exercise 2

➤ *Read each paragraph to find the topic.*

Consequences of an Aging Population

1.   The average age of the population of many countries is getting older. That means that businesses in those countries must adjust to older customers. In fact, many companies are working to respond to the special needs of the elderly. One example of this is the medical industry. New medicines and technologies are being developed especially for the health problems of older people. Another business that offers services for the elderly is the tourist industry. Many travel agents offer special trips for groups of older people. And, finally, there are many different kinds of products made for the elderly. These include everything from shoes and shampoos to magazines and furniture.

Topic:

Underline the topic sentence. Then circle the letter in front of the best statement of the author's main idea.

a. The medical industry is developing new medicines for the elderly.

b. New products and services are being developed by many companies.

c. Many companies are developing products and services for the increasing elderly population.

2.   In industrialized countries today, many elderly people suffer from depression. The main cause of this is loneliness. In the past, older people usually lived with other members of the family. They usually had some responsibilities around the home. For example, older women could help take care of the children or prepare meals. Older men could help their sons at work or around the house. These days, married children often prefer to live on their own, sometimes far away from their parents. Thus, older people may be cut off from family ties. They may feel cut off from the world around them. Life has changed so much so quickly that older people sometimes feel that they do not belong any more.

Topic:

Underline the topic sentence. Then circle the letter in front of the best statement of the author's main idea.

a. The elderly people in industrialized countries are often depressed because of loneliness.

b. Older people used to live with other family members and helped take care of the children.

c. Some elderly people may feel the world has changed too quickly for them.

Compare your answers with another student and make corrections if necessary.

exercise 3

➤ **Read each paragraph. Then work with another student and decide on the best main idea statement.**

Automobiles: Problems and Solutions

1.   The idea of a small electric car is not new. A number of different car manufacturers already sell such cars. But now a French company, Renault, has designed a very special kind of electric car. By pushing a button, you can make it fold up! The back of the car folds into the car body. These cars were designed mainly for use in cities. They have several advantages over regular cars. Their small size makes them much easier to drive around busy, narrow streets. They are also much easier to park in city parking spaces. Like other electric cars, these autos do not pollute the air. This is an important consideration these days when many cities have serious pollution problems.

   a. Electric cars do not pollute the air.

   b. The new folding electric car has many advantages over regular cars.

   c. Small cars are very convenient in narrow streets.

2.   Many studies have shown that it is better to wear your seat belt when you are traveling in a car. Seat belts greatly reduce the risk of death or injury in an accident. This fact is widely recognized and many governments have passed laws requiring seat belt use. However, many people still do not wear seat belts. Researchers have found several reasons for this. Some people feel uncomfortable with the seat belt. They are afraid of being trapped in the car in an accident. Others do not think that the seat belt can protect them. They believe that people have no power over their fate. Fate will decide whether they will have an accident and whether they will be injured or die. They think that wearing a seat belt or not will make no difference.

   a. In spite of the risks, some people do not wear seat belts.

   b. All new cars must now be equipped with seat belts.

   c. Some people feel uncomfortable wearing seat belts.

3.   The country with the most crowded roads is Italy. In 1992, there were an average of 101.1 vehicles (cars, trucks, and buses) per kilometer of road in Italy. This can be compared with the vehicles-per-kilometer ratios of other European countries. The ratio varies from 35.8 in France to 74.2 in Great Britain. In the United States, the ratio is 30.6. Part of the reason for Italy's higher ratio lies in its geography. Because much of the country is mountainous, there are fewer roads. Thus the traffic is more concentrated on those few roads. This fact has caused some serious problems. Many cities and highways are often blocked by terrible traffic jams. The heavy traffic has also meant a high accident rate for Italy. And finally, all those cars add to Italy's air pollution.

   a. Because of the mountains, there are fewer roads in Italy.

   b. Crowded roads create traffic jams, accidents, and air pollution.

   c. Italy's roads are the most crowded in the world.

Stating the main idea

exercise 4

➤ *The topic is given for each paragraph. Working with another student, write a main idea statement. Remember that it should be a complete sentence. It should cover the whole paragraph and not be too specific or too general.*

Interesting Inventions

1. After several decades, jogging is still a very popular activity in the United States. Many people like to go jogging early in the morning before work or after work in the evening. However, in the winter months especially, it may be dark during those hours. To help these joggers, a sports shoe manufacturer has invented a new kind of jogging shoe. These shoes have little red lights on the back of the heels. The lights are very small and lightweight. They are run by tiny batteries. With these new shoes, the jogger can feel much safer running along the road in the dark. The lights make the jogger much more visible to the drivers of motor vehicles. This may reduce the risk of accidents.

   Topic: A new kind of jogging shoe

   Main Idea:

2. If you have too much noise in your life, an American company has a special product for you! This product is a machine that can eliminate sound waves from the air. Machines like this are already in use in some very noisy factories. Soon there will be models for use in large trucks. Yet another model, the "personal quieting machine," is designed for use in homes or offices. It will be able to eliminate all kinds of unpleasant background noises, including street and airplane traffic. A quieter environment in the home could mean reduced stress and improved mental and physical health. A quieter office could allow greater productivity and job satisfaction.

   Topic: Quieting machines

   Main Idea:

3. Have you ever noticed how much of the potato is wasted when you peel it? When you are peeling just a few potatoes for your dinner, this does not matter, of course. But just imagine what happens when potatoes are peeled in factories. Industrial potato peelers, in fact, waste an average of 15% of the potato. In the largest factories, billions of pounds of potatoes are processed every year. This means a loss of millions of dollars annually. Now, new technology may bring an end to that loss. A special kind of laser potato peeler has been developed to eliminate almost all of the waste. However, this new peeler is not for everyone. Only the largest manufacturers will be able to afford to buy the new machine. Each one costs over a million dollars!

   Topic: A new laser potato peeler

   Main Idea:

exercise 5

> Read each paragraph. Then, working with another student, write the topic and a main idea statement. Remember: it must be a complete sentence!

Panda Bears in China

1.   The giant panda bear is a favorite of children and animal-lovers throughout the world. For many people, it also is symbolic of the sad situation for many other kinds of animals. Though so well known and loved, the panda is slowly dying out. At present, there are only about 1,230 wild pandas left in the world. They all live in China, in the forests of the Sichuan and Shaanxi provinces. Pandas used to be common in other areas. However, as the human population increased and the forests shrank, panda territory gradually disappeared. And so did the pandas. Now the Chinese government has created a number of "Panda reserves" to protect the pandas. Within these reserves, human settlement and tree cutting will be limited.

Topic:

Main Idea:

2.   A newborn panda is a tiny, helpless little creature. It looks like a little pink pig, and its eyes remain closed for three to four weeks. Pandas develop fairly slowly, compared to most animals. The babies are completely dependent on their mothers for a long time. In fact, they don't even begin to walk until they are about five months old. The only food they eat for at least a year is their mother's milk. That doesn't stop them from growing, however. Pandas may weigh over 55 pounds by the time they are a year old. Around that time, the young panda begins to eat bamboo, like its mother. This may not seem like a fattening food, but young panda bears gain weight quickly on this diet. By the time it is a year and a half old, a panda bear may weigh over 100 pounds.

Topic:

Main Idea:

3.   Chinese scientists recently had a chance to study a wild female panda bear with a newborn baby. She was a very loving mother. For 25 days, she never left her baby, not even to find something to eat! She would not let any other panda bears come near. She licked the baby constantly to keep it clean. Any smell might attract natural enemies that would try to eat the little panda. The mother held her baby in her front paws much the way a human does. When it cried, she rocked it back and forth and gave it little comforting pats. The mother continued to care for the young bear for over two years. By that time, the panda no longer needed its mother for food. However, it stayed with her and learned about the ways of the forest. Then, after two and a half years, the mother chased the young bear away. It was time for her to have a new baby, and it was time for the young panda to be independent.

Topic:

Main Idea:

exercise 6

➤ *Read each paragraph. Then, working with another student, write the topic and a statement. Remenber: it must be a complete sentence!*

Surprising Sources of Disease

1. People who work in large office buildings get sick more often than normal. They may have headaches, stomachaches, or sore, red skin. The reason for this lies in the buildings themselves. These large buildings usually have windows that cannot be opened. The same air stays in the building for a long time and becomes unhealthy. It may be full of chemicals that come from the furniture, the rugs, or the photocopy machines. Or it may be full of cigarette smoke. This unhealthy air causes "sick building syndrome," as doctors call this problem. In order to cure the people with this syndrome, it is necessary to treat the building. The answer is simple: more fresh air.

    Topic:

    Main Idea:

2. Did you know that you could get sick from a pet reptile? In the 1960s, little turtles were very popular as pets in the United States. Then doctors discovered that these turtles sometimes were sick with an infection called salmonella. People who touched the turtles could catch this infection and become seriously ill. In 1975, the U.S. government banned these turtles as pets. Now doctors think that people, especially small children, can get the same infection from another kind of pet: the iguana. The iguana is a reptile like a turtle and has recently become a favorite pet in many American homes. The government may have to ban these animals, too. For now, doctors say that people should wash their hands very carefully after touching an iguana.

    Topic:

    Main Idea:

3. Do you like your meat nicely browned, or even a little black on the outside? If you do, you should perhaps change your tastes. Scientists have found that meat cooked this way can cause cancer. One hamburger or one steak will not give you cancer, of course. But you should probably not eat browned meat every day. This is especially true for children. Children who grow up on a regular diet of browned hamburgers have a much higher risk of cancer. This risk can be prevented by cooking meat in another way. Adding soybeans to the hamburger meat also removes the factors that cause cancer.

    Topic:

    Main Idea:

exercise 7

➤ *Read each paragraph. Then, working with another student, write the topic and a main idea statement. Remember: it must be a complete sentence!*

People's Ideas About World Geography

1.   What happens when you ask someone to draw a map of the world? The results can be very interesting. Few people, in fact, have a very accurate idea of what the world looks like. You might expect some mistakes in the positions of the countries. After all, this is a task that requires a certain skill with a pencil and a good memory. But many people do not even know the relative size of the continents. They tend to enlarge them or make them smaller, according to their point of view. For this reason, the home continent is often drawn too large. A Brazilian, for example, tends to enlarge the continent of South America, while a Vietnamese enlarges Asia.

Topic:

Main Idea:

2.   Another common error is the tendency to make Europe too large and Africa too small. People from all parts of the world tend to draw the world this way, including the Africans! There are several factors that may be involved here. One factor may be the influence of old maps made with the "Mercator projection." This technique for drawing maps makes areas nearer the North Pole, including Europe, seem extra large. Other areas in the middle, such as Africa, seem smaller than reality. However, the Mercator maps also enlarge Greenland and Canada, and people usually do not make mistakes about their size. Thus, a better explanation must lie in people's ideas about the relative importance of the continents. The size of Europe tends to be exaggerated because of its importance in people's minds. Similarly, Africa becomes smaller because people feel it is unimportant.

Topic:

Main Idea:

3.   Ignorance about the African continent has led to some enormous errors in map making. One of the errors now seems quite incredible. In the late 18th century, a European explorer reported seeing mountains in southern Mali. From that report, a map maker drew in a long line of mountains. These "Kong Mountains," as he called them, appeared on almost all maps of Africa in the 19th century. They seemed to be an important feature of the continental geography. European politicians and traders made decisions based on their belief in the existence of these mountains. Finally, in the late 1880s, a French explorer proved that there were no mountains in that part of Africa. Only then did the "Kong Mountains" disappear from maps of Africa.

Topic:

Main Idea:

exercise 8

> **Read each paragraph. Then, working with another student, write the topic and a main idea statement. Remember: it must be a complete sentence!**

The Exxon Valdez Oil Spill

1.   On March 24, 1989, an enormous ship called the Exxon Valdez was traveling along the coast of Alaska. It was carrying about 50 million gallons of petroleum from the Alaskan oil fields. In Prince William Sound, the captain ran the ship aground. Some of the ship's tanks broke open and about 10.8 million gallons of petroleum poured out into the sound. It took three years and over 10,000 workers to clean up the oil. In the court case about the accident, the judges decided that the Exxon Company was responsible. The company had to pay $900 million for damages. Even that large sum was not enough to pay for all the workers, equipment, and research that was necessary. The total cost of the clean-up effort was about $2.5 billion.

Topic:

Main Idea:

2.   A tourist passing through Prince William Sound today probably would see no sign of the 1989 oil spill. The coast is once more a spectacular, wild place with clean water and beaches. However, to a more experienced eye, the scenery is not quite the same as before. For one thing, the beaches are too clean. The workers used hot water to clean oil off the rocks and sand. But in the process they also killed many kinds of marine plants. Rockweed, for example, is a brown plant that grows on rocks and in shallow water. Before the clean-up, it was very common along that coast, but afterwards it almost completely disappeared. Another difference is the decrease in the bird population. Over a half million birds died as a direct result of the oil spill. Certain kinds of ducks and ocean birds were especially unfortunate. Researchers guess that their populations declined by up to 70-80%.

Topic:

Main Idea:

3.   As scientists study the effects of the Valdez oil spill, they are discovering new problems. The oil not only caused the immediate deaths of many animals. It also had longer term effects on many other animals. The harbor seal (a marine mammal) is one example. At first, scientists hoped that the seals would stay away from the areas where there was oil. But instead, the seals swam right through the oil and came out on oily beaches. Scientists noted that these seals seemed sick, and in fact many disappeared. At an earlier counting in 1975, there were about 13,000 harbor seals in Prince William Sound. After the spill, there were only about 2,500. Research on the bodies of dead seals showed that they suffered some brain damage. This may have caused the seals to become confused and drown. The oil also seems to have affected the ability of female seals to have healthy babies. In the year after the oil spill, there were many more deaths than usual among baby seals.

Topic:

Main Idea:

Patterns of Organization

➤ *Try to memorize all of the groups of numbers below. After 60 seconds, your teacher will tell you to turn the page and write the numbers from memory.*

a.	3	6	9	12	15
b.	1	2	9	12	17
c.	1	4	7	10	13
d.	2	5	6	11	19
e.	4	6	8	10	12

Try to remember the groups of numbers. Do not look back. Write the numbers here:

a. _____

b. _____

c. _____

d. _____

e. _____

After you have written as many of the numbers as you can remember, look back and check your work.

Did you remember all of the groups of numbers?

Which groups were the easiest to remember?

Why were they easier?

What made the other groups difficult to memorize?

Compare your answers with another student. Do you agree?

The importance of patterns

Since the beginning of history, people have looked for patterns in the world around them. They looked at the mountains and saw the outlines of people's faces. They looked at the stars and saw animals and gods.

Scientists say that it is human nature to look for patterns in what you see. Your brain is always trying to make sense of the world around you. It tries to fit everything into some kind of recognizable shape or pattern that has meaning for you. A pattern makes it easier for your brain to understand and remember information. (Can you recognize and describe the patterns in the exercise above?)

In this chapter, you will learn to recognize four basic patterns that writers often use in developing their ideas. Finding the pattern helps you find the main idea. Thus, looking for patterns is a way to improve your comprehension while reading.

Four common patterns

Listing of related ideas or examples

In this pattern, the writer's main idea is stated in the form of a generalization. This is followed by a list of supporting details.

Example:

People have many different ideas about what makes a great vacation. <u>Some</u> people like to go for long walks in the forest, where they won't see anyone for days. <u>Others</u> prefer to spend their holiday in an exciting city. There they can visit museums, theaters, and good restaurants. <u>Still others</u> enjoy the fresh air at the seashore. They can spend their days at the beach and listen to the ocean waves at night. <u>A few people</u> decide to stay at home and do some major household projects. They might spend their vacation painting a porch or washing all the windows in their apartment.

The main idea in this paragraph is: *People have many different ideas about what makes a great vacation.*

How many different ideas about vacations does the author mention?

Look at the underlined words. They will tell you each time the author lists another way to spend a vacation. These underlined words are *signal words*. They function somewhat like traffic signals. Each signal calls your attention to something—in this case, the author's examples.

Sequence

In this pattern, the writer's main idea includes a series—events or steps that follow one after another.

Example:

Albert Einstein was born <u>near the end of the 1800s</u> in Ulm, Germany. He graduated from the University of Zurich in Switzerland <u>at the age of 26</u>. <u>Fourteen years later</u> he won the Nobel Prize for Physics. <u>For the next ten years</u> he lived in Germany. <u>Then, in the early 1930s</u>, he had to leave Germany because of Hitler and the Nazi Party. He moved to the United States, where he lived <u>until the time of his death at the age of 74</u>. He lived a long and productive life.

In this paragraph, the main idea is: *Albert Einstein lived a long and productive life*. The *signal words* help you notice important events in his life.

Comparison/Contrast

In this pattern, the writer's main idea explains similarities and/or differences.

Example:

Visitors see <u>some similarities</u> between New York and San Francisco. <u>Both</u> cities, for example, are exciting cultural centers. They are <u>equally</u> attractive to people from many parts of the world. The cities are <u>also alike</u> because they both have many beautiful buildings, large, lovely parks, and grand bridges. <u>On the other hand</u>, the two cities have <u>important differences</u>. <u>One difference</u> is the lifestyle. New Yorkers are always in a hurry and are much less friendly than residents of San Francisco. The streets in the California city are very clean, <u>unlike</u> New York, where the streets are often dirty. <u>Another major difference</u> is safety: San Francisco has much less crime than New York.

The main idea of this paragraph is: *There are both similarities and differences between New York and San Francisco.* The *signal words* call your attention to each similarity or difference the author mentions.

Cause-Effect

When the main idea is that one event or action causes another, authors use the cause-effect pattern.

Example:

In 1989, the Exxon Valdez oil tanker spilled millions of gallons of oil in Alaska's Prince William Sound. Biologists who have studied the local wildlife have noted the <u>consequences</u> of the spill. It has <u>resulted in</u> a great decline in the number of birds in the area. The spill also <u>has caused</u> many young harbor seals to suffer from brain damage and death. Killer whales also felt the <u>impact</u> of the spill. Since 1989, more than one third of the whale population has disappeared.

The main idea of this paragraph is: *The oil spill in Alaska resulted in many harmful effects on animals.* The *signal words* call your attention to each cause or effect the author mentions.

exercise 1

➤ **Each of the sentences below is written in one of the four patterns. Working with another student, guess the name of the pattern of each sentence. Write the letters of the pattern on the line in front of each sentence.**

Use these abbreviations:

L—Listing   S—Sequence   CC—Comparison/Contrast   CE—Cause/Effect

_____ 1. Nicole and Brigette woke up very early on the morning of the international roller skating competition and ate a quick breakfast.

_____ 2. The roller skating rink in Miami was much larger than the rink in their home town in France.

_____ 3. Among the competitors, there were skaters from Japan, Korea, Australia, Russia, Argentina, and many other countries.

_____ 4. Since the competition was taking place in the United States, the largest group of competitors was American.

_____ 5. The competition began in mid-morning with free skating for couples, and the first scores were posted after lunch.

_____ 6. A young Korean couple won this category because they worked so perfectly together.

_____ 7. Nicole and Brigette felt that the French couple had given a much livelier performance than the Korean couple.

_____ 8. Nicole was competing in several categories, including women's free skating, women's school figures, and pair skating.

_____ 9. After they had finished competing, the two girls stayed to watch the couples competitions.

_____10. They had both won some prizes, so they left the skating rink feeling very happy and excited.

Listing

In a listing pattern, the writer's main idea is a general statement that is followed by a list of supporting details. Some signal words for the listing pattern (many others are possible):

a few	other (s)	another	first
several	many	in addition	second
numerous	a variety	besides	third
the main	for example	one	last

Example:

In the following paragraph, the main idea and the signal words are underlined. Working with another student, write out the main idea. Then write examples next to the signal words on the lines below.

In the past few years, <u>scientists have found several new fuels to replace gasoline for automobiles</u>. <u>One of these fuels</u> is methanol, a form of wood alcohol. It can be used in many cars in almost the same way that gasoline is used. Natural gas is <u>another</u> alternative fuel for cars. However, cars that burn this fuel must be equipped with special tanks of natural gas. <u>A third</u> alternative, and perhaps the best, is electricity. Cars fueled by electricity have no engine at all, though they do have to carry large batteries.

Main Idea:_____

_____

Signal Words	Examples
One of these	_____
Another	_____
A third	_____

exercise 2

➤ **Read each paragraph. Look for the signal words and underline them. Then write the main idea, the signal words, and the examples on the lines below. Compare your work with another student.**

Electronic Mail

1.   E-mail (electronic mail) uses computers for communication. It has several important advantages over phones and regular mail. The main advantage of e-mail is that it takes very little time to send and receive messages. From your computer, you can contact someone far away (or in the next office). Seconds later, they have your message. If they are at their computer, you can get a response instantly, too. Another reason people like to use e-mail is that for just a few cents you can send a message to someone in another part of the world. You don't have to worry about the time difference or slow mail delivery. Your message is sent immediately, and your friends or colleagues can send a response at their convenience. Lastly, e-mail allows you to send a single message to many people at the same time.

Main Idea: _____

_____

Signal Words   *Examples*

_____   _____

_____   _____

_____   _____

2.   Communicating by e-mail is becoming increasingly popular for many reasons. First, it is a popular way to send messages among people who do not like to use the telephone. Second, it is useful for sending suggestions or requests. The person who receives them has time to think about their response. Also, e-mail messages always look the same, no matter who sends them. This means you don't have to worry about the quality of your letter paper. Furthermore, e-mail messages are uniform. They give no clues to the sender's age, gender, race, or physical condition. In addition, they do not give away the sender's feelings or emotional condition.

Main Idea: _____

_____

Signal Words   *Examples*

_____   _____

_____   _____

_____   _____

_____   _____

_____   _____

3.   One advertising executive explained why he preferred not to use e-mail. He gave a variety of reasons for why it was not useful for his business. The main reason was that he had no time to learn to use the system. Aside from that fact, he disliked e-mail because he felt that it was too impersonal. In addition, he said it was too fast and easy. He preferred a means of communication that encouraged a more careful and thoughtful style of work. He felt, too, that you lose a lot of information with e-mail. Since you do not hear the sender's voice, you can tell nothing about them as a person.

Main Idea: _____

_____

Signal Words   *Examples*

_____   _____

_____   _____

_____   _____

exercise 3

➤ *Look again at some paragraphs that you have already read. When you read them this time, notice that the author used a listing pattern. Look for the main idea, the signal words, and the examples. Compare your work with another student.*

Locate these paragraphs:

1. Page 82, Exercise 3, paragraph 3

    Main Idea: _____

    _____

    Signal Words   *Examples*

    _____   _____

    _____   _____

    _____   _____

2. Page 86, Exercise 7, paragraph 3

    Main Idea: _____

    _____

    Signal Words   *Examples*

    _____   _____

    _____   _____

    _____   _____

    _____   _____

    _____   _____

3. Page 88, Exercise 9, paragraph 2

    Main Idea: _____

    _____

    Signal Words   *Examples*

    _____   _____

    _____   _____

    _____   _____

exercise 4

➤ *On a separate paper, write a paragraph which begins with one of the sentences below. Make the first sentence your main idea. Use signal words for the listing pattern to complete the paragraph.*

After you have written the paragraph, read it aloud to another student. Find out if your ideas are clear and interesting. Then rewrite the paragraph.

a. I would like to have a job as a _____ because...

b. Grandmothers are important for several reasons...

c. The most important invention was _____ because...

d. We need to protect the environment because...

e. The best features of my hometown are...

Sequence

This pattern is used for the organization of two kinds of material:

- events ordered by time
  Examples: history, biography

- steps in a process
  Examples: the steps in an experiment; directions for building something

The important idea is that things happen in a certain order. Some signal words for the sequence pattern:

first	next	last	after	at last
finally	later	before	while	at the same time

Other signal words for this pattern are dates, years, times of the day, seasons, and plain numbers.

Example a: Chronological Order (time)

Franklin D. Roosevelt, the thirty-second president of the United States, served his country for most of his life. He was the only president to be elected four times. He was born in Hyde Park, New York, on <u>January 30, 1882</u>, and he began his studies at Harvard in <u>1903</u>. In <u>1905</u>, he married Eleanor Roosevelt, a distant cousin, and they had six children. <u>After</u> serving in the New York State Senate, Roosevelt worked in Washington as Secretary of the Navy until <u>1921</u>. <u>At that time</u>, he became very ill with polio and lost the use of his legs. <u>In 1928</u>, Roosevelt ran for governor of New York. <u>After</u> serving two terms as governor, he was elected to the presidency <u>in 1933</u>. Roosevelt died in office on <u>April 12, 1945</u>.

Main Idea:_____

_____

➤ *Note that each underlined word signals another period of time in President Roosevelt's life. Write the events that follow each signal word:*

Signal Words	*Events*
January 30, 1882	_____
1903	_____
1905	_____
After	_____
1921	_____
At that time	_____
In 1928	_____
After	_____
in 1933	_____
April 12, 1945	_____

Example b: Steps in a Process

Making orange juice concentrate from fresh oranges is done entirely by machines. First, oranges are dumped onto a moving belt. They travel into a machine which washes them with detergent. Next they are rolled into juicing machines, where seven hundred oranges per minute are split and squeezed. Then the rinds (the skin of the oranges) are thrown out the end of a long tube. At the same time, the juice goes through small holes in the bottom of the tube. Next, the juice goes into another machine called the finisher. There, the seeds and other tiny objects are removed. Last, the juice goes into large tanks, where most of the water is removed.

Main Idea:_____

_____

Again, note the signal words. Each underlined signal word points to a step in the process of making orange juice concentrate. Write the steps in the process that follow each signal word.

Signal Words	*Steps*
First	_____
Next	_____
Then	_____
At the same time	_____
Next	_____
Last	_____

exercise 5

➤ **Read each paragraph. Look for the signal words and underline them. Then write the main idea, the signal words, and the examples on the lines below. Compare your work with another student.**

Travel

1.   A trip to another country requires a certain amount of planning. First, you must decide where you would like to go. Next, you need to look at maps and books about those places. When you have decided where to go, you should find out how to get there. An agent can tell you about ways to travel and the cost. Then, you should find out what kind of documents you will need to enter the country. In the meantime, you may want to find out the language spoken there. If you don't already know it, you might want to learn a few important words and phrases. Finally, you should make a packing list to make sure you bring everything necessary for a pleasant trip.

Main Idea: _____

_____

Signal Words   *Examples*

_____   _____

_____   _____

_____   _____

_____   _____

_____   _____

2.   In the last seventy-five years, air travel has become the primary means of long-distance transportation around the world. The airplane was adopted for passenger service in Europe in 1919. Later, in 1927, people in the United States began to travel by air. In those days, people flew in small, two-engine propeller planes. Each plane carried 21 passengers and flew at about 305 km/hr. By 1950, planes could carry up to 100 passengers at about 480 km/hr. In 1989, the United States airlines alone carried about 452 million passengers, mostly on high-speed jet aircraft. The modern jetliner of the 1990s can carry more than 300 passengers at a speed of more than 885 km/hr.

Main Idea: _____

_____

Signal Words   *Examples*

_____   _____

_____   _____

_____   _____

_____   _____

_____   _____

3.   No matter where you travel by plane, the process is usually the same. You arrive at the airport at least an hour before the plane is scheduled to leave. Right away, you show your tickets and your passport to the agent. You get a seat assignment and check your suitcases. Then, you go to the gate where you will board your plane. As you walk there, you may stop to buy magazines and candy or make a last-minute telephone call. When you arrive at the gate, your carry-on bags are examined by a special x-ray machine. You must also walk through a metal-detector. Finally, an agent announces that it is time to board your plane, and you are on your way.

Main Idea: _____

_____

Signal Words	*Examples*
_____	_____
_____	_____
_____	_____
_____	_____
_____	_____
_____	_____

exercise 6

➤ **Read each paragraph. Underline the signal words and the examples. Then write the main idea on the lines below. Compare your work with another student.**

Famous African-Americans

1.   Kareem Abdul-Jabbar was a basketball star in the United States. When he was born in New York City in 1947, his parents named him Ferdinand Lewis Alcindor, Jr. He studied at the University of California at Los Angeles (UCLA) in the late 1960s. At that time, he led the university's basketball team to three championships. It was also during his college years that he converted to the Muslim faith. He changed his name to Kareem Abdul-Jabbar. In 1969, Kareem began his professional basketball career as a center on the Milwaukee Bucks team. Later, in 1975, he joined the Los Angeles Lakers. When he retired in 1989, Kareem held several all-time records in basketball. He had also been named "most valuable player" six times.

Main Idea: _____

_____

2.   Maya Angelou, an African-American author, had many difficult experiences while she was growing up. Born in 1929 in Long Beach, California, her original name was Marguerite Johnson. Her parents separated when she was three. Then she and her brother went to live with their grandmother in Stamps, Arkansas. Later on, she lived for a while with her mother and grandmother in St. Louis, Missouri. When she was only eight years old, Maya experienced abuse from her mother's boyfriend. Wherever

she lived, she was often badly treated because of racial prejudice. But her life was also shaped by the strong influence of love. In her childhood, she learned of love from her grandmother and her brother. As she grew older, she also began to love literature. After junior high school, Maya went to live with her mother in San Francisco. There, in 1945, she graduated from high school. A few months later, she had a baby son, who became the center of her life. In later years, Maya included all of these experiences in her novels, plays, and poems. She has received many honors as a writer and spokeswoman for Afro-Americans. But perhaps her greatest honor came in 1993. President Bill Clinton asked her to write the official poem for his inauguration. Then she read the poem aloud at the ceremony in front of the American public.

Main Idea: _____

_____

3. Spike Lee, an African-American film director, is one of the most noted people in his field. Born in Atlanta, Georgia in 1957, Spike's middle-class family moved to Brooklyn, New York, when he was two years old. His father, jazz musician Bill Lee, and his mother, Jackie, an art teacher, had five children. The Lees provided a loving and stable home for their family. Spike's interest in movies began as a youngster. After graduating from Morehouse College in Atlanta, he studied filmmaking at New York University. Soon after that, he made his first feature film, "She's Gotta Have It" with a budget of only $200,000. Since the success of that movie, Lee has written, produced, and directed five more films. All of them are extremely controversial and extraordinarily popular with both black and white audiences. One of Lee's latest achievements was to be invited to teach film at Harvard University.

Main Idea: _____

_____

exercise 7

➤ **Look again at some paragraphs that you have already read. When you read them this time, notice that the author has used a sequence pattern. Look for the main idea, the signal words, and the examples. Compare your work with another student.**

1. Page 83, Exercise 4, paragraph 1

Main Idea: _____

_____

Signal Words	*Examples*
_____	_____
_____	_____
_____	_____
_____	_____

2. Page 95, Exercise 5, paragraph 2

Main Idea: _____

_____

Signal Words   *Examples*

_____   _____

_____   _____

_____   _____

_____   _____

_____   _____

_____   _____

exercise 8

➤ **Read the following article. Pay special attention to the order of steps in making a submarine sandwich.**

Hot Subs for Lunch

The name may be different in other parts of the world. But in Boston, they are known as "subs," or submarine sandwiches. Their name is due to their shape, long and narrow like a submarine. A sub sandwich is one of the most popular lunch items in town.

The best way to find out about subs is to go to a sub shop. There, these delicious treats are a specialty. You will find huge ovens right behind the counter, because a real sub is served hot.

The sub sandwich maker usually says, "What kind of sub do you want?" The customer might answer, "Large Italian."

The expert begins his work of art. He takes a large, long bread roll from a plastic bag under the counter. He slices it lengthwise and puts in layers of meat and cheese. For the Italian sub, he'd include Genoa salami, mortadella sausage, other cold meats, and Provolone cheese.

Leaving the sandwich open, the sandwich chef places it on a metal tray. Then he slides it into the hot oven. He bakes it until the meat is warm and the roll is toasty. When the cheese has melted a bit, he knows it's time to take it out. Then he calls out, "What do you want on your large Italian?"

"Everything," is the reply. "Everything" means that he adds mayonnaise, salt, pepper, olive oil, and a sprinkling of oregano. But that is not all. He also puts in lots of chopped pickles, onions, and hot peppers. He tops it off with sliced tomatoes and crunchy chopped iceberg lettuce.

Finally, taking the sandwich in his hand, the sandwich maker folds the two sides together. He carefully slices it in half and wraps the finished product in waxed paper.

"For here or to go?" he asks. No matter where you eat it, you can be sure that you will enjoy lunch that day!

➤ *How did he make the submarine sandwich? Below are the steps he followed in making the sandwich. But they are out of order. Write the number of the steps in the correct order. Do not look back. Work with a group of three or four other students.*

1. He piles sliced meat and cheese on it.

2. He adds lots of chopped pickles.

3. He places it on a metal tray.

4. He wraps it in waxed paper.

5. He folds the two sides together.

6. He takes a large, long bread roll from a plastic bag.

7. He slices the roll in half lengthwise.

8. He asks, "For here or to go?"

9. He calls out, "What do you want on your large Italian?"

10. He allows it to bake until the meat is warm.

The correct order of the steps:_____

_____

Comparison—Contrast

This is the pattern a writer uses to show how two things are similar and/or different.

A *comparison* can include:
- only similarities
- similarities *and* differences.

A *contrast* includes only the differences.

Some signal words for the comparison-contrast pattern:

Signals of difference:

however	but	unlike	on the other hand
in contrast	while	although	conversely
instead	yet	rather	different from
more than	less than		

Comparative forms of adjectives and adverbs are also used to signal difference (older, faster).

Signals of similarity:

like	both	similarly	in the same way
as	same	also	in common

Example a: Comparison (Similarities and Differences)

<u>Both</u> New York City and Paris depend on vast subway lines to transport their millions of commuters. In <u>both</u> cities, the subways are often crowded, especially at rush hours. <u>Another likeness</u> is the terrible noise level in the trains. <u>A further similarity</u> is that the two subway systems both cover a wide area at little expense for commuters. <u>However</u>, the differences between the two are quite striking. <u>While</u> subway stations in New York range from plain to ugly, Paris stations are generally attractive. Many of the French stations are filled with works of art. In Paris, the subway trains are clean and they run every few minutes. <u>On the other hand</u>, New York's trains can sometimes be less clean and reliable.

Does this paragraph include similarities, differences, or (both)?

Main Idea:_____

_____

Signal Words   *Examples*

Both   _____

both   _____

Another likeness   _____

A further similarity   _____

However   _____

While   _____

On the other hand   _____

Example b: Comparison (Similarities)

Can you think of anything that Ukraine and Japan have in common? Not much, except for one surprising aspect of their cooking. Ukrainians are fond of a dish called *pilmeni.* It is made of pieces of flat pastry folded around a spicey meat filling. The Japanese make a dish that is remarkably like it, only they call it *gyoza.* In both countries, furthermore, people like to eat their *pilmeni* or their *gyoza* with sauce. The Ukrainians use sour cream and the Japanese use soy sauce.

Main Idea:_____

_____

Does this paragraph include (similarities), differences, or both?

Signal Words   *Examples*

in common   _____

like it   _____

both   _____

Example c: Contrast (Differences)

    When the first baby arrives in a household, everything changes. <u>While before</u>, the mother needed an alarm clock in the morning, now the baby decides when she should wake up. <u>Formerly</u>, the parents spent their evenings watching TV or reading, <u>but not now</u>. All their free time is spent admiring their infant. <u>In contrast</u> to pre-baby days, their life is more carefully planned. <u>While they used to</u> go out to see friends whenever they wanted to, that is not possible <u>any more</u>. If they want to go out without the baby, they must arrange for a babysitter. <u>Unlike</u> the neat and tidy rooms of the past, these days their apartment is full of baby things. Their friends have even noticed a <u>difference</u> in the topic of conversation: it's always about the baby!

Main Idea:_____

_____

Does this paragraph include similarities, (differences), or both?

Signal Words	*Examples*
While before	_____
now	_____
Formerly	_____
not now	_____
In contrast	_____
While they used to	_____
any more	_____
Unlike	_____
difference	_____

exercise 9

➤ *In these paragraphs, the signal words are not underlined. Read each paragraph. Underline the signal words. Then write the main idea and the signal words and examples on the lines below. Compare your work with another student.*

Modern Versions of Familiar Machines

1.   The latest kind of vending machine is nothing like the vending machines of the past. Like the old machines, the new ones are a quick and convenient way to buy food. But the new machines have been improved in several important ways. The old machines worked with coins that were sometimes "swallowed" without providing your food. The new machines, however, work with plastic cards that can be used many times without error. The food supplied by the old machines was usually not very good: stale pastries or tasteless sandwiches. In contrast, the new machines sell all kinds of delicious meals. They may offer fresh, oven-baked pizza, espresso coffee, or fresh pasta. In general, these new machines sell more interesting and better-tasting food.

Main Idea: _____

_____

Does this paragraph include similarities, differences, or both?

Signal Words   *Examples*

_____   _____

_____   _____

_____   _____

_____   _____

2.   The so-called "portable" computers of just a few years ago were heavy machines. They weighed about 15 pounds and were really designed to stay in one place. The idea of traveling with an old "portable" was out of the question. It would not even fit under an airline seat. Present-day laptop computers, however, are totally different. These "portables" are really meant to be carried around. They are sometimes even called "notebooks." Unlike the heavy monsters of the past, the laptop computers weigh only about five pounds. They can fit easily into a briefcase. In spite of their size, though, they have much more memory capacity than the older computers. Surprisingly, the laptops also have larger screens than the older models.

Main Idea: _____

_____

Does this paragraph include similarities, differences, or both?

Signal Words   *Examples*

_____   _____

_____   _____

_____   _____

3.   The next big technological change will be the shift from gasoline to electric-powered automobiles. In some ways, the cars are quite similar. Like gasoline cars, the electric vehicles provide convenient, private transportation. The interior of the two vehicles is much the same. Steering, brakes, and wheels are not different. On the other hand, there is a major difference. Unlike gasoline cars, the electric vehicle is totally silent. In contrast to the sound of the ignition in a gasoline engine, the sound of starting an electric car is "click." There is no engine sound, either, in the electric car.

Main Idea: _____

_____

Does this paragraph include similarities, differences, or both?

Signal Words   *Examples*

_____   _____

_____   _____

_____   _____

_____   _____

exercise 10

> *Read each paragraph. Underline the signal words. Then write the main idea and the signal words and details on the lines below. Compare your work with another student.*

Ideas about Education

1.　　High school graduates are sometimes nervous about attending college, because they fear that everything will be different. In fact, there are some important similarities between college and high school. In both places, academic success depends on being a responsible student. This means attending classes regularly, doing your homework, and studying new materials carefully. Similarly, social success in college is like high school. If you have had friends in high school, chances are you will have friends in college, too. College also resembles high school in student activities. Musical groups, sports teams, special interest clubs, and other activities are found in both institutions.

Main Idea: _____

_____

Does this paragraph include similarities, differences, or both?

Signal Words　　　　　　　　*Examples*

_____　　　_____

_____　　　_____

_____　　　_____

2.　　The University of Bologna in northern Italy is different from most North American universities. One important difference is its age. Founded in the tenth century, it is the oldest university in Europe. Its ancient halls give students a strong sense of history. This is in sharp contrast to the usual attitude of American students who study in newer surroundings. The University of Bologna is different, as well, because of its location. While North American universities are often located outside the city center, Bologna's campus is in the heart of the city. Unlike the American university campus, there are no trees or open spaces near this old Italian institution. Instead, students meet on the streets, in cafes, and in the courtyards of the historic buildings.

Main Idea: _____

_____

Does this paragraph include similarities, differences, or both?

Signal Words　　　　　　　　*Examples*

_____　　　_____

_____　　　_____

_____　　　_____

3.   In Russia, there is a strong tradition of learning foreign languages. This has led to the development of specialized foreign language schools. In many ways, these schools are similar to other Russian public schools. They are comparable in one very important way: the students do not have to pay for their education. The schools also teach similar subjects. However, their differences are quite noticeable. One major difference is that most of the school subjects are taught in a foreign language (French, German, or English). Second, the students are different. Unlike the students in regular Russian-language schools, students are selected to attend these schools. Quite often they come from families with higher levels of education. The greatest difference lies in the language abilities of the students. In contrast to other Russian children, they learn to express themselves fluently in a foreign language.

Main Idea: _____

_____

Does this paragraph include similarities, differences, or both?

Signal Words	*Examples*
_____	_____
_____	_____
_____	_____
_____	_____
_____	_____
_____	_____

exercise 11

➤ **Look again at some paragraphs that you have already read. When you read them this time, notice that the author used a comparison-contrast pattern. Look for the main idea, the signal words, and the examples. Compare your work with another student.**

1. Page 81, Exercise 2, paragraph 1

   Does this paragraph include similarities, differences, or both?

   Main Idea: _____

Signal Words	*Examples*
_____	_____
_____	_____
_____	_____
_____	_____

2. Page 82, Exercise 3, paragraph 2

Does this paragraph include similarities, differences, or both?

Main Idea: _____

_____

Signal Words   *Examples*

_____   _____

_____   _____

_____   _____

_____   _____

exercise 12

 Using some of the signal words for comparison-contrast, write a paragraph about one of the following topics. You can write about similarities, differences, or a combination of similarities and differences. Read your paragraph aloud to another student. Ask for suggestions on how you might make it clearer and/or more interesting. Then rewrite it.

a. The United States and another country

b. Movies and real life

c. Being a student and being a full-time worker

d. Male friends and female friends

e. Business management in my country and another country

Cause-Effect

This is the pattern which is used to show how one event or condition is caused by another.

Identifying Causes and Effects

Causes and effects are part of our daily lives. Therefore, this pattern is found very often in history books, science texts, and novels. It is important to recognize the cause-effect pattern when you read. But it is not as easy as the other patterns.

Example:

I forgot my umbrella this morning.
I was caught in the rain.

What happened first?

Next?

> forgot umbrella ————————————→ caught in the rain
>   (cause)   (time passes)   (effect)

A cause-effect sentence does not always put the cause first!

    a. Because I forgot my umbrella, I was caught in the rain.
             (cause)   (effect)

    b. I was caught in the rain <u>because</u> I forgot my umbrella.
          (effect)   (cause)

In both sentences, *because* is the signal word. It stays with the part of the sentence that tells the cause, even if the cause comes after the effect in the sentence. In order to understand a cause-effect pattern, always ask, "What happened first?" Then you will know the cause.

exercise 13

➤ **A. Study the following pairs of words and phrases. In each pair, which comes first in time? Which causes which? Draw an arrow from the cause to the effect in each pair. Work with another student.**

Example:

viruses ───────→ infectious diseases

1.	AIDS	HIV
2.	epidemics	bacteria
3.	coughs	colds and flu
4.	improperly stored food	food poisoning
5.	slow infant development	poor nutrition
6.	skin cancer	too much exposure to the sun
7.	swimming in pools	ear infection
8.	heart trouble	diet high in fat
9.	lung cancer	cigarette smoking
10.	skiing	broken leg

➤ **B. For each pair above, write a sentence. Begin each sentence with the word or phrase in the left-hand column.**

- If the arrow goes from left to right (───→), use these cause-effect signal words:

cause(s)	lead(s) to	is the cause of	results in
can cause	produces	gives rise to	brings about

- If the arrow goes from right to left (←───), use these cause-effect signal words:

is due to	is the result of	is caused by
results from	is produced by	is a consequence of
follows	can be caused by	can result from

Example: *Viruses can cause infectious diseases.*

1. _____
2. _____
3. _____
4. _____
5. _____
6. _____
7. _____
8. _____
9. _____
10. _____

exercise 14

➤ **Read each sentence. Underline and label the cause (C) and the effect (E). Draw an arrow from the cause to the effect. Work with another student.**

Example: <u>Carbon dioxide emissions</u> produce <u>global warming</u>.

C ————————————→ E

1. Coal-burning factories cause acid rain.

2. Stricter anti-pollution laws can lead to higher prices for consumers.

3. The death of lakes and streams can result from acid rain.

4. Forests have become diseased due to acid rain.

5. Coal burning also results in higher levels of sulfur dioxide in the air.

6. Higher infant death rates can result from sulfur dioxide pollution.

7. Coal burning causes the exterior walls of buildings to decay.

8. Strict anti-pollution controls may cause coal miners to lose their jobs.

9. Special equipment in coal furnaces can greatly reduce the amount of pollution that comes out of the chimney.

10. Pollution from carbon fuels can be decreased by encouraging the development and use of solar energy.

Multiple Causes or Effects

In many situations, there is not just a single cause and a single effect.

Example a: Sometimes a single cause can produce many effects. In the following paragraph, what is the cause?

What are the effects?

In 1992 Hurricane Iniki hit the Hawaiian Island of Kauai. As a result, all telephone lines were out of order, the airport was closed, and thousands of homes were damaged. Hotels were washed away, and tourists' holidays were ruined. Many Kauaians lost their jobs.

Example b: Sometimes a single effect is the result of several causes. In the following paragraph, what is the effect?

What are the causes?

The Frozen Yogurt Company closed its shop in the center of town. There really was no other choice. The poor economy meant fewer customers and higher prices for supplies. Bills for electricity and water seemed to go up every month. And then the landlord decided to double the rent.

Example c: Sometimes a single cause leads to a single effect which leads to another effect and another. This could be called a "chain reaction," with all the causes and events linked together. Notice how one thing leads to another in this paragraph:

> During the war in Vietnam in the 1970s, many villages were destroyed. People were left homeless, so they moved to the city. The cities were often overcrowded, with little hope for a good life. This led many people to leave their homeland and move to the United States. Now, many schools and colleges in the United States are expanding their English language programs.

War in Vietnam ⟶ Villages were destroyed ⟶ People were homeless ⟶ People moved to cities ⟶ Cities became crowded, no hope ⟶ People moved to the U.S. ⟶ U.S. needs more English language programs

exercise 15

> **A. Here are two possible causes for the effects listed below. Write the letters of the effects which should go with each cause. Some of the effects can be used twice. Work with another student. Be prepared to explain your answers.**
>
> Cause 1: *Learning a new language*   Effects:
>
> Cause 2: *Living in a new city*   Effects:
>
> Possible effects:
>
> a. Many headaches
> b. Meeting interesting people
> c. Feeling in danger
> d. Spending a lot of money
> e. Going to the language lab
>
> f. Feeling confused
> g. Understanding others' ideas
> h. Doing homework
> i. Finding a new job
> j. Getting married

> **B. Here are two effects which have multiple causes. Write the letters of the causes which you think should go with each effect. Some of the causes can be used twice. Work with another student. Be prepared to explain your answers.**
>
> Effect 1: *Many animals have become extinct.*   Causes:
>
> Effect 2: *Many cities are overcrowded.*   Causes:
>
> Possible causes:
>
> a. Smaller rain forests
> b. Use of chemical fertilizers
> c. Carbon-dioxide emissions
> d. Lack of job opportunities on farms
> e. Polluted rivers
> f. Wars
> g. High birth rates
> h. Too many hunters

exercise 16

➤ **Read each paragraph. Underline the signal words. Then write the main idea and the cause(s) and effect(s) on the lines below. Compare your work with another student.**

Ear Infections in Children

1.   Doctors have noticed an increase in the number of children who are treated for ear infections. This could mean that more children get infections than in the past. Such an increase could be caused, in part, by an increased use of day care. In day-care centers, little children can catch infections from each other.

Main Idea: _____

_____

Cause(s):   Effect(s):

2.   A young child's untreated ear infection can lead to serious consequences. The infection can spread to the throat and cause a general illness. It can also do permanent damage to a child's hearing ability. Perhaps the least-known consequence of untreated ear infection involves language development. Language learning depends on good hearing. Children with frequent or untreated ear infections cannot hear well. The result is a delay in their ability to speak and use language effectively.

Main Idea: _____

_____

Cause(s):   Effect(s):

3.   The greater numbers of reported ear infections could result from social and economic factors. Parents may be more aware of the importance of treating the condition. Doctors may have more time for such simple ailments, now that more dangerous diseases are controlled by immunization. And there may be economic causes. Some doctors who are paid for each visit might have an economic interest in paying attention to ear infections. Economic factors may influence parents as well, since some health centers charge very little for visits. Thus parents are encouraged to bring in their children more often for lesser problems, such as ear infections.

Main Idea: _____

_____

Cause(s):   Effect(s):

exercise 17

➤ *In these paragraphs, you may find some "chain reactions." Read each paragraph. Then write the main idea and the cause(s) and effect(s) below. Compare your work with another student.*

How Diseases Spread

1.   When people move from one city or country to another, the spread of diseases may result. People often bring in germs which may not have been present there before. These new germs can spread quickly and cause previously unknown diseases. If a germ is completely new to a region, people have no natural protection against it. They become ill more easily and die more often. In turn, newcomers may catch diseases which were not present where they came from. If they go back, they may carry the disease with them and start an epidemic there, too.

   Main Idea: _____

   _____

   Cause(s):   Effect(s):

2.   Changes in heating systems of buildings can also lead to disease. In the 1970s, there was a worldwide shortage of heating oil. To save fuel, hotels in the Unites States lowered the temperature in their heating systems. This lower temperature was just perfect for a deadly germ which grows in heating pipes. When the heated air was blown into the rooms of a hotel, it carried the germs. Many visitors became ill and several died.

   Main Idea: _____

   _____

   Cause(s):   Effect(s):

3.   Pollution of the oceans can also result in the spread of disease. Phosphates and nitrates from fertilizers plus human waste eventually flow into the oceans. These pollutants result in the increased growth of tiny plants called *algae*. These plants provide a home for cholera, a deadly disease. The infected algae can stick to ships, which then carry the cholera germs all around the world. Germs of the disease recently rode on ships going from India to South America. There, thousands of people have died from the resulting epidemic of cholera.

   Main Idea: _____

   _____

   Cause(s):   Effect(s):

exercise 18

➤ *Apply your knowledge of the cause-effect pattern in the following paragraphs which you have already read. For each paragraph, write the main idea, the cause(s) and effect(s).*

1. Page 86, Exercise 7, paragraph 2

   Main Idea: _____

   _____

   Cause(s):   Effect(s):

2. Page 96. Exercise 6, paragraph 1

   Main Idea: _____

   _____

   Cause(s):   Effect(s):

3. Page 98, Exercise 8, paragraph 3

   Main Idea: _____

   _____

   Cause(s):   Effect(s):

Recognizing patterns

The opening sentences of a passage often give you clues about the pattern of the whole passage. If you can guess what the pattern will be, you will be able to follow the author's thinking better. You will also be able to find the important ideas more quickly.

exercise 19

➤ *Each of the sentences in this exercise is a possible beginning for a newspaper article. Working with another student, decide which pattern you think the author would use in the article. Then write the letters of that pattern beside the sentence.*

L—Listing   S—Sequence   CC—Comparison/Contrast   CE—Cause/Effect

_____ 1. The success of Milan's soccer team is due in large part to good management and good luck.

_____ 2. Making a pizza at home can be quick and simple if you follow these steps.

_____ 3. The industrial Italy of today is a far different place from the rural Italy of just a generation ago.

_____ 4. The Mafia would never be so powerful in Italy if the Italian government hadn't helped it in some way.

_____ 5. Italian society has undergone a number of profound changes in recent years.

_____ 6. The only way to save the artistic treasures of Italy is to drastically reduce the number of cars in Italian city centers.

_____ 7. The career of Francesco Guccini—one of Italy's most loved pop/folk singers— began in a cafe in Bologna.

_____ 8. Changes in life style have brought changes in the eating habits of many Italians.

_____ 9. The standard of living of most Italians today is not very different from that of their European neighbors.

_____10. Applying for citizenship in Italy is a complicated bureaucratic process that may take over a year.

exercise 20

➤ *Each of the sentences in this exercise is a possible beginning for a newspaper article. Working with another student, decide which pattern you think the author would use in the article. Then write the letters of that pattern beside the sentence.*

L—Listing   **S—Sequence**   **CC—Comparison/Contrast**   **CE—Cause/Effect**

_____ 1. The high cost of newspapers in some countries is one simple reason why fewer people read them.

_____ 2. While television reporting may be more immediate, newspaper reporting is often far more complete.

_____ 3. Do your children watch too much television? Here are a few simple steps for limiting television viewing without causing a major family battle.

_____ 4. When radio was at its height, it was the focus of much family and social activity.

_____ 5. One sure way to create a poor reader is to put a child in front of a television set all day.

_____ 6. The technology of television certainly has come a long way since its invention over fifty years ago.

_____ 7. Recent research has shown that violence on television can cause violent behavior among children.

_____ 8. Television advertising is far more effective than advertising in magazines or newspapers.

_____ 9. Television has had an enormous influence on politics in recent decades.

_____10. The first television advertisements from the 1950s would now seem very simple and obvious to us.

exercise 21

➤ *In each paragraph, there is a different pattern and a missing sentence. Working with another student, decide what the pattern is and which sentence fits best. The missing sentences are listed below.*

L—Listing   **S—Sequence**   **CC—Comparison/Contrast**   **CE—Cause/Effect**

1.   For the tourist in Italy, Bologna has many advantages over the more popular city of Florence. First of all, there are far fewer tourists there. This means that museums and monuments are much less crowded. Since there are few foreigners, you can also get a much better idea of how Italians live. Furthermore, the Bolognese tend to be more friendly to visitors than the Florentines.

Sentence: _____   Pattern: _____

2.   Bologna's Etruscan origins go back at least 2,400 years. It became a Roman city in the 2nd century B.C. With the fall of the Roman Empire, it came under Byzantine rule. Then it fell to the armies of northern barbarians, called the Longobards. Bologna became an independent city-state in about 1000. In 1507, the city came under the rule of the Roman Catholic Church. This ended with the arrival of Napoleon and the French army in 1796. Then, in 1859, the city joined the Kingdom of Savoy, which became the Kingdom of Italy in 1861.

Sentence: _____   Pattern: _____

3.   Bologna's progressive, or leftist, city government is the result of a number of historical factors. Many centuries of sometimes brutal rule under the Popes undoubtedly influenced the Bolognese. During those years, they learned to distrust the Church and all established power. By the early 20th century, there was already a strong leftist movement in Bologna. The conservative parties further lost influence in the 1920s and 1930s. At that time, they supported the Fascists and the Nazis. The leftists, on the other hand, gained in influence in those years.

Sentence: _____   Pattern: _____

4.   In their fondness for Bologna, the Bolognese have given their city a number of nicknames. To some, it is known as Bologna "the red." This name comes in part from the strong leftist political tendencies of the city. To others, it is Bologna "the wise" because of its university. The oldest university in Europe, the University of Bologna is still an important intellectual and cultural center. And finally, some like to think of Bologna as "the fat," a paradise for food lovers. And indeed, the local cooking tends towards richness and plenty—delicate stomachs be careful!

Sentence: _____   Pattern: _____

Missing sentences:
a. In 1816, Bologna was once again ruled by the Church, with the help of the Austrian Empire.
b. It also comes from the many red-toned buildings in Bologna that give the city a unique coloring.
c. The porticos lining Bologna's streets make them far more pleasant for walking than Florence's narrow and noisy streets.
d. Medieval Bologna was an independent city-state, and the Bolognese developed a long-lasting love of independence and self-government.

exercise 22

➤ *In each paragraph below, there is a different pattern and a missing sentence. Working with another student, decide what the pattern is and which sentence fits best. The missing sentences (plus one extra) are listed below.*

1.   Archaeologists believe that the first people to eat corn lived in central Mexico 5,000 years ago. They gathered a kind of corn that grew wild in much of Central America. The cultivation of corn made possible the great Indian civilizations, from the Aztec to the Zuni. By the time Europeans arrived, corn was cultivated all over North and South America. Curious about this new grain, Columbus brought some seeds back to Europe. Within a century, people were growing corn in many parts of Europe, Asia, and Africa.

   Sentence: _____   Pattern: _____

2.   The cultivation of corn in the United States has changed dramatically in the past century. Farmers used to grow corn in small fields of a few acres. Now corn farms may be as large as 6,000 acres. Before the age of machines, farmers had to pick each ear of corn by hand. It might take several days to harvest 10 acres of corn. Now, however, huge harvesting machines can pick hundreds of acres of corn in a day. While corn growing used to be a way of life for many families, now it is big business.

   Sentence: _____   Pattern: _____

3.   In modern life, corn has many uses. Corn is also hidden in many other foods: cookies, bread, or beef. A large part of the corn production in the United States, in fact, goes to feed beef cattle. But corn is not just a food. It is also used in the production of all kinds of things, from glue to hand lotion and paint. Recently, manufacturers have begun to use corn to make a new type of plastic for garbage bags. In many places, cars are now powered by a mixture that contains ethanol, a fuel made from corn.

   Sentence: _____   Pattern: _____

4.   Genetic engineering is bringing about some important changes in the production of corn. It has allowed scientists to develop plants that produce larger and more numerous ears of corn. This makes it possible for farmers to harvest far more corn per acre of land. In the near future, genetic engineering may develop types of corn that are resistant to certain diseases. This will help farmers save millions of tons of corn that are lost every year to disease. Scientists are also working on kinds of corn that can be cultivated in dry or very hot areas. Genetics may furthermore soon develop a kind of corn that contains more protein and is also more nutritious. All these changes mean that corn will be able to feed more people around the world.

   Sentence: _____   Pattern: _____

Missing sentences:

a. This will help farmers save millions of tons of corn that are lost to disease every year.
b. We eat corn in many forms, from popcorn to corn oil, corn flour, and corn syrup.
c. Before a thousand years had passed, they had learned to cultivate corn.
d. For the Hopi Indians, corn is a symbol of life.
e. It took a family several long days of hot, hard work to harvest a few acres of corn.

exercise 23

➤ *In each paragraph below, there is a different pattern and a missing sentence. Working with another student, decide what the pattern is and which sentence fits best. The missing sentences (plus one extra) are listed below.*

1.   Sir Isaac Newton worked on many important scientific problems of his day. His best known written work is *Principia,* the book that explained his law of universal grav-itation. He is famous as well for his development of the laws of motion. However, he also made important discoveries about optics and the nature of color. His other work included experiments and writings on astronomy, chemistry, and logic.

Sentence: _____   Pattern: _____

2.   Isaac Newton was born in England in 1642. He began his studies at Trinity College, Cambridge University, in 1661. In 1665, when the plague (a terrible disease) struck England, Newton left the university and returned home. The next few years in Woolsthorpe were the most productive in his life. However, his most famous book, *Principia,* was not published until 1682. In honor of his work, he was made director of the English Mint in 1699. Sir Isaac Newton died in 1727 and is buried in Westminster Abbey.

Sentence: _____   Pattern: _____

3.   Although the two men were geniuses, Isaac Newton and Albert Einstein have very little else in common. True, they both did their best work before the age of 26. However, that is the only similarity between them. Newton cared about the public's opinion of him, and he did not like improper behavior. Einstein, on the other hand, enjoyed being different and did not care what others thought. Newton spent his later years in a comfortable job with the government, while Einstein remained a full-time scientist.

Sentence: _____   Pattern: _____

4.   Newton did most of his best work between 1665 and 1668, during his stay in Woolsthorpe. Many historians and scientists have wondered how he managed to pro-duce so many brilliant ideas in such a short time. It is probable that he had begun to develop his theories earlier while at university. Then, in the peace and quiet of Woolsthorpe, those ideas took form. No one will ever know exactly what inspired his most creative thinking. It is certain, however, that his genius is still felt today.

Sentence: _____   Pattern: _____

Missing sentences:
a. Present-day physicists have discovered limits to the mechanical universe which Newton described.
b. Popular belief says that a falling apple gave Newton the idea of the law of universal gravitation.
c. In addition, he invented differential and integral calculus.
d. Newton was described as a man who never smiled, but Einstein was well known for his sense of humor.
e. In fact, by the age of 26, he had already completed most of his best scientific work.

exercise 24

> *In every essay, book chapter, or magazine, it is possible to find a single overall pattern for the whole text. However, individual paragraphs in the text may have different patterns. In this exercise, you will look for patterns in a passage about Hawaii on page 227. Number the paragraphs. Working with another student, answer these questions:*

1. What is the overall pattern of this reading?

2. What are some signal words that helped you decide on this pattern?

3. What are the pattern for each of these paragraphs? Explain your answers.

   Paragraph 1:

   Paragraph 3:

   Paragraph 5:

   Paragraph 7:

Skimming

What is skimming?

Skimming is high-speed reading that can save you lots of time. You skim to get the general sense of a passage or a book. What would you do if you found yourself in these situations?

1. You want to find out a little about the recent elections in France. There is a long newspaper article on the subject, but you don't have time to read it all.

2. You need some information about the theories of Sigmund Freud. You have found many books about Freud and now you need to know which will be most useful.

3. You went to a movie last night and you thought it was terrible. You notice a review of that movie in a magazine today. You want to find out quickly if the reviewer agrees with you.

4. You are reading a detective story and you are in a hurry to find out who the murderer is.

The answer is the same for all these situations: *skim.*

How do you skim?

You should read only the words that will help you get the sense of the text. The following passage shows what parts you should read. These are the parts that usually give the author's ideas or opinions.

Read the first sentences or paragraph quite carefully. The beginning often contains general information about the rest of the text.

If the text is long, you might also read the second paragraph. Sometimes the first paragraph is only an introduction and the second paragraph contains the main idea.....
....
........After that, you should look at the beginning of each paragraph ....
....
......................................maybe read a few words...
...................................in the middle ....
....Usually the topic sentence is at the beginning.
But sometimes it may be at the end...
....
.... skip some paragraphs...
not important.......................................
You should usually read the last paragraph more carefully. The author often summarizes the main idea at the end. These are the general rules about skimming. And this is all the text you need to read when you skim!

Guidelines for Effective Skimming

- Always work as fast as you can. Don't let details slow you down.

- Always keep in mind your reason for skimming.

- Be flexible when you are skimming. How much you skim in a passage depends on your purpose and on the passage.

Skimming Book Reviews

One way to find out about a book is to read a review of the book in a newspaper or magazine. Book reviewers usually tell something about the subject of the book and give their opinion. However, sometimes they do not state their opinion directly. They give some hints about it and let the reader infer it.

exercise 1

 Here is a book review of The Year of the Turtle. *Read the questions and then skim the review for the answers. Work as quickly as you can. (Not more than 30 seconds for the skimming!) Compare your answers with another student.*

1. Is this a good book to give as a birthday present to a six-year-old boy?
   Why or why not?

2. Would you like to read this book?
   Why or why not?

The Year of the Turtle is the work of an artist of great talent. It is also the product of a great love for nature in general and turtles in particular.

David Carroll's enthusiasm for turtles began early. When he was only a boy he started catching them in the lake near his home. Since then, his life has been filled with turtles: he has spent 40 years studying them and fighting for their protection. He knows turtles as no one else does and he brings us his knowledge in admirable, clear language.

The book follows a turtle through the four seasons of the year. In a gentle, but vivid tone, he brings us into the life of the pond and the river. Not only the turtle, but also the other animals of these wetlands take part in his story. The frogs, fish, beetles and beavers all are described with great care and great skill.

Carroll also draws a very clear picture of the present situation for the turtle. In fact, many kinds of turtles are disappearing from the United States and other parts of the world. This is happening because their homes in the wetlands are being destroyed. All too often, wetlands are filled in so that houses and factories can be built. This means the loss of turtles and of their whole world.

exercise 2

➤ *Here are eight short descriptions of books on the opposite page. Read the questions and then skim the book descriptions for the answers. Work as quickly as you can. (Not more than one minute for the skimming!) Compare your answers with another student.*

1. Which book do you think would be most useful to you and why?

2. Which book is the most interesting to you and why?

3. Which books would you recommend to someone who is interested in the environment?

4. Which books would you recommend to someone who is interested in health?

5. Which book would you recommend to someone who is interested in how technology affects our lives?

Books

State of the World 1993—Lester R. Brown et al. Earth will have 92 million more inhabitants—a number equal to the entire population of Mexico—by this time next year, but the planet is incapable of supporting them, the authors argue. Over the past decade, State of the World has highlighted environmental and economic dilemmas soon to confront the planet's burgeoning population before most people ever realized these predicaments existed. Topics in this all-new edition range from reviving coral reefs to supporting indigenous people and dealing with water scarcity—issues so globally important that this edition has been translated into 27 languages. As always, the authors present solutions to the problems they describe and offer forecasts for the future. Norton, 1993, 268 p., paperback, $10.95.

Reversing Memory Loss: Proven Methods for Regaining, Strengthening, and Preserving Your Memory—Vernon H. Mark with Jeffrey P. Mark. The authors, a former chief of neurosurgery at Boston City Hospital and a co-author of Brain Power, outline new tests, diagnoses, and treatments for memory loss. They emphasize that as many as 30 percent of the cases diagnosed as Alzheimer's disease may instead trace to other, treatable problems. They also cite depression, stress, substance abuse, and over medication as increasingly common causes of memory loss and discuss cases of brain damage or disease that can be helped, if not completely reversed. Originally published in hardcover in 1992. HM, 1992, 244 p., paperback, $9.95

Where There Is No Doctor: A Village Health Care Handbook—David Werner with Carol Thurman and Jane Maxwell. A first-aid guide written especially for the villager but also useful for anyone who cannot get immediate health care. It contains basic treatments for common illnesses such as diarrhea, toothache, colds, and flu, as well as graphic chapters on childbirth, skin diseases such as impetigo and scabies, and nutritional disorders such as acid indigestion and rickets. An extensive chapter on first aid details treatments for burns, bites, and lacerations. Special emphasis is given to children, their diseases, and possible complications following birth. A glossary and extensive index conclude the book. Hesperian Found, 1992, 446 p., illus., paperback, $14.00.

Extinction: Bad Genes or Bad Luck?—David M. Raup. In this thought-provoking overview of what we know and don't know about the causes of species extinction, Raup examines Earth's five major episodes of mass extinction, investigating several suspects—including sea-level rise, global cooling, volcanism, and meteorites—and presenting some startling new claims. He concludes with a discussion of whether extinction results from some inherent fault in the organism ("bad genes") or just bad luck. The book is written in a clear, conversational style for the lay reader. Originally published in hardcover in 1991. Norton, 1992, 210 p., paperback, $9.95

A Dog Is Listening: The Way Some of Our Closest Friends View Us—Roger A. Caras. Even though it is believed to be the first domesticated animal in the world, the dog's behavior, senses, and interpretations of the world mostly elude humans. As the owner of more than 50 dogs during his lifetime, Caras has spent a great deal of time studying the behavior and physiology of his own animals and has made a career of writing about his perceptions. He details the world through a dog's eyes and examines the capabilities of the dog's senses, which can be sensitive enough to detect human epileptic seizures before they happen. The history and habits of canines through the ages are also discussed. Originally published in hardcover in 1992. Fireside, 1993, 239 p., b&w photos and illus., paperback, $11.00

Eat for Life: The Food and Nutrition Board's Guide to Reducing Your Risk of Chronic Disease—Catherine E. Woteki and Paul R. Thomas, eds. This authoritative and easy-to-read book for consumers is the product of a consensus of nutrition scientists in their effort to determine healthful and unhealthful eating habits. The heart of the book is a nine-point dietary plan to reduce the risk of diet-related chronic diseases, such as heart disease, cancer, osteoporosis, and obesity. The book includes practical recommendations for building healthful eating patterns, as well as tips on shopping, cooking, and eating out. Originally published in hardcover in 1992. Harper-Perennial, 1993, 179 p., paperback, $10.00.

The Twenty-Four-Hour Society: Understanding Human Limits in a World That Never Stops—Martin Moore-Ede. As director of the Institute for Circadian Physiology, Moore-Ede has devoted his life's work to examining how the body clock works and the effect 24-hour technology has on the physiology of humans. Some of the biggest accidents of modern industrial times have occurred at night, including the Exxon Valdez oil spill and those at Three Mile Island and Chernobyl. The author contends that this may be because the humans in charge were suffering sleep deprivation and exhaustion, which may have hindered their performance. Guidelines for how we may better organize our work schedules and monitor alertness are included, as are ways to combat jet lag and sleep disorders faced by those with hectic and erratic schedules. Addison-Wesley, 1993, 230 p., hardcover, $22.95.

Lifespan: Who Lives Longer and Why—Thomas J. Moore. Many commonly held beliefs about lifestyle and longevity get debunked here. For example, the author, a fellow at the Center for Health Policy Research at George Washington University, argues that the age of your mother and father has more influence on your lifespan than regulating cholesterol levels and weight watching. Moore feels that the threat of the influenza virus—which kills 100,000 people in the United States in a bad year and has killed a million people in a single year twice in this century—should receive more serious attention among populations. A discussion of what people really need to concentrate on to live longer is included, in addition to updates on current longevity research. S&S, 1993, 318 p., hardcover, $23.00.

exercise 3

➤ *Skim the review of* Typical American, *a novel by Gish Jen. Read the questions and then skim the review for the answers. Work as quickly as you can. (Not more than* **two minutes** *for the skimming!) Compare your answers with another student.*

1. Is this a good book for an 11-year-old girl?
   Why or why not?

2. Does this seem like a good book for vacation reading?
   Why or why not?

3. Is this a good book to read if you are interested in romance?
   Why or why not?

4. Did the reviewer think this was a good book?
   How can you tell?

TYPICAL AMERICAN

by Gish Jen
296 pp. New York: Plume/Penguin Books. $10.00

When Yifeng leaves Shanghai province for graduate study in America, he vows to himself that he will not return home until he has his doctorate. Furthermore, he will do calisthenics daily, not eat too much, and have nothing to do with girls, since girls, as everyone knows, are the ruin of even the best scholars, who "kissed, got syphilis, and died without getting their degrees."

This is the humorous, yet heartbreaking tone of a fine first novel about the immigrant experience. From his arrival in New York, we follow poor Yifeng—who soon becomes Ralph Chang—as he struggles to make sense of the strange and mysterious rites of American life.

Short, plump, and with ears that stick out, he meets his first temptation in the form of the secretary of the foreign students' office at the university. That proves a disappointment, Ralph fails to keep up with the bureaucratic requirements of being a foreign student, and

he takes to a clandestine existence, nearly succumbing to loneliness and hunger.

However, a lucky coincidence brings him together again with his ambitious sister, Theresa, who has fled before the communist take-over in China. Through Theresa he meets Helen, also from Shanghai, who has been brought up to be the perfect Chinese wife. They marry and the three of them set out together to conquer the American dream.

Their roller coaster ride through the vicissitudes of American life runs from the merry, to the absurd, to the pathetic and, finally, very nearly ends with tragedy. Through it all, they try to reconcile their Chineseness with the Americanness all around them.

At times, they are swept up by enthusiasm for things American—as when Ralph decides he wants to learn how to drive, or Helen finds her dream house, a split-level with a kitchen nook. But their enthusiasm is always quickly tempered by their awareness of the cultural distance that separates them from Americans. "Typical American" becomes the family's favorite expression for the "uncivilized" ways they encounter—"typical American use-brute-force" or "typical American no-morals". And when they get into trouble—as when they're swindled into building on unbuildable property —they fall back on Chinese maxims and Chinese ways of thinking.

This book will inevitably be compared with *The Joy Luck Club,* also about the Chinese-American experience, but it will not suffer from the comparison and in many ways may be a superior novel. It is far more consistent, with a tighter narrative construction and a more uniformly crafted style. The writing is elegant, while at the same time extremely witty, and the story is told with a poignancy and sympathy that keeps us involved all the way through.

Though Ralph is not always a likable character—his plodding obtuseness can sometimes be exasperating—we pity him, trapped as he is in his belief that "a man is what he made up his mind to be." We also come to feel affection and admiration for the two women in his life, so determined in the way they try to cope with the disasters he brings on them.

As with so many novels about the American dream, this one ends with delusion. Even in this land of opportunity, where the possibilities seemed limitless, Ralph finally realizes that "a man was as doomed here as he was in China." "A man was the sum of his limits; freedom only made him see how much so. America was no America."

But the bleakness of this realization is offset by the final images of the novel. We close the book with a smile as we picture Theresa, as Ralph does, wearing an her improbably orange bathing suit and splashing in the inflatable swimming pool.

---

exercise 4

> *Skim the review of* **Beastly Behaviors: A Watcher's Guide to How Animals Act and Why** *on page 138. Read the questions and then skim the review for the answers. Work as quickly as you can. (Not more than* **two minutes** *for the skimming!) Compare your answers with another student.*

1. Is this a good book for a friend with two young children who love animals?
   Why or why not?

2. Is this a good book for someone who wants to know about farm animals?
   Why or why not?

3. Does the author of this book like zoos?
   Why or why not?

4. Does this sound like a book you would like to read?
   Why or why not?

Book reviews

Beastly Behavior: A Watcher's Guide to How Animals Act and Why
Janine M. Benyus
Illustrated by Juan Carlos Barberis
Addison-Wesley, $29.95

This book should be in the bookcase or backpack of every nonprofessional zoophile, amateur ethologist, armchair naturalist, creature watcher or even just fond relative of young zoo fans. A long introductory essay, "How Animals Behave: A Primer," describes in precise but lively prose the primary activities common to all mammals, birds and reptiles, among them sleeping, communicating, fighting, yawning, grooming, moving, courting, copulating and parenting. Of course we advanced primates have added a few flourishes, but it is sobering to realize how adequately these few words also describe most human behavior. The great differences between, and sometimes within, most species are not in what they do but how they look. This is one of the great charms of nature, but a mystery too since the variations in diet, climate, predators, habitat or history do not quite seem to account for the extravagant extremes in size, structure and ornament of moose and mouse, flamingo and wren, or even borzoi and Chihuahua.

Each of the 20 short subsequent chapters is devoted to a creature of particular appeal, menace, oddity or beauty, such as the panda, crocodile, penguin or peacock. Every section is adorned with detailed drawing, and a chart of "Vital Stats" gives taxonomy, typical size, weight, longevity, and also habitat, a subject on which Benyus has written several guides. A paragraph or two deals with some unique aspect of that animal—like the zebra's handsome camouflage, the crane's courtship dance—as well as with the creature's role in history or myth or the talismanic value of its horns, ears, tusks or tail. A somber theme is the rapid decline of these wild animals whose tribes have been decimated by pesticides, hunting, poaching and, most inexorably, shrinking habitat.

Benyus often explains the animal's variant on basic behavior patterns: for example, after the male ostrich scrapes out a shallow nest, both the "major hen" and the others in the harem lay their eggs. Then the male and the major hen laboriously hatch them "while the minor hens walk away scot-free." She also notes such colorful pastimes as neck wrestling, knuckle walking, mud wallowing, whisker stropping and feather painting. Even such variations and diversions, however, like the more obviously crucial activities, are presented as survival maneuvers or reproductive strategies—techniques for saving oneself or perpetuating one's genes. Benyus stresses this bleak sociobiology in her introduction. But then, moving from the general to the specific, she cannot entirely avoid a hint of affectionate anthropomorphism (who can—or should?) in the sections on the gentle elephants and sociable zebras, the playful penguins and sea lions—or the dolphins, those clever creatures who nonetheless seem so fond of us.

Any compact compendium of basic animal information provides a great service, but it helps to have it served up so attractively. Along with the drawings and witty paragraph headings, sidebars brighten the pages: for the lion chapter, "A Mane is a Mixed Blessing" and "What do Males do, Anyway?" Small sketches show how to read each species' body language, to tell a grin from a snarl. The author's scientific descriptions are often enlivened with colloquial comments: on the subject of breeding—a major concern for zoos and naturally for most animals, as well—she says of pandas: "Females can be picky and, because the world's captive community is so limited, finding a compatible mate can be like dating in a very small town."

"The world's captive community" of course means the network of zoos, a subject on which Benyus, like so many animal lovers, is ambivalent. After a grim history of early menageries in a preface called "What's New with Zoos?" she moves on to praise some modern zoos, especially for exhibits designed to duplicate natural habitats. Their animals are healthier and happier than the shabby, moth-eaten, autistic camels and lions one remembers from city zoos of the past. At their best, she suggests, such zoos can provide wholesome entertainment and useful education. Moreover, like most modern zoo directors, she sees the zoo as a Noah's Ark: the very existence of many endangered species may depend on breeding in captivity for later release. There have already been some successes of this kind: the vanishing but now reestablished golden lion tamarin and Arabian oryx. Even so, in a concluding chapter called "Zoo Critique," Benyus laments that many zoos are inadequate or worse: she provides a detailed checklist for evaluating your local zoo, and a chart of how to reform or even close down a serious offender.

But at last there is hope of reconciliation among those who regard zoos as educational, those who condemn them as prisons for animals, those who praise them as nurseries for endangered species, and the many others who find zoos depressing but dread the loss of beauty and the loneliness of a world in which one might never see a live wild animal larger than a raccoon. This common ground is the BioPark. Michael H. Robinson, director of the Smithsonian's National Zoological Park, who calls the conventional zoo "an anachronistic entity," has worked for years to promote this concept of "a holistic form of bioexhibitory portraying life in all its interconnectedness." A BioPark is a large, natural, protected environment containing most of the birds, mammals, insects, trees, flowers and minerals indigenous to a certain region, such as an African savanna—or even several of these extended "exhibits" in one vast area. The antizoo U.S. Humane Society last summer urged the establishment of 6 to 12 large regional BioParks containing native wildlife. An in November 1992, "Amazonia," a tropical rain forest environment, opened at the National Zoo, and Cleveland opened its own large BioPark.

Audrey C. Foote is a Washington, D.C. freelance writer and translator.

Skimming news stories and magazine articles

exercise 5

A. Read the questions and then skim the news story for the answers. Work as quickly as you can. (Not more than two minutes for the skimming!) Compare your answers with another student.

1. What has happened to the three children from South Carver?

2. What do the people in South Carver think about the situation?

3. What do you think will happen to them?

THE BOSTON MAIL • Sunday, February 12, 1995

All-night search for 3 missing children in South Carver

by Ellie Nashima

SOUTH CARVER - Several hundred people—police, firefighters and volunteers—searched a large area of swampland and woods for three children who disappeared yesterday afternoon.

The children, Seth and Cindy Erland, 7 and 5, and their cousin Bruce McCaffy, 11, were last seen playing near the Erland's home on Kingston Street at about 3:30 p.m. and were reported missing about four hours later, said Carver Police Sgt. Dan Preston.

The rescue efforts were hampered by winds of 20 to 30 m.p.h. and rain mixed with sleet and snow. Temperatures last night hovered around freezing and police expressed concern about the physical condition of the children.

The searchers formed human chains to try to cover all of the 4- by 5-mile area of the swamp. The search teams included State Police, Civil Defense officials, Carver, Plymouth and Middleboro police officers and firefighters, Coast Guard officers, and several hundred volunteers from as far away as Brockton and Attleboro. Up to seven bloodhounds and German Shepherds were being used in the search, along with floodlights and infrared lights from the Coast Guard helicopter.

By late last night, there was no sign of the children or their belongings. Earlier, some footprints had been seen in the snow which may have been made by the children, but they were washed away by the rain.

Seth is 4' 4" tall and weighs about 60 pounds. He has light brown hair and was wearing a navy jacket with red stripes.

Cindy is 4'3" and weighs about 55 pounds. She has long brown hair and was wearing a purple jacket with a pink hood.

Bruce is about 4'10" and weighs 85 pounds. He has short, brown hair and was wearing a red jacket and jeans.

A fourth child was playing with them in the woods during the afternoon, according to the police. The boy reported that they had all fallen into the swamp. He had taken a different route in getting out and had become inadvertently separated from the group.

The boy, whom police said is about 11 years old, managed to find his way home. He arrived at about 5:00 p.m. and reported the other children missing. Though he was wet and cold, he did not require medical attention.

The boy also said that the Erland's dog had been with the children when they fell into the swamp. The dog returned home alone at about 6:00 p.m.

Carver Police Chief Anthony Marino warned of the danger of searchers getting lost. Some parts of the swamp are "up to our shoulders," he said.

The children may have headed east towards the beacon from the Plymouth Municipal Airport. Marino added: "We're looking at trouble here. That's the worst part of the swamp they might have gone into."

Richard Erland, the father of Seth and Cindy, was out with the searchers. Though all search efforts so far had been fruitless, he was still hopeful: "Those children know the woods well and the two boys have some wilderness training from Boy Scouts." He believed that the children may have found some shelter from the bad weather.

However, Paul Mahoney, a neighbor, said "Those kids could be pretty lost. It'd be impossible to stay on a path in the dark. I've gotten lost there myself."

Ken Thatcher, 22, of Plymouth, one of the volunteer searchers, said that the children faced extreme conditions. "They're wet, and it's real cold out there. We've got to get to them soon."

> **B. Now you will skim another news story on the same subject. Read the questions and then skim the news story for the answers. Work as quickly as you can. (Not more than two minutes for the skimming!) Compare your answers with another student.**

1. How did the story end?

2. How did the children feel in the night?

3. Was it easy to find them?

4. How did their parents feel in the end?

THE BOSTON MAIL • Monday, February 13, 1995

Carver children safe after night in swamp

SOUTH CARVER - Cold, wet and scared, the three children who were lost all last night in a remote corner of an icy swamp were found this morning by a team of searchers. The discovery brought an end to a massive rescue operation involving hundreds of local and state officials and volunteers.

The children had spent the night on a small mound of high ground, hugging each other and their dog for warmth and comfort. Seth and Cindy Erland, 7 and 5, and their cousin Bruce McCaffy, 11, were found by two Carver police officers and a local hunter at 8:15 a.m.

"Come here, kids," shouted John Haggerty, when he saw them. "Come and give me a hug."

Haggerty, who fell twice into water over his head, had been out all night wading through what he called, "a vicious swamp."

"It was a very emotional moment," he said, speaking from his hospital bed where he was being treated for mild hypothermia. "We were all so happy to see each other."

The rescuers led the children back through a mile of swamp, with Cindy in police officer Dave Madeiros' arms, to an ambulance. They were rushed to Plymouth Hospital, where they were treated for exhaustion, mild hypothermia. and muscle injuries to the legs, the result of exposure to the freezing air and water.

Seth Erland, who was wearing sneakers, had also developed severe blisters after giving his dry socks to his sister, Cindy.

Hospital officials said they were to remain there overnight for observation, but added that their condition was satisfactory. The children asked for hamburgers and french fries soon after their arrival.

The police, who made use of the most sophisticated equipment in their 18-hour hunt for the children, were surprised to learn that the Erland's dog, Bonnie, had broken away from her leash during the night and found her way back to the children.

Bruce McCaffy's mother, Paula, commenting on all the high-technology rescue equipment, wondered why no one had ever thought of using Bonnie, who is half German shepherd and half Labrador retriever, to try to find the children—a Lassie-style rescue.

The dog had accompanied the children and their friend, Tom Pritchard, 11, when they tried to take a short cut home through the woods. They took the short cut because they were afraid they would be late getting home, they said.

Only Pritchard and the dog made their way safely home on Sunday. Throughout the night, in the rain, sleet, and snow, the area was searched, with helicopters, floodlights and trained tracking dogs.

Paula McCaffy said that she had never given up hope, but she admit-ted, "we were pretty worried about those kids." There was a chance the children might not survive the night in the severe weather conditions.

In the end, while others searched with their high-technology devices, dogs , sirens, etc., it was simple instinct and common sense that led the three rescuers to the children.

After talking to Pritchard, the rescuers tried to figure out which direction the boys may have taken, and then struggled through some of worst areas of the swamp, shouting the children's names until they got an answer.

It came from Bruce, who came to the edge of some higher ground. He led the rescuers back to the other children, to where they had all spent the night under some pine trees.

Bruce said that they had been very afraid at times during the night, but they had never given up hope. He knew from his scout training that they should stay in one place after they got lost. At one point they heard a Coast Guard helicopter just overhead, but they had no way of making themselves seen or heard. Richard and Sally Erland, though much fatigued from the night's strain, expressed their thanks for all the efforts to save their children.

Sam Erland, grandfather to all of the children, summed up the family's feelings: "We couldn't be happier. We're so elated, we're up there in the clouds."

Skim the article from a travel magazine about "jet lag." (Jet lag is your body's reaction to a long plane trip across time zones.) Read the questions and then skim the article for the answers. Work as quickly as you can. (Not more than two minutes for the skimming!)

1. According to this article, is jet lag worse when you travel eastward or westward?

   Why?

2. What causes jet lag?

3. What can you do to minimize jet lag?

4. Is there any quick cure for jet lag?

OVERCOMING JET LAG

Experts give recommendations on what works and what doesn't in trying to escape the effects of crossing time zones.

BY MONICA BROOKS

The day before a long flight you are frantically doing last-minute chores and errands, packing, and reading guide books. Then, on the plane, you have several drinks with dinner and stay up late watching the movie. After a brief nap, it's time for breakfast and a morning arrival in, let's say, Paris or Rome. Adrenaline flowing, you spend the entire day sightseeing and taking pictures. By evening, exhaustion has set in, and the next morning, you can hardly wake up before noon. Jet lag has taken hold.

Most people who travel by air across multiple time zones fall victim to this affliction of modern air travel. They may suffer from any of a number of unpleasant symptoms, including insomnia, fatigue, nausea, sleepiness, and lethargy.

According to Dr. Harriet Minsky, professor of psychology at Montreal University, the symptoms of jet lag vary from person to person, and also vary according to how far a traveler has flown. Recovery from jet lag also varies, with some sufferers feeling better gradually and others experiencing alternative days of feeling better or worse.

Dr. Minsky points out that there are three primary causes of jet lag, and of these, two are avoidable. First, people often wear themselves out getting ready for a trip, so they are already exhausted when they get on the plane. Second, long-distance travelers often have a couple of drinks to pass the time. The alcohol can cause stomach distress and interfere with getting a good night's sleep.

The third and unavoidable cause of jet lag is the fact that long distance air travel upsets your internal biological clock. Dr. Alvin Lacy, chief of general medicine at Northern Medical College, explains that our inner clock controls our cycle of sleeping and waking.

The brain takes its cues from the amount of light and other features in the environment. Without environmental cues, the brain tends to set its biological clock to a longer day. This means that, for most travelers, the effects of jet lag are less severe on trips toward the west, because the travel is following the sun. In traveling toward the east, the body must adjust by shortening its day, going against the body's natural tendency. This explains why trips from west to east often result in greater suffering from jet lag.

Individuals are not all affected to the same degree by jet lag. For example, "night owls," people who are usually most alert and lively late at night, are less likely to feel the effects of jet lag. Younger people suffer less than older travelers. In terms of personality types, extroverts (people who are sociable and like to be in groups) tend to suffer less than introverts.

Many people believe that there must be some quick and easy cure for jet la—and, in fact, all kinds of cures have been popularized, from vitamins to special diets, but research has shown that none of these are very effective.

However, Dr. Minsky assures travelers that if they follow certain common sense strategies, they will overcome jet lag more quickly.

• Get plenty of rest and eat healthy meals prior to taking a long flight.

• On the plane, set your watch to your destination's time immediately. Then allow that time to guide your behavior. During the trip, eat and sleep according to the new time zone.

• Once you arrive, begin to follow a normal routine for that time zone. Try not to take naps. Set an alarm clock to wake you in the morning. Spend time outside during the day, and sleep at night.

• Avoid sleeping pills, alcohol, or other drugs that you do not normally use.

exercise 7

 Skim the following essay about the future from **Time** *magazine. Read the questions and then skim the article to find the answers. Work as quickly as you can. (Not more than three minutes for the skimming!) Compare your answers with another student.*

1. Is this writer hopeful or discouraged about the future?
   How can you tell?

2. What are some negative effects of population growth, according to this author?

3. What does this author say must be done to avoid disaster?

Too Many People

IF THE ENVIRONMENT IS ALREADY THREATENED BY OVERPOPULATION, WHAT WOULD THE WORLD BE LIKE WITH TWICE AS MANY INHABITANTS? YOU WOULDN'T WANT TO BE THERE.

BY EUGENE LINDEN

THE STATE OF THE ENVIRONMENT in the later part of the next century will be determined largely by one factor: human population. If the species doubles its numbers by 2050, to nearly 11 billion, humanity may complete the devastation that accelerated so steeply in this century. Such unabated expansion in our numbers would continue to soak up the world's capital and prevent the poorer nations from making the necessary investments in technological development that might deter continued population growth.

If the worst occurs, countless millions will become environmental refugees, swamping the nations that tried to conserve their soil, water and forests. The great-grandchildren of today's young people would have to share the planet with only a ragged cohort of adaptable species dominated by rats, cockroaches, weeds, microbes. The world in which they survived would consist largely of deserts, patches of tropical forest, eroded mountains, dead coral reefs and barren oceans, all buffeted by extremes of weather.

The best hope for both humanity and other life-forms would be to cut human propagation in half, so the world's numbers do not exceed 8 billion by mid-century. (The only event in which the earth would achieve zero population growth or even shrinkage would be some environmental or social catastrophe.) The huge run-up in human numbers has foreclosed most options and shortened the amount of time available to come to grips with rising threats to the environment, contends systems analyst Donella Meadows, co-author of *Beyond the Limits*, which updates the controversial 1972 blockbuster *The Limits to Growth*. In the past, says Meadows, there were always new frontiers for exploding populations, as well as empty lands to accept wastes. No longer: most suitable areas have been colonized, most easy-to-find resources are already being exploited, and most dumping grounds have filled up. "If humans manage brilliantly starting very soon," Meadows believes, "it is possible the world might look better than it does now."

Still, for centuries humanity has confounded doomsayers by finding new supplies of food and energy. In the early 1970s some environmentalists interpreted temporary rises in food and oil prices to mean mankind was again pushing the limits of earthly resources, yet surpluses returned in later years. Julian Simon, among other economists, argued that this revealed a basic problem with the limits-to-growth argument. Price rises caused by scarcities, he argued, will always stimulate human ingenuity to improve efficiency and find new resources.

In the intervening years, however, there has been evidence that the market often fails to react as quickly as problems demand. The world took 15 years to respond to signs of ozone depletion in the upper atmosphere, but because ozone-destroying chemicals take 15 years to migrate to that stratum, the real delay amounts to 30 years. Moreover, these chemicals can remain in the atmosphere as long as 100 years. In addition, market forces often work perversely to hasten the demise of species and resources. The increasing appetite for bluefin tuna among sushi lovers and health-conscious diners has vastly increased the market price of the fish. But instead of dampening demand, the principal effect has been to encourage further fishing, to the point that the total number of the magnificent pelagic fish in the Atlantic has dropped 94% since 1970.

Demographers refer to such collisions between rising demand and diminishing resources as "train wrecks." As the world adds new billions of people in even shorter periods, such potential conflicts happen almost everywhere. With most of the world's good land already under the plow, a population of 11 billion human beings would probably have to make do with less than half the arable land per capita that exists today. That would set the stage for disaster, as farmers stripped nutrients from the soil, exacerbated erosion and gobbled up water and wild lands.

If population keeps building at the current rate, the most ominous effect is that millions of life-forms will become extinct. Humans, no matter how well behaved, cannot help crowding out natural systems. A survey of 50 countries by environmental researcher Paul Harrison showed that habitat loss, the most important factor leading to extinctions, rises in direct proportion to the density of the individuals that make up various species. Big animals often range over hundreds of square miles and increasingly collide with settlements. Smaller species, which make up most of nature's diversity, are affected by human activities in countless ways. Frogs, for example, are gradually disappearing around the world, perhaps because airborne pollutants are destroying their eggs. The crucial question is whether humankind can afford to exterminate large numbers of other species without ruining the ecosystems that also sustain us.

The world could avoid this question by reducing the burden placed on the biosphere by rising human numbers and the lifestyles of rich nations. To do so, however, would require countries to treat these threats far more seriously than they did at the Summit in Brazil last June. The affluent nations must move their economies more rapidly toward patterns of production and consumption that recognize the limits of what the earth can provide and what wastes it can accommodate. The poorer nations must make monumental efforts to remove incentives for people to have large families. This will require massive social change, including better education and improved access to family planning. with each passing year, it becomes more likely that the fastest-growing nations will be forced to adopt coercive measures, as China has, if they are to stabilize their numbers.

IF NONE OF THIS TAKES PLACE, what might the earth look like? Author Meadows predicts that at its best, the typical landscape might resemble the Netherlands: a crowded, monotonous tableau in which no aspect of nature is free from human manip-ulation. Other analysts look to the history of island cul-tures because they tend to reveal how the environment and humans respond when burgeoning populations put stress on an isolated ecosystem.

Easter Island in the Pacific provides a cautionary exam-ple. When Europeans first landed there in 1722, they found 3,000 Polynesians living in extremely primitive conditions on the island amid the remnants of a once flourishing culture. The story of Easter Island is one of ecological collapse that began around the year 1600, when a swollen population of 7,000 stripped the island of trees, depriving inhabitants of building materials for fishing boats and housing. As the populace retreated to caves, var-ious clans warred over resources, then enslaved and later cannibalized the vanquished. By the time Europeans arrived, the beleaguered survivors had forgotten the pur-pose of the great stone heads erected during Easter Island's glory days.

The tropical island of Mauritius in the Indian Ocean presents a more hopeful case study, according to environ-mental historian Richard Grove of Cambridge University. Mauritius is nearly as densely peopled as Bangladesh, yet manages to support healthy ecosystems and a booming economy. Nearly 200 years ago, the island's French settlers became alarmed by the cutting of ebony forests that caused severe erosion and had led to the extinction of the dodo bird. By the end of the 18th century, the locals had developed a full set of environmental controls, including strict limits on tree cutting. In recent years, Mauritius has launched a successful education effort to stabilize popula-tion growth. The country now ranks among the most prosperous in Africa. "I would be much less pessimistic about the future if the rest of the world could act like Mauritius," says Grove.

The world no longer has the leisure of the two cen-turies Mauritius took to develop a conservation ethic. In the past, natural forces shaped the environment. Now, unless a new round of volcanism erupts worldwide or a comet courses in from outer space, human activities will govern the destiny of earth's ecosystems. It may soon be within human power to produce the republics of grass and insects that writer Jonathan Schell believed would be the barren legacy of nuclear war. If humanity fails to seek an accord with nature, population control may be imposed involuntarily by the environment itself. Is there room for optimism? Yes, but only if one can imagine the people of 2050 looking back at the mad spasm of consumption and thoughtless waste in the 20th century as an aberration in human history.

Skimming encyclopedia entries

 exercise 8

➤ *Skim the articles about Eleanor Roosevelt from two different encyclopedias. Read the questions and then skim both articles to find the answers. Work as quickly as you can. (Not more than three minutes for the skimming!) Compare your answers with another student.*

1. Which article tells you more about the personal life of Eleanor Roosevelt?

2. The author of one of these articles has written a book about Eleanor Roosevelt. Which one do you think it is?

3. Does Eleanor Roosevelt sound like the typical woman of her time? Why or why not?

4. What effect did Franklin Roosevelt's illness have on Eleanor's life?

ROOSEVELT, ANNA ELEANOR [rŏ´zə vəlt] (1884-1962), wife of Franklin Delano Roosevelt, thirty-second president of the United States, and a political personality in her own right. She influenced not only domestic legislation but also the activities of other nations as a U.S. delegate to the United Nations and as a goodwill ambassador abroad. Eleanor Roosevelt was born in New York City on Oct. 11, 1884. Elliott, her father, was the younger brother of Theodore Roosevelt and her mother, Anna Hall, was a direct descendant of Chancellor Robert R. Livingston, who administered the oath of office to George Washington. Eleanor was orphaned at age ten and raised by her grandmother, Mary Hall, in upstate New York. She grew to be almost 6 feet (1.8 meters) tall with brown hair and blue eyes. For a short time she studied with tutors, then at fifteen the painfully shy girl went to England where she spent three years at Allenswood, a private school outside London. On her return home in 1902, she made her debut, joined the Junior League, and taught calisthenics and dancing at a settlement house in the slums of New York City.

Eleanor Roosevelt

Her father was a godfather to her distant cousin, Franklin D. Roosevelt of Hyde Park, N.Y., with whom she played as a child. They met occasionally as they were growing up, formed a serious attachment for each other in 1903, when Franklin was at Harvard, and married in 1905 despite his mother's opposition. Her uncle, Pres. Theodore Roosevelt, gave the bride away.

During the early years of her husband's political career, she had six children; five sons and a daughter. Her second son died at six months of influenza.

Mrs. Roosevelt first became aware of politics in 1911 when her husband served in the New York State Senate. She found it distasteful, though she later enjoyed the social and charitable activities that went into being the wife of the assistant secretary of the U.S. Navy during President Wilson's administration. It was only after her husband was paralyzed by poliomyelitis in 1921 that she developed an interest in politics. Tutored by Louis Howe, Franklin D. Roosevelt's political mentor, she became politically active and participated in several women's organizations involved with social legislation. It was Howe's intention to use her to reawaken her crippled husband's interest in the outside world. He taught Mrs. Roosevelt to speak in public and analyze political situations, and helped her to write magazine articles on women's problems.

However, once her husband returned to the political arena, she did not fade into the background. In 1926, she started a furniture factory at Hyde Park to help the unemployed. The next year she became assistant principal and taught American history and literature at Todhunter School in New York. In 1928, when her husband ran for governor in New York, she served as director of women's activities for Alfred E. Smith in his presidential campaign against Herbert Hoover.

During Franklin's two terms as governor, Eleanor Roosevelt served as his "legs and eyes," and made many inspections of state institutions at his request. She expanded this activity after he became president in March 1933. For this and several other activities, Mrs. Roosevelt became known as the most controversial first lady in history. Not content with restricting her role to that of White House social hostess, she advised her husband, helped foster legislation, such as the National Youth Administration, spoke her mind publicly on issues, and prodded all levels of government to improve housing, education, health, and the status of minority groups. She also wrote *My Day,* a syndicated column running in 140 papers, a monthly magazine column, and several books, as well as making lecture tours that covered 50,000 miles a year. All the profits from these ventures were donated to charity.

During World War II, Mrs. Roosevelt continued inspections for her husband and made goodwill tours at his request to England, the South Pacific, and the Caribbean zone. She also visited dozens of military camps inside the United States and reported her findings to the President. For a short time, 1941-1942, she held her only official government job, as assistant director of the office of civilian defense under Fiorello La Guardia.

When her husband died on Apr. 12, 1945, Eleanor Roosevelt told reporters: "The story is over." However, she accepted an appointment from President Truman later in the year to serve as a member of the U.S. delegation to the United Nations. During this period, she took special interest in refugee matters and was chairman of the Human Rights Commission of the UN Economic and Social Council. Fellow American delegates to the UN General Assembly's first session at London in January 1946 credited her with winning the fight to save 1,000,000 refugees from being forcibly returned to Communist countries. Mrs. Roosevelt was instrumental in writing and passing the Declaration of Human Rights.

She left the United Nations in 1952, but returned in 1961 when Pres. John F. Kennedy appointed her a U.S. delegate to the 15th session of the UN General Assembly. In the intervening years she became active again in Democratic Party politics. During the presidential elections of 1952 and 1956, she campaigned for Adlai E. Stevenson. At the 1960 Democratic convention, she pressed for a Stevenson-Kennedy ticket. In 1959, she joined in a drive to consolidate the Democratic reform movement in New York City. Her superabundant energy found many outlets, including newspaper and magazine columns, radio and television appearances, and lecture tours. She died on Nov. 7, 1962, in New York City, and was buried next to her husband at Hyde Park.

ALFRED STEINBERG

ROOSEVELT [rō´zə vəlt] **Eleanor** (1884-1962), one of America's great reforming leaders, who had a sustained impact on national policy toward youth, blacks, women, the poor, and the United Nations. As the wife of President Franklin D. Roosevelt, she was the country's most active First Lady. But she was also an important public personality in her own right.

Early Life. Anna Eleanor Roosevelt was born in New York City on Oct. 11, 1884. Her parents Elliott and Anna Hall Roosevelt, were members of socially prominent families, and she was a niece of President Theodore Roosevelt. She had an intensely unhappy childhood. Her mother, widely known for her beauty, called Eleanor "granny," and her father, whom she adored, was banished from the family because of alcoholism. Her parents died when she was young, and she was raised strictly by her grandmother Hall. Her childhood and adolescent experiences left her with a deep sense of insecurity and inadequacy and a craving for praise and affection.

She first attended private classes and at the age of 15 was sent to Allenswood, a finishing school near London. With the encouragement of the headmistress, Marie Souvestre, the shy girl emerged as a school leader. She returned to New York in 1902 to make her debut in society, but soon

Eleanor Roosevelt

sought to escape its rituals through work with the city's poor at a settlement house. On March 17, 1905, she married her distant cousin Franklin D. Roosevelt. She was given in marriage by President Theodore Roosevelt.

Wife and Mother. In the next 11 years Eleanor Roosevelt gave birth to six children, one of whom died in infancy. In the bringing up of her children, she submitted to the domination of her formidable mother-in-law. After her husband's election to the New York state Senate in 1910, she performed the social role expected of the wife of a public official. As the wife of the assistant secretary of the navy during World War I, she pitched into war work with the Red Cross.

Personal Independence. The end of the war coincided with a grave personal crisis, the discovery of her husband's love for another woman. Eleanor and Franklin Roosevelt were reconciled, but when they returned to New York in 1921 she determined to build a life of her own. She had become active in the League of Women Voters, the Women's Trade Union League, and the women's division of the Democratic party. Her personal emancipation was completed after Roosevelt was stricken with polio in 1921.

Eleanor Roosevelt was determined to keep alive her husband's interest in public affairs. Encouraged and tutored by Louis Howe, Roosevelt's close adviser, she became her husband's political stand-in. By 1928, when Roosevelt returned to the political wars as a candidate for governor of New York, she had become a public figure in her own right. In 1926 she helped found a furniture factory in Hyde Park to aid the unemployed. In 1927 she became part owner of the Todhunter School in New York City, serving as vice principal and teaching history and government.

First Lady. When her husband became president in 1933, she feared the move to the White House would make her a prisoner in a gilded cage. But as First Lady, she broke many precedents. She initiated weekly press conferences with women reporters, lectured throughout the country, and

had her own radio program. Her syndicated newspaper column, *My Day*, was published daily for many years. Traveling widely, she served as her husband's eyes and ears and became a major voice in his administration for measures to aid the underprivileged and racial minorities.

In 1941 she made her one venture while her husband was president into holding public office herself, as co-director of the Office of Civilian Defense. But she resigned following criticism of some of her appointments. During World War II she visited troops in England, the South Pacific, the Caribbean, and on U.S. military bases.

Later Years. When her husband died on April 12, 1945, Eleanor Roosevelt assumed that the "story was over." However, she went on to 17 more years of notable public service, perhaps the most satisfactory of her career. She was appointed a member of the U.S. delegation to the United Nations by President Harry Truman in December 1945. As chairman of the Commission of Human Rights she was instrumental in the drafting of the UN Declaration of Human Rights. She resigned from the United Nations in 1952, but was reappointed by President John Kennedy in 1961. She remained active in Democratic party politics and was a strong supporter of Adlai Stevenson in the presidential campaigns of 1952 and 1956 and at the Democratic convention in 1960.

In her later years Eleanor Roosevelt presided over her large family at Val-Kill, her home at Hyde Park. She kept up a voluminous correspondence and a busy social life. "I suppose I should slow down," she said on her 77th birthday. She died the next year on Nov. 7, 1962, in New York City, and was buried in the rose garden at Hyde Park next to her husband. Her many books include *This Is My Story* (1937), *This I Remember* (1949), and *On My Own* (1958).   JOSEPH P. LASH
Author of "Eleanor and Franklin"

Further Reading: Hansen, William P., and Haney, John, eds. *Eleanor Roosevelt* (Chelsea House 1987); Lash, Joseph P., *Eleanor and Franklin* (Norton 1971); Lash, Joseph P., *Eleanor: The Years Alone* (Norton 1972).

exercise 9

➤ **Skim the articles about AIDS from two different encyclopedias. Read the questions and then skim both *articles to find the answers. Work as quickly as you can. (Not more than three minutes for the skimming!) Compare your answers with another student.***

1. Which article begins with a brief history of AIDS in the United States?

2. Which article gives more information about the transmission (spreading) of AIDS?

3. If you were writing a report about AIDS, which of these articles would be more useful to you?

   Why?

4. Do these articles give any hope that a cure will be found soon for AIDS?
   Explain:

5. In skimming the articles, did you find out something about AIDS that you did not know before?
   Explain:

AIDS, acronym for acquired immune deficiency syndrome, a progressive, degenerative disease of several major organ systems, including the immune and central nervous systems. The disease is caused by the human immunodeficiency virus type 1 (HIV-1). AIDS was first identified in 1981.

The initial symptoms of infection often resemble influenza or mononucleosis and appear days or weeks after exposure. These symptoms usually disappear after several weeks. A prolonged symptom-free period may last ten or more years after initial infection. Progressive failure of the immune function, evidence of substantial and increasing damage to the brain and spinal column, and profound weight loss characterize the later stage of the disease. Death often results from infections that occur once the immune system fails or from wasting, cancer, or destruction of the brain.

Infection in infants follows one or two courses. About one-half of the children infected at birth fail to thrive, experience multiple severe infections during the first several months of life, and die within the first year. Other infants exhibit only minor symptoms and survive for six to ten years or more.

The virus can be transmitted sexually from men to women, from women to men, and from men to men. The use of condoms reduces the frequency of heterosexual transmission by greater than 90%.

The virus can be transmitted from mother to child before birth, at birth, and possibly by breast feeding after birth. About one-third of children born to infected mothers are infected by age three months.

The AIDS virus can also be transmitted by blood transfusions, organ transplants, and artificial insemination. The virus is very efficiently transmitted by means of shared needles or syringes, and it remains active in dried blood for many weeks. The virus is very rarely if ever transmitted by means other than those described above, including saliva.

Infection is commonly diagnosed by the detection of an immune reaction to the virus, determined by measuring antibodies. Antibodies often appear within six weeks of infection, and they persist throughout the course of the disease. A very small number of infected people remain free of antiviral antibodies for more than a year after infection. Infection can also be diagnosed by detection of viral proteins or viral nucleic acids.

It is estimated that as of the early 1990s between 10 and 20 million people are infected worldwide. The most severely infected region is central Africa. The epidemic is well established in North and South America, Europe, Australia, India, and Southeast Asia.

HIV-1 belongs to a family of viruses called retroviruses. These small RNA viruses convert their genetic information from RNA to DNA on infection and insert the DNA form of the genetic material into the genetic material in the chromosomes of the host cell. The virus's genetic material cannot be removed from these chromosomes. Consequently, a person infected with HIV-1 remains infected for life. In addition to the information required to make new virus particles, HIV-1 makes at least seven additional proteins. Some govern the rate of virus replication. Others increase the infectious nature of the virus.

Several features of the virus's life cycle render it resistant to vaccines. The virus can infect cells at the mucosal surface, which makes prevention difficult. Infected cells may harbor the virus's genetic information without producing viral proteins; such cells cannot be recognized by the immune system. The surface of the virus particle is heavily coated with sugar molecules that are identical to those of the host cell and cannot be recognized by the immune system. Moreover, HIV-1 viruses isolated from different individuals vary in their immunological properties, and they may even vary within a single infected person. Although attempts to create vaccines that overcome such difficulties are in progress, no vaccine has yet been shown to prevent infection.

AIDS treatments include the use of antiviral drugs to slow the rate of HIV-1 replication. Other treatments are designed to prevent or treat opportunistic infections and cancers that result from a deficient immune system. Nucleoside analogues, including azidothymidine (AZT), dideoxyinosine (DDI), and dideosycytosine (DDC), show some promise for delaying onset of terminal symptoms. Genetic therapies as well as new antiviral drugs directed against specific viral proteins such as the protease, the tat protein, the envelope glycoprotein, and DNA polymerase are currently being evaluated.

Viruses similar to HIV-1 have been isolated from humans and nonhuman primates. The human immunodeficiency virus type 2 (HIV-2), prevalent in some West African countries, induces an AIDS-like disease, although with a longer latent period and lower probability of disease. Simian immunodeficiency viruses (SIVs) have been isolated from some Africans, but not Asian or New World, nonhuman primates.

WILLIAM A. HASELTINE, Dana-Farber Cancer Institute and Harvard Medical School

ACQUIRED IMMUNE DEFICIENCY SYN-DROME (AIDS), a human disease that ravages the immune system, undermining the body's capacity to defend itself against certain microbial organisms. It usually leads to death from multiple infections in a few months to several years from the time of onset. The disease was first identified in 1980 among homosexual men in New York and California, and by mid-1993 it had stricken more than 315,000 persons in the United States alone, causing nearly 195,000 fatalities. There were growing numbers of cases in Europe, Africa, Asia, and Latin America as well, and about 14 million people worldwide were believed to be symptomless carriers of the disease. Although male homosexuals continue to constitute a major portion of the victims in many countries, the risk groups also include a growing number of both male and female intravenous drug abusers and infants of mothers afflicted with the disease. In addition, there is some heterosexual transmission of AIDS. The disease has also occurred among hemophiliacs, who receive clotting factor derived from the pooled blood of many donors.

Signs and Symptoms. The chief manifestations of AIDS are the presence of rampant "opportunistic" infections that do not cause disease in normal individuals, and the appearance of a skin neoplasm, or abnormal growth, known as Kaposi's sarcoma, which until recently in the United States and Europe was a rare, relatively benign, condition in elderly men. The most common early symptoms of AIDS include fever, weight loss, enlarged lymph nodes, skin eruptions, and shortness of breath. As the disease progresses, there may be drastic wasting, nausea, diarrhea, neurological and visual impairment, and mental disturbances. These symptoms are the result of the infection caused by any of a number of different viruses, bacteria, fungi, and protozoa. For example, one fungus, Pneumocystis carinii, causes a type of pneumonia that is common among AIDS patients but is otherwise rare.

Diagnosis. Abnormalities of cellular immunity in AIDS typically include a change in the distribution of certain types of thymus-derived (T) lymphocytes, those white blood cells that modulate the immune response. (See also IMMUNITY; The Immune Response.) While characteristic of AIDS, this disturbance can be seen in other diseases and thus cannot be used as a diagnostic test by itself. Many other blood tests point to widespread disruption of immune function in AIDS.

Treatment. While no effective treatment for the underlying immune deficiency has been developed, management of some of the secondary infections, neoplastic processes, and other complications is possible and may improve longevity and quality of life. The drug azidothymidine, or AZT, has been shown to prolong the lives of some AIDS patients.

Transmission. The transmission of AIDS occurs through infected blood or body fluids by sexual contact or the use of contaminated needles in the intravenous injection of drugs.

Transmission of the disease through blood transfusions has caused alarm. However, a test has been developed that has enabled blood banks to screen their supplies of blood from contamination with the AIDS virus. The possibility that AIDS could be transmitted through casual contact, such as by sharing dining utensils or bathroom facilities has caused widespread public alarm despite reassurances to the contrary from public health professionals.

Cause. The cause of AIDS is a virus called human immunodeficiency virus, or HIV. The origin of the disease and the nature of its appearance in the United States are uncertain. It has been suggested that the causative agent of AIDS might have been introduced from Haiti or Africa, locations in which numerous other infectious diseases, such as malaria and amoebic dysentery, are endemic. In 1992 and 1993, a small number of AIDS-like illnesses occurring without evidence of HIV infection were under study.

The Center for Disease Control and Prevention in Atlanta, the National Institutes of Health, the Pasteur Institute in Paris, and independent investigators are working to find a drug or drugs to combat the AIDS virus, and are conducting studies to clarify the immunology and epidemiology of the disorder. Scientists are also testing vaccines that may eventually be effective in preventing the AIDS infection. *See also* BLOOD: Blood Transfusion; HOMOSEXUALITY.

FREDERICK P. SIEGAL AND MARTA SIEGAL

Making Inferences

What is an inference?

Sometimes the topic of a text may not be stated anywhere directly. You must look for clues and try to guess what the passage is about. This is called making an inference.

Example: Try to infer what "it" is in this passage.

> I found **it** in the middle of the sidewalk on my way home from school one spring morning. **It** was very tiny and it was hardly breathing when I picked **it** up. I fed **it** raw meat and other treats for several weeks. Soon, **it** became strong and started to hop around. One day, someone left a window open. When I came home from work, I discovered that **it** had disappeared.

What is "**it**?"

Underline the ideas in the paragraph which helped you to make this inference.

The ability to make inferences is very important in reading. You often need to infer the topic or main idea of a text, the author's opinion, or other information.

Inferring missing information

There are many situations in real life when you need to make inferences. Below are some exercises based on real situations. Try to use the information that is given to guess what is missing.

exercise 1

➤ *On the next page is a postcard from a friend. The postcard got wet, so you couldn't read the postmark or the first line. Where has your friend gone for her vacation? Who is with her? Discuss your inferences with another student.*

exercise 2

➤ *Also on the next page is a notice that came in the mail. The notice was torn and some words are missing all along the edge. Who is the notice from? What is it about? Discuss your inferences with another student.*

exercise 1

[Postcard front — handwritten message:]

Dear ~~Carmen~~
~~...~~ ~~...~~ in ~~...~~
~~...~~ ~~...~~ a quiet, pleasant city. Not much of a nightlife for Sarah. She was hoping to meet some other people her age. But everyone here is very nice and they all speak excellent English. Now we're driving north, through the lakes. The scenery is just lovely. You should see Arnie with his camera! He's taken hundreds of pictures. The evenings are especially beautiful, with this strange light until midnight. We never feel like going to bed. In a few days we'll be in the land of the midnight sun. Arnie and Sarah send their love.

Carmen Garza
14 Palomino St.
Juarez, TX
78216

exercise 2

To Parents of Students at

On Tuesday, October 11, parents of all students in the ... will be held at 8:00 in Room 1... attendance is requested.

At the meeting we will i... school committee. We will also ... the lunch program and the schoo... ask questions or to make sugges... matters.

There will be time afterwa... teachers or school officials. W... the 11th.

Yours sincerely,

George Bindershaft

George Bindershaft, Principal

Making inferences from conversations

Have you ever overheard part of a conversation and tried to imagine what it was about? If so, you were making inferences. In the following exercises, you will practice inferring information from short dialogues.

If you find words you do not know, skip over them. Look for the clues that will help you answer the inference questions.

➤ **Read the conversation and try to infer the answers to the questions below.**

Example:

A: Excuse me. Do you live around here? Is this Elm Street?

B: No, this is Maple Ave.

A: Maple Ave?... Oh, dear. I really don't understand this! I'm looking for Elm St. and I thought this was it.

B: No, no. Elm St. isn't anywhere near here.

A: But wasn't that the high school back there?

B: No, that was the town hall.

A: Oh. Then I really *am* confused. Can you take a look here and show me where I am?

B: Sure. Let's see... You're over here. See? This is Maple Ave. and here's the high school. Now, if you want to get to Elm St. you'd better take the bus...

1. Who are these people?

    A visitor from out of town and someone who lives there

2. What are they talking about?

    Where they are—the visitor is lost and wants to know where she is on the map

3. Are they men or women? How can you tell?

    It is impossible to tell.

exercise 3

➤ **Read this conversation and infer the answers to the questions below. Discuss your inferences with another student.**

A: Why is he taking so long?

B: He has to get changed, you know. He's got all that make-up to take off.

A: Well, we've been here forty minutes now. It's cold out here. Are you sure we're at the right door?

B: Yes, I'm sure. Come on. Let's not give up now. I've just got to see him close up.

A: They say he's really quite ugly.

B: Oh, no, that's not true. I've seen him on TV a couple of times. He's got the cutest smile.

A: Well, I don't know. I'm just about frozen. If he doesn't come out in another two minutes, I'm going home.

B: Oh, look! Here he comes. Quick, where's your pen?!?

1. Where are these people?
2. What are they doing?
3. Who are they talking about?
4. Are they men or women? How can you tell?

exercise 4

➤ **Read this conversation and infer the answers to the questions below. Discuss your inferences with another student.**

A: Excuse me. Would you mind turning down the music, please?

B: What's that?

A: I said, could you please turn the music down! My whole apartment is rattling!

B: Oh. Is that better?

A: A little better. It is after midnight.

B: Ah, come on. It's still early. It's my birthday, you know, so I asked a few friends over.

A: Well, that's very nice, but I've got to get up early tomorrow.

B: But it's Sunday tomorrow. What do you have to get up for so early?

A: That's none of your business. The rules say no noise after 11:00. So if you're going to continue, I'll have to call the police.

B: Oh, all right. Don't get so uptight about it all.

1. Where are these people?
2. Who are they?
3. What are they talking about?
4. Are they men or women? How can you tell?

exercise 5

➤ **Read this conversation and infer the answers to the questions below. Discuss your inferences with another student.**

A: For here or to go?

B: To go.

A: Large or small?

B: Uh… small.

A: Light or black?

B: Black.

A: Sugar?

B: Yes, two please.

A: Want a bag?

B: No, thanks.

A: OK, that'll be seventy-five.

B: Here you are.

A: Bye now.

B: Bye.

1. Where are these people?

2. What are they talking about?

3. Are they men or women? How can you tell?

exercise 6

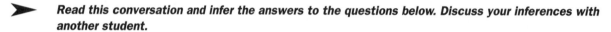

➤ **Read this conversation and infer the answers to the questions below. Discuss your inferences with another student.**

A: So how was it?

B: Terrible.

A: Really? You were so excited about going.

B: I know, but I tell you, I'm glad to be back.

A: What happened?

B: First of all, there was the weather. It rained every day. Not just a little, but all day! There we were with these gorgeous beaches and no sun!

A: I guess you didn't get much of a tan.

B: Look at me! I'm as pale as I was before.

A: At least you must have gotten some rest.

B: Rest! The second day we were there, my husband got sick. He was sneezing and coughing for three days and nights. And then I caught his cold. I felt just awful for another three days.

A: Well, how was the food?

B: That was the only nice thing about the whole week. Except that we were too sick to enjoy it half the time. Anything new here in the office?

A: Not much. It's been a slow week.

1. Where are these people?

2. What is their relationship?

3. What are they talking about?

4. Are they men or women? How can you tell?

exercise 7

➤ **Read this conversation and infer the answers to the questions below. Discuss your inferences with another student.**

A: Fill it up, please.

B: Regular or Super?

A: Regular.

B: Want me to check the oil?

A: No, that's all right.

B: What about the windshield. Need a cleaning?

A: Sure. Go ahead.

B: OK.

A: How much?

B: Ten-fifty.

A: Here, put it on my Visa.

B: We don't take credit cards.

A: No credit cards! Hope I've got the cash. Let's see, let me look in my jacket pocket. No.... oh here, that makes ten. I must have another fifty cents on me somewhere.

B: Don't worry about it.

A: Really, I'm sorry. I thought I could use my Visa.

B: That's OK. You can give it to me next time.

A: Thanks a lot.

1. Where are these people?

2. What are they talking about?

3. Are they men or women? How can you tell?

exercise 8

> *Read this conversation and infer the answers to the questions below. Discuss your inferences with another student.*

A: Is this the kind of thing you're looking for?

B: It's hard to tell. You see, she's got very definite ideas.

A: How about a nice little item like this?

B: Hmmm. You'd think I'd know by now. I mean, it's been thirty-seven years since we married. But every year I have the same problem! Those do look nice, but they're a bit too old-fashioned. She doesn't think of herself that way, you know.

A: Then what about these. They're more classic.

B: No, no. She's not the classic type. Something more modern.... Those over there. That's what she'd like.

A: The ones with all the colors? We usually sell those to, well… to younger women.

B: She's fond of color. Always has been. Says I'm so dull in my business clothes....

A: Shall I gift wrap it?

B: No, that's not necessary. I'll just put the box in my pocket.

1. Where are these people?

2. What are they talking about?

3. What did "B" put in his pocket?

4. How old is "B"?

Making inferences from short stories and plays

The authors of novels, stories or plays often do not explain everything about characters or situations. The reader must infer the author's meaning from the descriptions or the dialogues. In the following exercises you will practice making inferences about characters and situations.

Remember that you do not need to understand every word. If you find words you do not know, skip over them. Read quickly for the clues that will help you infer the answers to the questions.

exercise 9

➤ **Read the following passage from "A Domestic Dilemma," a story by Carson McCullers. (A "dilemma" is a problem with no easy solution.) Working with another student or a group of students, try to infer the answers to the questions below. Then underline the words or phrases that helped you.**

A Domestic Dilemma

The children were in the living room, so intent on play that the opening of the front door was at first unnoticed. Martin stood looking at his safe, lovely children. They had opened the bottom drawer of the secretary and taken out the Christmas decorations. Andy had managed to plug in the Christmas tree lights and the green and red bulbs glowed with out-of-season festivity on the rug on the living room. At the moment he was trying to trail the bright cord over Marianne's rocking horse. Marianne sat on the floor pulling off an angel's wings. The children wailed a startling welcome. Martin swung the fat little baby girl up to his shoulder and Andy threw himself against his father's legs.

'Daddy, Daddy, Daddy!'

Martin set down the little girl carefully and swung Andy a few times like a pendulum. Then he picked up the Christmas tree cord.

'What is all this stuff doing out? Help me put it back in the drawer. You're not to fool with the light socket. Remember I told you that before. I mean it, Andy.'

The six-year-old child nodded and shut the secretary drawer. Martin stroked his fair soft hair and his hand lingered tenderly on the nape of the child's frail neck.

'Had supper yet, Bumpkin?'

'It hurt. The toast was hot.'

The baby girl stumbled on the rug and, after the first surprise of the fall, began to cry; Martin picked her up and carried her in his arms back to the kitchen.

'See, Daddy,' said Andy. 'The toast—'

Emily had laid the childrens' supper on the uncovered porcelain table. There were two plates with the remains of cream-of-wheat and eggs and silver mugs that had held milk. There was also a platter of cinnamon toast, untouched except for one tooth-marked bite. Martin sniffed the bitten piece and nibbled gingerly. Then he put the toast into the garbage pail.

'Hoo—phui—What on earth!'

Emily had mistaken the tin of cayenne for the cinnamon.

'I like to have burnt up,' Andy said. 'Drank water and ran outdoors and opened my mouth. Marianne didn't eat none.'

'Any,' corrected Martin. He stood helpless, looking around the walls of the kitchen. 'Well, that's that, I guess,' he said finally. 'Where is your mother now?'

'She's up in you alls' room.'

Martin left the children in the kitchen and went up to his wife. Outside the door he waited for a moment to still his anger. He did not knock and once inside the room he closed the door behind him.

Emily sat in the rocking chair by the window of the pleasant room. She had been drinking something from a tumbler and as he entered she put the glass hurriedly on the floor behind the chair. In her attitude there was confusion and guilt which she tried to hide by a show of spurious vivacity.

'Oh, Marty! You home already? The time slipped up on me. I was just going down—'

1. What are the relationships among the four characters here?

2. Where are they?

3. What has happened just before this passage?

4. Which character do you think expresses the author's point of view?

5. What do you think will happen after this in the story?

exercise 10

➤ *Read the passage below from "The Day Mr. Prescott Died," a story by Sylvia Plath. Working with another student or a group of students, try to infer the answers to the questions below. Then underline the words or phrases that helped you.*

THE DAY MR. PRESCOTT DIED

'That,' said Liz after a drag of her cigarette, 'is the last glass Pop drank out of. But never mind.'

'Oh…, I'm sorry,' I said, putting it down fast. All at once I felt very much like being sick because I had a picture of old Mr. Prescott drinking his last from the glass and turning blue. 'I really am sorry.'

Ben grinned 'Somebody's got to drink out of it someday.' I liked Ben. He was always a practical guy when he wanted to be.

Liz went upstairs to change then, after showing me what to get ready for supper.

'Mind if I bring in my guitar?' Ben asked, while I was starting to fix up the potato salad.

'Sure, it's okay by me,' I said. 'Only won't folks talk? Guitars being mostly for parties and all?'

'So let them talk. I've got a yen to strum.'

I made tracks around the kitchen and Ben didn't say much, only sat and played these hillbilly songs very soft, that made you want to laugh and sometimes cry.

'You know, Ben,' I said, cutting up a plate of cold turkey, 'I wonder, are you really sorry.'

Ben grinned, that way he has. 'Not really sorry, now, but I could have been nicer. Could have been nicer, that's all.'

I thought of Mama, and suddenly all the sad part I hadn't been able to find during the day came up in my throat. 'We'll go on better than before,' I said. And then I quoted Mama like I never thought I would: 'It's all the best of us can do.' And I went to take the hot pea soup off the stove.

'Queer, isn't it,' Ben said. 'How you think something is dead and you're free, and then you find it sitting in your own guts laughing at you. Like I don't feel Pop has really died. He's down there somewhere inside of me, looking at what's going on. And grinning away.'

'That can be the good part,' I said, suddenly knowing that it really could. 'The part you don't have to run from. You know you take it with you, and then when you go any place, it's not running away. It's just growing up.'

Ben smiled at me, and I went to call the folks in. Supper was kind of a quiet meal, with lots of good cold ham and turkey. We talked about my job at the insurance office, and I even made Mrs. Mayfair laugh, telling about my boss Mr. Murray and his trick cigars. Liz was almost engaged, Mrs. Prescott said, and she wasn't half herself unless Barry was around. Not a mention of old Mr. Prescott.

---

1. Who are the main characters in this story?

2. Where are they?

3. What happened before this passage in the story?

4. What do you think will happen next?

 exercise 11

> **Read the passage from A Streetcar Named Desire, a play by Tennessee Williams. Working with another student or a group of students, try to infer the answers to the questions below. Then underline the words or phrases that helped you.**

A Streetcar Named Desire

Act I, Scene 4

BLANCHE. And that—that makes it all right?

STELLA. *(Rises)* No, it isn't all right for anybody to make such a terrible row, but—people do sometimes. *(Leans over chair by dressing-table.)* Stanley's always smashed things. Why, on our wedding night—soon as we came in here—he snatched off one of my slippers and rushed about the place smashing the light-bulbs with it.

BLANCHE. He did—what?

STELLA. *(Arranging dressing-table chair to face mirror, as she sits in it.)* He smashed all the light-bulbs with the heel of my slipper! *(Laughs.)*

BLANCHE. *(Crossing to above dressing-table.)* And you—you let him—you didn't run, you didn't scream?

STELLA. I was sort of—thrilled by it. *(Rises, moves stool below armchair into place, then moves to L. of doorway.)* Eunice and you had breakfast?

BLANCHE. *(In front of dressing-table.)* Do you suppose I wanted any breakfast?

STELLA. There's some coffee left on the stove. *(Crosses U.)*

BLANCHE. *(Below dressing-table.)* You're so—matter of fact about it, Stella.

STELLA. *(Below radio table, holding up some loose wires.)* What other can I be? He's taken the radio to get it fixed. *(Gurgles pleasantly.)* It didn't land on the pavement, so only one tube was smashed.

BLANCHE. And you are standing there smiling!

STELLA. *(Puts wires back on radio table.)* What do you want me to do? *(Moves screen to head of bed—folds and stacks it there.)*

BLANCHE. *(Sits on bed.)* Pull yourself together and face the facts.

STELLA. *(Sits beside Blanche on bed—at Blanche's L.)* What are they, in your opinion?

BLANCHE. In my opinion? You're married to a madman.

STELLA. No!

BLANCHE. Yes, you are, your fix is worse than mine is! Only you're not being sensible about it. I'm going to do something. Get hold of myself and make a new life!

STELLA. Yes?

BLANCHE. But you've given in. And that isn't right, you're not old! You can get out.

STELLA. *(Slowly and emphatically.)* I'm not in anything I want to get out of.

BLANCHE. *(Incredulously.)* What—Stella?

STELLA. *(Rises. Crosses below to door between rooms.)* I said I am not in anything I have a desire to get out of. *(Surveys mess in living-room.)* Look at the mess in this room!

---

1. What are the relationships among the three characters?

2. Where are they?

3. What happened before this passage?

4. Which character do you think expresses the author's point of view?

5. What do you think will happen after this in the story?

exercise 12

➤ **Read the passage below from A Roomful of Roses, *a play by Edith Sommer. Working with another student or a group of students, try to infer the answers to the questions below. Then underline the words or phrases that helped you.***

A Roomful of Roses

NANCY: I'm sorry—Bridget. (*Reaching toward her in an impulsive gesture of affection*) Darling, I do want you to stay. More than anything in the world, I want you to stay. We all want you— won't you think about it? Just during the next few days, think about it. Hard.

BRIDGET: No! It's utterly impossible!

NANCY: Are you so happy at home?

BRIDGET: Why do you ask me that?

NANCY: I want you to be happy somewhere. If not with me, then somewhere else.

BRIDGET: You don't have to worry about that. I am happy. Terribly.

NANCY: And you like your school?

BRIDGET: I love it. The only thing I don't like—I don't like this conversation. And if it's all right with you, I'll dress for dinner now.

NANCY: Oh, baby—you don't have to be so lonely.

BRIDGET: Listen! Don't say a thing like that to me. Don't you dare to be sorry for me!

NANCY: Bridget!

BRIDGET: Don't you dare! You have no right! (*She starts up the stairs.*)

NANCY: *Bridie!* You come back here. Don't ever speak to me in that tone again. I don't care what you think I have done to you, you are never to speak to me in that way again. Do you understand?

BRIDGET: Yes.

NANCY: All right. Now come over here and sit down.

BRIDGET: I have nothing to say.

NANCY: But I have something to say. I've been waiting a long time to say it, so I hope...I want you to understand, that no matter how you feel toward me, you are a deep and important part of my life. I love you very much.

BRIDGET: Is that all?

NANCY: No. No, it isn't. There is something else. I knew—you would feel resentful and hurt...But I didn't dream it would be like this. I've tried in every way I know to reach you. I've stayed awake nights trying to think of a way—some way—of reaching you...

BRIDGET: Of breaking me down, you mean.

NANCY: Yes, if you want to put it that way. Bridie, you're a little girl still. In many ways a very little girl. But soon—you will be a young woman. (*Bridget starts to rise.*) Now wait! It's for your own sake I'm saying this. It's for you. Bridie, don't let the fact that there was something very bad in your life once be the most important thing about you. Don't blame everyone you meet for something that happened a long time ago.

BRIDGET: May I go to my room now?

NANCY: Do you really hate me so much?

BRIDGET: No, I don't hate you. I don't feel anything about you at all. Just blankness. And I want to keep it that way.

BRIDGET: Bridie, it wasn't all *my* fault—what happened wasn't all my fault! I've never told you this before, but your father was—Oh, dear.

BRIDGET: I don't care *whose* fault it was! You were the one who ran away!

NANCY: Not from you! I wanted you with me. I tried—you know I tried—I didn't run away from you.

BRIDGET: You ran away from Dad and me. Why? Because you liked Jay better?

NANCY: No—things aren't that simple.

BRIDGET: Then *why?*

NANCY: Bridie, listen—there are things you won't understand until you are older, but try—try to understand this—the love I have for Jay is love your father did not want from me. And it has nothing whatever to do with the love I feel for you.

BRIDGET: You're too late, Mother. I don't care anymore. That's funny. I call you Mother. But it's only because I don't know what else to call you. To me you aren't my mother. As far as I'm concerned, my mother is dead. And I used to wish you had died. Oh, how I wished...I'd lie awake in bed at night and pretend that you had died. Sometimes it seemed so real—and I'd cry... All right, now you know what I really feel about you. Do you still want me to stay?

NANCY: More than ever.

BRIDGET: You're crazy!... (*She turns and runs up the stairs.*)

---

1. What is the relationship between these two characters?

2. Where are they?

3. What can you tell about the past?

4. What do you think will happen after this in the story?

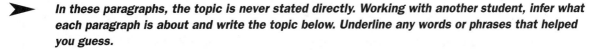

Inferring topics and main ideas

exercise 13

➤ *In these paragraphs, the topic is never stated directly. Working with another student, infer what each paragraph is about and write the topic below. Underline any words or phrases that helped you guess.*

1.   In the early days, people thought it would have a positive effect on family life. It brought the whole family together in one room. It also put an end to the usual family quarrels. Everyone stayed quiet and just listened, for a change. But now it is clear that not all the effects are positive. Some researchers believe that it prevents parents and children from having normal relationships. The members of the family may be sitting together, but most of the time no one talks. No one relates to anyone else in the room. The only communication that happens is one-way: from the actors to each individual. And this brings up another problem. Many children spend most of their free time this way. That means that they have no idea of what family life can be. The picture they get of a family—from what they see—is false and too simple. It leaves out many negative aspects and many uncertainties. This may mean that they may not be able to tolerate real family life with all its complexities.

Topic:

How can you tell?

2.   Some of us have done this hundreds of times—we sometimes think we could do it in our sleep. But if it's your first time, don't worry. It's really a very simple procedure. First you sort everything into piles. It's better to separate things carefully at this point or you can cause real damage. Then when one pile is ready, let technology work. Be sure you follow the directions. And remember that it is better not to do too many things at once. Mistakes can be expensive. The next step depends on your equipment. You may be able to put technology to work again. Or you may have to use old-fashioned methods and take it outside. In any case, it will eventually be time to make piles again and put everything where it belongs. And then you are done—for now. All too soon the time will come to repeat the whole procedure again!

Topic:

How can you tell?

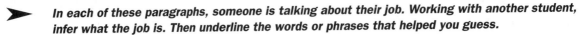

exercise 14

➤ *In each of these paragraphs, someone is talking about their job. Working with another student, infer what the job is. Then underline the words or phrases that helped you guess.*

1. "The minute you climb in, you start feeling excited. There's nothing so exciting for me, not even a jet plane. You get in and start up and off you go. And then you've got to pay attention every minute. There's always someone doing something crazy who's likely to end up under your wheels. I sometimes think it's a miracle if I can get all the way there with no accidents. You've always got to be thinking ahead. There's a lot of people in this job who have stomach problems from the tension. They lose their hearing too, because of the noise. You've got to be tough on this job, you know."

    Job:

2. "My day starts at four o'clock in the morning. That's when my feet hit the floor. I'm at work at five-thirty and I finish at two in the afternoon. In between I do a lot of walking. I wear out a lot of shoes each year—maybe four or five pairs. And my poor feet, at the end of the day they're really hurting. The other problem is the dogs. Sometimes you can make friends with them and they'll follow you around. But other times, they can be mean. I've been bitten a couple of times. I can't say as I care much for dogs any more. But it's not all bad, my job. One thing I like is the way you meet a lot of people. You learn all about their private lives, too. It never gets boring."

    Job:

3. "The most important thing is to understand people. You've got to know what they're thinking. If you can figure that out you can get them to do anything. They come in with an idea about what they want. You get them talking about themselves, about what they like. If it's a man, you talk about baseball, or something like that. If it's a woman, you ask her about fashions. That way they get comfortable with you. You ask them a lot of questions and get them saying yes. Then they just get into the habit of saying yes. In the end you can put them into anything you want, if you're really good. They need a little car for the city; you send them home with a truck. Of course, I wouldn't really do that. It wouldn't be right. You've got to sell on this job, but you also have to be fair. It's not fair to take advantage of people too much. There are some people in this business who'd do anything. But I don't believe in that."

    Job:

exercise 15

➤ **In these paragraphs, the writer does not state the main idea directly. Working with another student, try to infer the main idea and write it below. (Remember that the main idea is always a complete sentence.) Underline the words or phrases that helped you.**

Sleep: An Important Part of Life

1. Are you sometimes a little tired and sleepy in the early afternoon? If so, you are not the only one. Many people feel this way after lunch. They may think that eating lunch is the cause of their sleepiness. Or, in summer, they may think it is the heat. However, the real reason lies inside their bodies. At that time—about eight hours after you wake up—your body temperature goes down. This is what makes you slow down and feel sleepy. Scientists have tested sleep habits in experimental situations where there was no night or day. The people in these experiments almost always followed a similar sleeping pattern. They slept for one long period and then for one short period about eight hours later.

    Main Idea:_____

    _____

2. In many parts of the world, people take naps in the middle of the day. (A nap is a short, daytime period of sleep.) This is especially the case in warmer climates, where the heat makes work difficult in early afternoon. Researchers are now saying that naps are good for everyone in any climate. First of all, a daily nap means a more rested body and mind and many health benefits. In countries where naps are traditional, people tend to suffer less from stress and stress-related problems such as heart disease. Another benefit of taking naps is improved job performance. In jobs where public safety is involved, a nap can make an important difference. Studies have found, for example, that airplane pilots make fewer mistakes if they take regular naps.

    Main Idea:_____

    _____

3. Many working people, unfortunately, have no time to take naps. Though doctors may recommend taking naps, employers do not allow it! If you do have the possibility, however, here are a few tips about making the most of your nap. Remember that the best time to take a nap is about eight hours after you get up. A nap too late in the day may only make you feel more tired and sleepy afterward. This can also happen if you sleep for too long. A nap that lasts too long may also make it difficult for you to sleep at night. If time is a problem, try a short nap—even ten minutes of sleep can be helpful. Some people, in fact, find that they do not need to sleep at all. They feel rested and more awake after just lying down for a while.

    Main Idea:_____

    _____

exercise 16

Book reviewers usually tell something about the subject of the book and give their opinion. However, sometimes they do not state their opinion directly. They give some hints about it and let the reader infer it.

➤ ***Read the book reviews below and try to infer the reviewer's opinion of the book.***

1.   This modern cowboy story is set in 1949. It follows three young men on a wild ride on horseback out of Texas and into northern Mexico. Their adventure takes them out of twentieth century America and into a totally different world. Here, it is still possible to live with horses and nature. There are the bad guys and good guys, as in the classic films. But the book is not just a rewrite of a John Wayne movie. The characters are convincing and the descriptions of the natural world are truly brilliant. The style is ambitious—we are reminded of Faulkner—and it could easily have become terribly stylized. But this author has the skill to make it work. The masterly writing and action-filled plot keep the reader's attention throughout. We hope the second volume that the author promises will be as satisfying as this.

What is the reviewer's opinion of this book?

How do you know?

Does it sound like something you would like to read?

Discuss this with another student. Do you agree?

2.   One of the oldest themes in literature is the love triangle. This theme has inspired some of the world's classics. However, it has also inspired some very poor writing. This first novel unfortunately falls in the second category. The situation is not new: a man falls in love with his best friend's wife. At first the characters are interesting and the reader begins to like them. But that interest soon dies out. The characters talk on and on but nothing ever seems to happen. And their conversation is all on the same topic: themselves. The ending is tragic, or at least it is supposed to be. But by the time we get to the end of the book, we don't really care about these people. I suggest this author take up banking, or some other career that doesn't require too much imagination!

What is the reviewer's opinion of this book?

How do you know?

Does it sound like something you would like to read?

Discuss this with another student. Do you agree?

Summarizing

What is summarizing?

Summarizing is the retelling of the important parts of a passage in a much shorter form.

Why summarize?

- To make sure you have understood something.
- To explain the sense of a passage to someone else.
- To review texts for examinations.

What does a good summary include?

- A good summary includes the main ideas and the major supporting points.
- A good summary does *not* include minor details, repeated details, or the reader's opinions.

Summarizing sentences

Summarize a sentence by taking out the unnecessary words. Use summary words to take the place of groups of words about the same topic. Keep only the words which tell the main point of the sentence. Use as few words as possible.

Example:

The tall cowboy put the saddle on his horse, untied him from the fence, waved good-bye and rode off into the sunset.

Summary: The cowboy left.

Explanation: You can leave out the word *tall*, since that is not an important fact. All of the things that the cowboy did (put saddle on horse, untied him, waved good-bye, and rode off) can be summarized in one word: left.

exercise 1

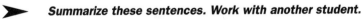

▶ **Summarize these sentences. Work with another student.**

1. After she turned on the oven, Michiko mixed the sugar, flour, eggs, milk, oil, and vanilla in the new blender, poured the batter into the buttered pans, and put the cake in the oven.

   Summary:

2. As the bus rolled into her hometown, Liz looked around at the familiar streets and shops which she had not seen for two years.

   Summary:

3. Serge put on his raincoat, picked up his umbrella from the table near the door, turned off the lights, put out the cat, and got ready for his ten-minute walk to the bus stop.

   Summary:

4. When the Chen family returned from their vacation, they found the back door broken open, the television set missing, and all the food in their freezer gone.

   Summary:

5. In Natasha's library you can find mysteries, novels, biographies, travel books, how-to manuals, science fiction thrillers, and reference books.

   Summary:

6. With her new credit card, Yoko bought groceries at the supermarket, shoes at the department store, and a new set of tires for her sports car at the auto supply store.

   Summary:

7. During the summer along the Charles River in Boston, you can go rollerblading, running, biking, or sailing, or you can have a picnic, listen to a concert, or watch a movie.

   Summary:

8. After clearing away the old leaves and branches, Bill dug up the hard ground, mixed in fertilizer and new soil, raked it all smooth, and planted the seeds.

   Summary:

9. When they heard the weather forecast, the islanders closed the windows, put tape across the glass, moved all of their plants and chairs indoors, and stocked up on bottles of fresh water.

   Summary:

10. Sue put her pens and pencils neatly in a row, turned on the radio, stacked her English books on the desk, got herself a soda, and sat down in her desk chair.

    Summary:

Summarizing paragraphs

A paragraph summary should be as short as possible, but it must be a complete sentence.

The summary of a paragraph is the main idea of the paragraph. Often (but not always), the main idea is found in the topic sentence.

Step 1. Read the paragraph all the way through to be sure you understand it.

Step 2. Check to see if the paragraph contains a topic sentence.

- If the paragraph has a topic sentence, does it state the main idea of the paragraph? If so, you can use the topic sentence as the summary.

- If the topic sentence is not a good statement of the main idea, write a summary which states the main idea.

Step 3. Take out unnecessary words.

Example:

Shopping malls have produced a revolution in United States shopping and living habits in just 45 years. Before 1950, there were no malls, but now almost every city or region has at least one. In fact, shopping malls have become a part of daily life. Many people even think of them as social centers. In a way, malls have taken the place of Main Street. Shops and services which were once spread over several city blocks are now in one place at the mall. Busy householders can save time by doing their shopping at the mall. And people young and old, with time on their hands, often say, "Let's go to the mall!"

Topic sentence: *Shopping malls have produced a revolution in United States shopping and living habits.*

You can make this even shorter: *Shopping malls have changed United States culture.*

exercise 2

Summarize each of the following paragraphs. Follow the steps explained above. Use as few words as possible. Work with another student.

Shopping Malls in the United States

1. Although every shopping mall is a bit different in design, shoppers often quickly feel comfortable in a new mall. That is because malls usually share certain features. You can almost always find most of the following: a department store, a pharmacy, a toy store, a book shop, clothing shops for all ages, shoe shops, a bank, and places to eat. These businesses are all under one roof. Most malls are enclosed, so that shoppers never have to go outdoors once they get to the mall. A few malls sometimes also have doors to shops on the outside of the mall. Every mall is surrounded by a large parking area.

   Summary:

2.   Malls are not all exactly alike. In a suburb of Chicago, where many wealthy people live, malls are quite large and beautiful. One of these malls is two stories tall and houses about 50 businesses. These range from small specialty shops to large luxury department stores. The roof of the mall is made of glass and is twice as tall as the shops inside. Musicians play for the customers in the evenings, and trees and fountains are found in central seating areas. In a poor, rural town in southern Maine, however, a typical mall is plain and rather small. It might have a supermarket, a pizza parlor, a book and gift shop, a laundromat, and a bank. All its shops are found on one level, and the interior of the enclosed mall is plain and undecorated. Recorded music is piped in through speakers.

Summary:

3.   While shopping malls have changed American life, not all of their effects have been positive. Most of the shops and services found in malls are parts of large corporations. These businesses have taken away customers from smaller shops in the area and forced them to close. That has meant fewer individually owned businesses and less local control over jobs. In addition, malls are harmful to the environment. They have sometime been built on land that is important for the survival of birds and wild animals. Wherever they are built, they cover large areas with buildings and parking lots— instead of trees or grass. Thus, they contribute to the general loss of nature. And finally, malls are usually far from any town center, so people must use cars to get there. This results in increased air pollution and heavy traffic on the roads near the mall.

Summary:

exercise 3

➤   *Summarize each of the following paragraphs. Follow the steps explained on page 169. Use as few words as possible. Work with another student.*

The Challenger Disaster

1.   By 1984, NASA, the United States space program, had carried out many successful flights of the space shuttle. In fact, Americans were beginning to take the whole NASA program for granted. Then, the president announced that the next shuttle would carry a school teacher into space. Hundreds of teachers from all parts of the country applied for the job. They all wanted to be "the first teacher in space." During the next year, these adventurous educators were tested and examined and trained. At last, the choice was announced. A teacher from New Hampshire, Christa MacAuliffe, would be the first teacher-astronaut.

Summary:

2.   Many months of preparation and training followed the announcement. First, Christa went through intensive physical training. She had to be in top condition for the flight. Then she learned how to operate some of the delicate instruments on the Challenger space shuttle. Christa planned special lessons which she would teach from space. Finally. she trained with the other astronauts, so they could work as a team in space.

Summary:

3.   Everyone knows what happened on that terrible day in January, 1986. Early in the morning, the Challenger crew had a good breakfast and discussed their plans. They made sure they understood all of the work they would be doing during the flight. Later, they boarded a special van which carried them to the shuttle. The weather was rather cold, and some NASA officials wondered if they should put off the flight. After some discussion, they decided to go ahead. The Challenger took off over the Atlantic Ocean in Florida. Minutes later, it exploded in the air. All of the crew members died in the crash.

Summary:

Summarizing short passages

Step 1. Read the passage all the way through.

Step 2. Go back to the beginning and underline the topic sentence in each paragraph. If you cannot a find topic sentence, write a short summary of the paragraph.

Step 3. Put the sentences from the paragraphs together. Connect them with signal words or other connecting words. (Remember, signal words and connecting words tie ideas together. Examples: *and, but, however, first, next, then, because.*)

exercise 4

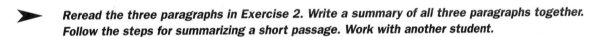

> **Reread the three paragraphs in Exercise 2. Write a summary of all three paragraphs together. Follow the steps for summarizing a short passage. Work with another student.**

exercise 5

 Reread the three paragraphs in Exercise 3. Write a summary of all three paragraphs together. Follow the steps for summarizing a short passage. Work with another student.

exercise 6

Summarize this short passage. Work with another student. When you have finished, compare your work with another pair of students.

A New Way to Visit the Wilderness

People who are looking for outdoor adventure often go to Maine. This state in the northeastern United States contains large areas of wilderness. There you can enjoy a new and exciting sport: white water rafting. In the past, this sport was practiced only in the western states. But now, several outdoor travel companies offer weekend rafting trips. They provide guide service, equipment, and even food and they invite people who have had no experience at all. Thus, city residents, too, can get a taste of wilderness. All they need to bring with them is a desire for adventure.

"White water" is the water of a river when it moves very fast over rocky areas. As the water fills with air bubbles, it looks white. The areas of white water are also the most exciting areas for rafters—and also the most dangerous. In fact, rafting guides must always be on the look for white water. And rafters must be ready to swim, because the raft can tip over in white water. For that reason, rafters should always wear special life vests that will keep them afloat.

Rafting is a sport that almost anyone can do. It does not require great physical strength. Sometimes, at very rocky parts of the river, rafters will need to walk for a while. They may also need to carry the rubber rafts at times, but these are very light. Paddling the boats is easy because they are going down river. The main activity is simply to enjoy the wonderful wild scenery.

Most rafting companies offer overnight trips that combine with camping. This kind of trip is ideal for a family with children over twelve. Several rafts of people will start out from a base camp. Their food supplies, sleeping bags, tents, and other necessities are sometimes packed onto the rafts. Or all the supplies might be brought by car to the next camp site. The guide often is also the cook for the group of rafters and may be quite a good chef. After a day of rafting, in any case, the food tastes good and sleep comes easily.

➤ *Write one sentence to summarize each paragraph.*

Paragraph 1:

Paragraph 2:

Paragraph 3:

Paragraph 4:

Now tie the sentences together to make one short paragraph. Write the final summary below. Use only the words which are absolutely necessary.

exercise 7

➤ *Summarize this short passage. Work with another student. When you have finished, compare your work with another pair of students.*

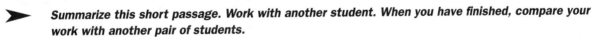

New Species in North America

Hundreds of different species of plants and animals have arrived in the United States. This number has increased greatly as international travel and business have increased. Some of these new "residents" have caused problems for agriculture or for the environment. The Mediterranean fruit fly, for example, arrived in California on some imported fruit in the 1970s. In its original home in the Mediterranean area, it had never caused much damage. In California, however, it multiplied very quickly. Soon the California fruit industry was in trouble. The government had to take serious measures, including using lots of chemicals to try to kill the flies. However, they have not managed to get rid of the fly altogether.

Another example of an animal that has recently settled in North America is the zebra mussel. This small shellfish was first discovered in the Great Lakes in 1986. It may have come over from Russia on a cargo ship. In a very few years zebra mussels had spread over all the Great Lakes and into many important rivers. They have grown into thick masses, covering many areas of lakes or river bottoms. They have also covered and closed up pipes for power stations and water treatment centers. Government officials say that the mussels have caused many millions of dollars worth of damage.

Sometimes the damage caused by an immigrant species is not measurable in dollars. It may not harm us directly, but it may change the environment. And that may cause problems for the plants or animals that were living there before. Loosestrife is a plant that came to North America some time in the 19th century. It may have been carried as seeds on the back of some sheep from Europe. Or someone may have brought the seeds to plant in their garden. In any case, loosestrife now grows along rivers and lakes all over North America. It is a pretty plant, with a purple or pink flower. But when a lot of loosestrife grows in one place, other plants cannot grow there. The birds and small animals that depend on those other plants cannot stay there, either. As loosestrife spreads, they may have trouble finding any place to live and they may begin to disappear.

Write one sentence to summarize each paragraph.

Paragraph 1:

Paragraph 2:

Paragraph 3:

Now tie the sentences together to make one short paragraph. Write the final summary below. Use only the words which are absolutely necessary.

Summarizing longer passages

When you summarize an essay, textbook chapter, or magazine article with many paragraphs, follow these steps:

Step 1. Read the passage all the way through.

Step 2. Go back to the beginning and number the paragraphs in the text.

Step 3. Divide the text into parts. Notice which paragraphs focus on the same idea. Part one, for example, will be Paragraph #1 to Paragraph #x. Part two will start with paragraph #y, and so forth.

Step 4. For each part, write a sentence which summarizes all the paragraphs in it.

Step 5. Tie all of those sentences together to form a summary, using signal words and other function words.

exercise 8

➤ *Summarize an article you have already read. Turn to the article titled "Picking Apples—A New England Tradition" on page 26. Follow the steps for summarizing a longer passage explained above. Work with another student. Use as few words as possible in your final summary.*

Step 1

Part 1: Paragraph 1–_____

Part 2: Paragraph _____–_____

Part _____: Paragraph _____–_____

Part _____: Paragraph _____–_____

Step 2: Write a very brief summary of each part here:

Part 1:

Part 2:

Part 3:

Part _____:

Step 3: Tie the summaries of the parts together to make one final summary. Use as few words as possible.

exercise 9

➤ Summarize the Reading Faster passage on page 223. Follow the steps for summarizing a longer passage. Work with another student. Use as few words as possible in your final summary.

Step 1

Part 1: Paragraph 1–____

Part 2: Paragraph ____–____

Part ____: Paragraph ____–____

Part ____: Paragraph ____–____

Step 2: Write a very brief summary of each part here:

Part 1:

Part 2:

Part 3:

Part ____:

Step 3: Tie the summaries of the parts together to make one final summary. Use as few words as possible.

exercise 10

Follow the steps for summarizing a longer passage. Summarize this magazine article. Work with another student. Use as few words as possible.

Better Homes in Gardens

by Marc Lecard

In the middle of winter, homes are sealed tight. Householders want to cut down on heating bills and save natural resources, so they make their homes air tight. They put special materials over windows and around doors to keep the heat in and the cold out. But while keeping the cold out, they keep in a surprising amount of air pollution.

The air in a typical home or apartment can have many different kinds of poisons in it. Some can even cause cancer. Certain chemicals are given off by furniture, building materials, and household products. Refrigerators and other household appliances add unhealthy chemicals to the air. And tobacco smoke contains even more poisonous fumes. Even breathing adds certain poisonous chemicals to the air, such as acetone and ethyl alcohol. Inside a tightly sealed building with poor ventilation, hundreds of air pollutants can be found.

But you don't have to stop breathing the air in your home! Cleaner air may be as close as your house plants! According to a NASA scientist, house plants can help keep indoor air breathable. This scientist, B.C. Wolverton, has been investigating the use of plants as living air filters for more than 20 years. His research developed from studies of the air in spaceships.

Wolverton found that some common house plants had an appetite for certain poisons in the air. Spider plants and Boston ferns love formaldehyde. Peace lilac takes in large amounts of a chemical called trichloroethylene. English ivy and chrysanthemums eat benzene.

Since he began his study, Wolverton has tested more than 40 plants for their ability to remove pollutants from the air. Among the most useful for average households, he says, are areca palm, golden pothos, Janet Craig plant, and corn plant. These plants are easy to grow indoors, require only low light, and clean the air effectively. He suggests using two or three plants for every 100 square feet of space.

Plants take in pollutants in the air through their leaves along with carbon dioxide in the process of photosynthesis. Tiny microscopic bugs (microbes) in the soil around the roots help break down the poisons so that the plants can feed on them. In fact, the way the roots feed on these broken-down pollutants is a part of the natural cleaning process. According to Wolverton, "Ninety percent of the work is done by the microbes."

Wolverton predicts that someday all homes and offices will have indoor gardens built into them. They will be a normal part of the design of the building's air control systems.

Step 1

Part 1: Paragraph 1–____

Part 2: Paragraph ____–____

Part ____: Paragraph ____–____

Part ____: Paragraph ____–____

Step 2: Write a very brief summary of each part here:

Part 1:

Part 2:

Part 3:

Part ____:

Step 3: Tie the summaries of the parts together to make one final summary. Use as few words as possible.

Thinking Skills

Introduction

If you want to read well in English, you must think in English as you read. If you think in another language and translate from the English, you will always have difficulty with comprehension. Understanding the words and the grammar is not enough. You need to be able to follow the *ideas* in English.

The exercises that follow will help you to develop your ability to follow ideas and think in English.

Example a:

In this example, the final sentence is not complete. Try to think of an ending which would complete the sentence logically. Then look at the four possible endings below the paragraph. Decide which is the best ending and circle the letter.

In the past, if you wanted to eat Japanese food, you had to go to Japan. Now, you can find Japanese restaurants all around the world, from New York to Rome or Sydney. In the same way, Italian food used to be found only in Italy. Now, Italian restaurants can be found everywhere, from Moscow to Tokyo or Sao Paulo. People everywhere are learning to enjoy the foods of other countries. Someday, it may be possible to

a. eat Italian food in Tokyo.
b. eat only traditional food in each country.
c. eat every kind of food in every country.
d. eat only Japanese food.

Which is the best ending?

Explanation: Ending *a* is not correct, because of the word *someday* in the last sentence. We know from the paragraph that people already eat Italian food in Tokyo.

Ending *b* is not correct because we know from the paragraph that many different kinds of food are available in most countries.

Ending *c* is correct because the main idea of the paragraph is that different national foods are being eaten in more and more countries.

Ending *d* is not correct, because it is the opposite of what the paragraph says.

Example b:

The "Potato Famine" was a terrible period in Irish history. In the early 19th century, many Irish people were very poor. They had little to eat except potatoes. Then, in the 1830s, a disease killed most of the potato plants in Ireland. With no potatoes to eat, millions of Irish people

a. got sick.
b. ate meat instead.
c. were much happier.
d. died of hunger.

Which is the best ending?

Compare your choice with another student. Explain how you got your answer.

Example c:

Coca Cola was invented in the United States at the beginning of the 20th century. By the 1950s and 1960s, it had become a popular drink and a kind of symbol of American culture. In the next decade, the Coca Cola company began exporting to Europe and other countries. The drink was soon in great demand around the world, but it was very expensive. That is no longer the case. There are now Coca Cola factories in many countries. In most places, a can of Coca Cola is no more expensive than other drinks. In fact, market research recently discovered something surprising. The country where a can of Coca Cola now costs the most is

a. the United States.
b. Switzerland.
c. China.
d. Australia.

Which is the best ending? Check your answer in the Answer Key on page 289.

Guidelines for Success on Thinking in English Exercises

1. Guess the meanings of unknown words. Do not translate from another language while you are reading. Words in another language can confuse you and prevent you from following the ideas in English.

2. Look for the main idea of the paragraph. The correct ending will follow the main idea.

3. Work quickly! Your first guess is usually your best guess.

4. Each time you work on these exercises, write the date in the right-hand margin. Try to do some exercises every week.

Thinking in English

➤ *Choose the best ending for each paragraph. The Answer Key is on page 289.*

1. Fog is a major cause of accidents on highways in some areas. Every year many thousands of people lose their lives because fog can dangerously reduce visibility. The drivers cannot see very far ahead so they

a. do not have time to avoid accidents.
b. go faster to avoid accidents.
c. have more time to read the signs.
d. do not have time to have accidents.

2.   The idea of a car that knows where to go may seem impossible. However, new technology may soon make this possible. Cars will have computers to tell drivers which roads have the least traffic. That way the drivers will not waste time in traffic jams. There will also be less pollution because the car engines will be running less. These new cars will be known as

a. "expensive cars."
b. "fast cars."
c. "traffic cars."
d. "smart cars."

3.   Scottish people like to think that golf is a Scottish sport. The game did not come from Scotland, however. It was first played in Holland in the 14th century. Only later did it become

a. popular with the Dutch.
b. popular in Scotland.
c. a real sport.
d. an Olympic sport.

4.   When Christopher Columbus sailed west from Spain in 1492 he wanted to reach Asia. He did not know there was another continent in between Europe and Asia. In fact, when he died he still believed that the land he had found was

a. Asia.
b. America.
c. Spain.
d. another continent.

5.   In the past, many people in western Ireland and the Scottish Highlands spoke Gaelic as their first language. Now only a few people speak Gaelic, and they are mostly from the older generation. The younger people

a. hardly understand any English.
b. don't like to speak with strangers.
c. often don't even understand Gaelic.
d. don't often speak with the older generation.

6.   When Europeans first arrived in North America in 1620 the forests were full of bears. There were more than half a million of these wild animals. Then the Europeans began to cut down the forests where the bears lived. They also began to hunt the bears. By 1900, there were very few bears left. Now, however, the bear population is about 200,000. The bears have begun to multiply again, thanks to

a. better hunting methods.
b. better foods for them.
c. better laws to protect them.
d. better laws to protect Europeans.

7.   The dog was the first domesticated animal. Very early in human history, people learned that a dog could help with hunting. Dogs also were good company for early man. We can say that the dog is man's "best friend" and his

   a. worst enemy.
   b. only friend.
   c. latest friend.
   d. oldest friend.

8.   For many years, alligator skin was popular in the United States for making fashionable leather shoes and purses. From 1870 to 1965 at least ten million alligators were killed in the United States for leather. Then, in 1967, the government made laws against hunting alligators. After that the alligator population began to grow again. Now there are

   a. no more alligators in the United States.
   b. fewer alligators than there were in 1967.
   c. more alligator skins for making shoes and purses.
   d. nearly two million alligators in the United States.

9.   It used to be fashionable for women to have very small waists. They often wore tight clothes around their middles to make them thinner. A woman with a very thin waist was said to be "wasp-waisted" because her body looked like the body of a wasp. The wasp is an insect with

   a. a large head and small body.
   b. a very thin middle.
   c. tight clothes around its middle.
   d. long, thin legs.

10.   The tulip is a flower that originally grew in Turkey. In the 17th century it became very popular in Holland. Some Dutch merchants became very rich by importing tulips. They sold them to the

   a. Dutch at very high prices.
   b. Turkish at very high prices.
   c. Turkish at very low prices.
   d. Dutch at very low prices.

11.   Most flowering plants bloom in the spring or summer. But there are some plants that also have flowers in the winter. One of these is the peony. Certain kinds of peonies can produce beautiful red or pink flowers even

   a. on the warmest days of the year.
   b. when other flowers are blooming.
   c. on the coldest days of the year.
   d. when it has no leaves.

12.   The yew tree grows very slowly and can live for hundreds of years. In southern England one year, a terrible storm blew down many tall, old yew trees. Some of these splendid trees were more than 300 years old. New yew trees have been planted, but they will

a. grow more quickly.
b. only live for a few years.
c. be tall and splendid only after many years.
d. never be as splendid as the old trees.

13.   In the past, North American forests were full of chestnut trees. People used chestnuts in cooking in many different ways. They also loved to cook chestnuts over a fire and eat them plain. Then in the early 1900s a disease killed almost all the trees. Now it is hard to find fresh chestnuts in the U.S. markets and usually they are

a. from North America.
b. without much flavor.
c. roasted over a fire.
d. imported from Europe.

14.   Evergreen trees never lose their leaves. For that reason these trees are sometimes associated with the idea of a life after death. In Italy, evergreens are usually the only kinds of trees that people plant

a. in graveyards.
b. along streets.
c. in long lines.
d. in gardens.

15.   Until recently the kiwi fruit was rare in most countries. All the kiwis came from far away New Zealand. They were transported a great distance and so they were expensive. Now many countries grow kiwis. The supply of this fruit has greatly increased and so

a. it has become even more expensive.
b. it is harder to get.
c. New Zealand has stopped producing it.
d. it has become less expensive.

16.   There are many ways to prepare eggs for eating. You can fry them, boil them or scramble them. Or, if the eggs are very fresh, you can even eat them without cooking them. Whatever way you choose to eat your eggs, however, you must

a. always break the shell first.
b. always cook them.
c. never cook them.
d. never break the shell.

17. Chocolate is one of the most popular sweets in the world. It is eaten as candy, in cakes, cookies, and puddings. In some places, however, it is also eaten in a non-sweet form. The Mexicans, for example, make a chicken dish with a spicy chocolate sauce. This sauce does not include

a. any chocolate.
b. any vitamins.
c. any sweetener.
d. any candy.

18. Legumes are a category of vegetable that includes beans, lentils, and peas. In many parts of the world legumes are an important basic food. They usually do not cost much and they are full of protein, vitamins, and minerals. Americans generally do not eat many legumes. Instead they spend a lot of money on meat. Meat has protein too, but it also has lots of unhealthy fat and cholesterol. In fact, many Americans would be healthier if they

a. ate more meat.
b. ate more legumes.
c. were richer.
d. spent less money on food.

19. Pigs have long been the most common animal for meat in many parts of the world. The reason for this is economic. The pig produces meat more efficiently than any other animal. For every 100 pounds of food, it produces 20 pounds of meat. In comparison, for example, cattle produce

a. more than 30 pounds of meat per 100 pounds of food.
b. twice as much meat per 100 pounds of food.
c. only about seven pounds of meat per 100 pounds of food.
d. nearly double the amount of meat per 100 pounds of food.

20. Vitamins are very important for good health. One vitamin that you need to have regularly is vitamin C. Certain fruits and vegetables are rich in this vitamin. Some examples are oranges, lemons, and grapefruits, as well as red peppers and tomatoes. Vitamin C can be destroyed by heat, so it is a good idea

a. to eat only cooked fruits and vegetables.
b. to eat only vegetables that have vitamin C.
c. to eat lots of uncooked fruits and vegetables.
d. never to eat uncooked fruits and vegetables.

21. Some kinds of birds fly great distances every year. In the fall, they leave their homes in the north and fly thousands of miles south. Then in the spring, they return to the north, to exactly the same place. Scientists do not really know how they do this. They believe that these birds must have

a. some way of speaking.
b. an especially rich diet.
c. some kind of map in their heads.
d. special feathers on their wings.

22.   Where there are people, there are almost always mice or rats. This is true in all parts of the world. These animals can be a real problem. They eat or damage supplies of food. They can also damage clothes and furniture in the home. Finally, they can carry many types of diseases to humans and other animals. Therefore, you should

a. keep a good supply of food in the home.
b. clean your clothes carefully.
c. boil all the water you drink.
d. keep your home free of mice and rats.

23.   Many scientists, including Charles Darwin, wondered why we cry tears. What is the biological or evolutionary purpose of tears? We could just as well cry without any tears falling. But, in fact, our eyes fill with tears. Scientists have proposed many theories about tears, but none of these theories has been proven. And so, in evolutionary terms,

a. the origin of tears remains a mystery.
b. Darwin explained the origin of tears.
c. there are many reasons for crying with tears.
d. only Darwin studied the origin of tears.

24.   We usually do not think of the night sky as a colorful scene. You don't see much color, in fact, if you look at the stars with just your eyes. But scientists with special equipment now have a different picture of what is in the sky at night. A new series of photographs shows

a. a black and white sky.
b. all kinds of bright colors in the night sky.
c. that the night sky has little color.
d. lots of new stars in the night sky.

25.   Many people are very afraid of snakes. It is true that poisonous snakes can make you very ill or even kill you. However, very few snakes are poisonous. Most snakes are harmless. In fact, they usually are afraid of people. If you meet a snake in your garden, it will probably

a. bite you.
b. slide quickly away.
c. stay and watch you.
d. come closer.

26.   Some of the most famous classical composers died quite young. Among these, for example, were Schubert and Mozart, who both died in their thirties. But not all composers have had short lives. Bach lived until age 65 and Haydn until age 69. Still others, like Verdi and Richard Strauss,

a. died at a very young age.
b. lived on into their eighties.
c. died while playing the piano.
d. were alive in the twentieth century.

27.   A popular children's song compares a star to a "diamond in the sky." The idea that stars look like diamonds is not new. But now scientists are saying that there may be real diamonds among the stars. These diamonds are certainly interesting for the scientists. But they are not going to make anyone rich, because

    a. only children can see them.
    b. only the scientists know where they are.
    c. they are too expensive.
    d. they are too far away.

28.   The telephone companies in the United States have a major problem: they are running out of numbers for their customers. The system now in use was invented in 1947. No one then had any idea how fast the population would grow. Soon there will be no more combinations left of the seven-digit numbers. People will have to start using

    a. the telephone less.
    b. shorter numbers.
    c. longer numbers.
    d. more expensive telephones.

29.   Exercising in your home may be good for your health, but it may not be good for your children. In 1990, about 13,000 children were hurt by exercise equipment. The exercise bicycle was the most common cause of injury. Many children lost a finger or a toe in the wheels of these bicycles. So if you have an exercise bicycle, you should

    a. let your children use it too.
    b. stop using it immediately.
    c. keep it outside.
    d. not let your children play with it.

30.   It may be possible in the future to choose the sex of your child. Researchers in France believe that they have found a way to influence the sex of the unborn child. They say that it depends on what the woman eats in the period before she gets pregnant. However, other researchers are doubtful about this theory. They say that the process is really much more complex. According to these critics, the new theory

    a. will change the way women eat.
    b. is much too complicated.
    c. does not deal with other factors.
    d. is influenced by the French peoples' love of good food.

31.   Long before there were airplanes, people wanted to be able to fly. Early scientists studied birds' wings to see how they worked. Then they tried to build wings of feathers. But when they actually tried to fly, they never

    a. spread their wings enough.
    b. stayed up for long.
    c. hurt themselves.
    d. fell to the ground.

32.   When people first began to try to fly in the 18th century, they used hot-air balloons. However, it was not really possible to control the balloons. They went wherever the wind was blowing. The idea of a real flying machine remained a dream for a long time to come. The dream finally came true in 1903. That year Wilbur and Orville Wright

    a. invented a new kind of engine.
    b. made their first successful flight in an airplane.
    c. flew across the Atlantic Ocean.
    d. wrote a book about their flying experiences.

33.   What would you do if you got lost in a desert? The most important thing is to find water. But where can you find drinking water in the middle of all that sand? The answer is simple: in the desert plants. In fact, the most common desert plant, the cactus, contains lots of good water. With the right method and some simple tools, you

    a. can get only a few drops of water a day.
    b. will get water that is undrinkable.
    c. will be able to find a drinking fountain.
    d. can get about a liter of water a day.

34.   Do you know what to do if someone falls off a small boat? The first thing to do is to throw out a life ring. Don't lose sight of the person. You should try to get close with the boat. At the same time, you must be very careful not to hurt the person in the water. Then you should try to help him or her climb back into the boat. This is not always easy, especially if

    a. the weather is warm.
    b. the person is hurt or cold.
    c. there are several people to help.
    d. the person is a good swimmer.

35.   In 1585, Sir Walter Raleigh tried to start the first English settlement in North America. However, the settlement was not successful. Many settlers became sick and others died of hunger or in battles with the Native Americans. When another ship came from England a few years later, the newcomers found that

    a. the settlement had grown.
    b. the settlers were not glad to see it.
    c. all the settlers were dead.
    d. the settlers had all married Native Americans.

36.   In different parts of the world, people build their houses of different materials. In areas where there is a lot of wood, houses are made of wood. In hot, dry areas with little wood, houses are often made of clay bricks. In the far northern areas, people even build their houses of ice. Generally,

    a. people prefer houses made of stone.
    b. wooden houses are dangerous because they can burn.
    c. people in some areas build their houses of leaves.
    d. people build their houses with whatever they can find.

37.   The population of the earth has been growing at a rapid rate. In 1700, there were about 500 million people in the world. By 1850, the population had grown to one billion. In the next 100 years, the population more than doubled. In 1950, it was

   a. less than a billion.
   b. about two and a half billion.
   c. over five million.
   d. just over a billion.

38.   The one cent coin in the United States has a picture of Abraham Lincoln on it. Lincoln, the 16th president of the United States, was one of the country's greatest presidents. He came from a poor family, however. He had to study on his own and work very hard as a young man. This was the reason why the government decided to put Lincoln's picture on the smallest coin. It would remind everyone that in America

   a. even someone from a poor family could become president.
   b. someone from a poor family could never become president.
   c. most of the presidents have come from poor families.
   d. there have been no presidents from poor families.

39.   Why do we grow old? This is a question that people have asked since the beginning of history. Now biologists are looking for scientific answers to this question. They think that aging is part of our genetic program. From the evolutionary point of view this makes sense. A person who can no longer have children is no longer useful to the species, so he/she

   a. grows old and dies.
   b. lives a long life.
   c. stops having children.
   d. has a genetic program.

40.   The Japanese love to eat raw fish. Dishes of uncooked fish, called sushi or sashimi, are prepared at most Japanese restaurants. Japanese cooks use many kinds of fish or shellfish for these dishes. Whatever kind of fish they use, however, it must always be very fresh. To prove that the fish is fresh, some restaurants will even serve

   a. fish cooked on a grill.
   b. fish that is still alive.
   c. whole fish.
   d. many unusual kinds of fish.

41.   Cars are the most important cause of air pollution in many cities. This is especially true in cities, such as Los Angeles, where most people go to work by car. In order to reduce pollution, the city must reduce the number of cars on the road. This is only possible, however, if people have another way to get to work. For this reason, many city governments are working to improve the

   a. highway system.
   b. quality of life.
   c. connections between cities.
   d. public transportation system.

42. Imagine a baby about five months old. It can cry and smile, it can eat and sleep, and it can dirty its diaper. Did you know that it can also count? That's not all—small babies are also able to add and subtract small numbers of things. This may be surprising news, but a psychologist has proven that it is true. Many people think that these abilities are learned at school. But this psychologist believes that they are

   a. not present until adulthood.
   b. learned only by five-month old babies.
   c. already present in small babies.
   d. very difficult for children to learn.

43. Until recently scientists thought that the first humans developed from our ape ancestors in Africa. According to this theory, these early humans then gradually moved to other parts of the world. Now there is new evidence for a different theory about the beginnings of humans. In 1990 scientists in China found the bones of two human heads from about one million years ago. These heads may mean that humans

   a. all developed in Africa
   b. didn't all develop in Africa.
   c. developed from apes.
   d. all looked alike.

44. Children who are left-handed tend to have more accidents than right-handed children. Doctors have two theories to explain this fact. One theory says that left-handed children may simply fall and bump into things more. Another theory, however, explains the accidents very differently. According to this theory, the problem is not with the children, but with the world around them. Most things, such as doors, cars, and toys are

   a. designed and used best by right-handed people.
   b. designed for left-handed people.
   c. not designed for right-handed people.
   d. made by people without children.

45. One of the most important principles in biology is that all living things must come from other living things. This principle was not discovered until the 18th century. Before that, people believed that life could come from other kinds of matter. For example, they thought that worms could come from meat. Then a scientist tried covering the meat so that flies could not land on it. No worms grew on the meat, since of course they really came from the

   a. scientist.
   b. cloth.
   c. flies' eggs.
   d. 18th century.

46.   Sixty-five million years ago, the age of the dinosaurs suddenly came to an end. The dinosaurs all disappeared from the earth. Scientists have always wondered why this happened. A new discovery in Mexico may give them the answer. The discovery is a huge circle 180 kilometers wide. This circle was probably caused by some very large object that hit the earth. When it hit, it may have caused changes in the earth's climate and sea levels. These changes may have

a. helped the dinosaurs to live longer.
b. been necessary for the dinosaurs.
c. killed the dinosaurs in Mexico.
d. been disastrous for dinosaurs.

47.   Frogs are not generally known for being good parents. The female frog usually lays her eggs and then goes away and the baby frogs grow up on their own. However, one kind of frog is different. This frog, either male or female, will stay with the eggs until the baby frogs are born. Then the parent will carry the babies on its back to a special kind of plant. It puts one baby frog in each of these watery flowers. And that's not all. Every day

a. the baby frogs grow larger.
b. the parents go swimming.
c. the father sleeps most of the day.
d. the parent brings food to the babies.

48.   Scientists wondered for a long time just how whales are related to land mammals. They believed that there must have been some kind of in-between mammal. It would have lived partly in the sea and partly on land. However, they had no evidence of such an animal. The discovery of "Pakicetus" seems finally to be proof of this theory. The bones of Pakicetus show that this large mammal lived 50 million years ago. It

a. was a kind of large fish.
b. found its food in the water but spent much time on land.
c. looked a lot like a whale.
d. lived far up in the mountains and ate mostly leaves.

49.   "Every time you eat a sweet, drink green tea." This is what some Japanese mothers used to tell their children. Modern dentists never took this advice very seriously, until just recently. But research shows that green tea really does help your teeth. It contains something that naturally kills the bacteria that damage teeth. This discovery was made by a Japanese-American chemist. He says he is planning to invent and sell

a. green tea toothpaste.
b. a new kind of sweet.
c. green toothbrushes.
d. a sweet toothpaste.

50.   An albino is an animal (or a person) that is born without any color. Albinos have pale, whitish fur or feathers, pink skin and pink eyes. Albinos are very rare in nature because they usually do not live very long. One reason for this is that they often become blind and cannot take care of themselves. Another reason is simply the color. A white animal

a. is not noticed by other animals, and so it is not disturbed.
b. can hide well in the snow all winter.
c. can easily find other animals and kill them.
d. usually cannot hide well, and so it can be easily caught by larger animals.

51.   In May 1990, 80,000 pairs of Nike athletic shoes fell off a ship in the Pacific Ocean. Ocean scientists were very interested when they heard about this. They tried to find out information about any of these shoes that got to land. In all, 1,300 pairs of shoes were reported along the coasts of the United States and Canada. From these reports they learned something about

a. certain rare sea birds.
b. the movement of ocean currents.
c. how to get free shoes.
d. the Nike shoe company.

52.   Most doctors now agree that mother's milk is better for babies than artificial milk. However, artificial milk has one advantage. It always tastes the same for the baby. Mother's milk, on the other hand, can change flavor. Certain foods may give the milk a strange taste. For example, if the mother eats cabbage or garlic, many babies will refuse her milk. Doctors have also discovered that babies may also refuse their mothers' milk after she has exercised a lot. After exercise, in fact,

a. the milk may have an especially sweet taste.
b. the mother may have extra milk.
c. the milk may have an unpleasant, sour taste.
d. there may be very little milk.

53.   Everyone knows that too much wine can have many bad effects on the body. Doctors discovered recently that a small amount of red wine may have at least one good effect. It may lower the level of cholesterol in the blood. However, new research now proves that this is not the result of the alcohol in the wine. Instead, scientists have learned that there is a special chemical that lowers cholesterol. This chemical is present in purple grape juice and perhaps in other grape products. So people with high cholesterol

a. should drink lots of wine.
b. should go to the doctor.
c. can get the same benefit without drinking wine.
d. should drink white wine.

54.   For centuries, men who work as coal miners have had many health problems. The worst of these problems is a disease called "Black Lung." It is caused by the coal dust in the mines. In the United States, until very recently, about one in every five miners got this disease. For these men, it meant poor health and a shorter life. Then in 1969, a new law forced the coal companies to improve the working conditions for miners. Since then,

    a. many more miners have gotten "Black Lung."
    b. the conditions in the mines have worsened.
    c. there have been many fewer miners in the mines.
    d. fewer miners have gotten "Black Lung."

55.   The connection between sunlight and cancer has been known for a long time. In 1894, German scientists claimed that too much sun could cause skin cancer. Then in 1928, an English scientist proved that this theory was true. Today, there are many kinds of skin cream to protect against the danger of skin cancer. Doctors advise everyone, especially young people, to use these creams when they stay in the sun. A recent study shows, however, that this advice is not being followed. In fact, most young people

    a. stay out of the sun.
    b. do not use these creams.
    c. use these creams.
    d. do not want to get cancer.

56.   Doctors usually say that people who are at risk for heart disease should be careful about their diet. They should not eat foods that have a lot of fat. That means they should not eat nuts, since nuts contain 70-90% fat. Recent research, however, has shown that this advice may be wrong. In fact, people who eat lots of nuts (peanuts, almonds, or walnuts) seem to have fewer heart problems. The scientists are not yet sure why this is true, but doctors may soon advise their patients

    a. to eat nuts in moderate amounts.
    b. to eat fat.
    c. never to eat nuts.
    d. to have fewer heart problems.

57.   The game of croquet was probably invented in France. In the 13th century, French villagers played something they called "paille-maille." From there, the game traveled to Ireland, where they called it "crooky." In the mid-19th century, some people in England began playing "croaky." It quickly became popular all around the world. Now it is played

    a. everywhere, from the United States to India and Australia.
    b. from the south coast of England to the north of Scotland.
    c. from one village to another.
    d. from the Middle Ages to our modern age.

58.   Checkers is a game that requires a lot of mathematical thinking. It's a very good game for computers to play. Some computer scientists in Canada made a computer program for checkers. Then they invited the world championship checkers player, Marion Tinsley, to play against their program. They wanted to see who was better at the game—computers or people. The computer managed to win two games, but Tinsley won four. The scientists concluded that

a. people are still better at some kinds of thinking.
b. computers are best at everything they do.
c. computers will never be able to beat Tinsley.
d. people will always win games like checkers.

59.   Theoretical physicists are known for their bad luck with equipment. Other scientists like to say that something breaks whenever a theoretical physicist walks into the room. One famous physicist, Wolfgang Pauli, was especially unlucky. There were many stories about him. A scientist in Gottingen, Germany was once surprised when some equipment in his laboratory suddenly broke. He couldn't understand why this had happened. Later, he heard that Pauli had been traveling by train that day through Germany. The train had stopped at the station in Gottingen

a. long after the equipment had broken.
b. long before the equipment broke.
c. at the very same moment that the equipment broke.
d. long enough for Pauli to drink some coffee.

60.   The Chinese were the first people to make books. They discovered how to make paper and how to print books in about 1300. At that time, there was almost no contact between Europe and China. One of the few Europeans to travel to China was Marco Polo. He visited China in the 13th century and may have seen some books. But neither he or any other European learned about books from the Chinese. The Europeans

a. quickly learned how to make books from Marco Polo.
b. never learned how to make books.
c. invented paper and printing on their own later on.
d. learned about books even before the Chinese.

61.   A bird feeder can provide you with an interesting new hobby — bird watching. Winter time is the best time for this hobby. Then the birds have trouble finding other food, so they will come to your feeder. If you put the feeder near a window, you can even watch them from inside your home. But once you have started feeding the birds, you should continue until spring. If you stop in the middle of the winter, the birds

a. will have more to eat.
b. may stay near the house.
c. may get cold.
d. may die of hunger.

62.   In many countries these days, it is rarely necessary to go inside a bank. You can do all your banking at automatic banking machines. You can use these machines when you are traveling, too. For example, let's say you arrive in Paris in the evening when the banks are closed. You need French money to buy dinner. You can use your own bank card in a French automatic banking machine. And in just a few seconds,

    a. you will be rich.
    b. it will take all your money from you.
    c. it will give you money from your own bank account.
    d. you can telephone to anywhere in the world.

63.   Sao Paulo is the largest city in Brazil and the second largest city in South America. The official population of the city is 10 million, but the real population is probably more like 13 million. This is partly because the city is growing very quickly. Every year hundreds of thousands of people move there. But there is another important reason for the difference between the official and the real population. Many very poor people in Sao Paulo do not have any place to live. When the government counts the population, these homeless people

    a. are often not counted.
    b. go to live somewhere else.
    c. are often counted twice.
    d. have nowhere to go.

64.   Over 15 million people cross the 25 mile-wide English Channel every year. Some of these people go across in airplanes, but most go across on boats. Huge ferry boats carry cars and trucks across, or there are smaller, faster boats for passengers. As of 1994, however, there is yet another way way to cross the Channel: through the "Chunnel." This is the name of the tunnel that connects England and France. The governments of the two countries had talked for years about digging such a tunnel. Now the "Chunnel" is a reality and England

    a. has become an island.
    b. is no longer connected to Europe.
    c. is no longer really an island.
    d. will have to dig another tunnel.

65.   According to Eugene Morton, a scientist, all animal sounds have certain things in common. Animals tend to make low, loud sounds when they are angry. And they tend to make high, softer sounds when they are fearful or friendly. Human beings can, of course, make many more kinds of sounds than most animals. But Morton believes that even human speech has the same features as other animal sounds. According to Morton, if you say, "I love you" your voice

    a. is naturally high.
    b. usually is very loud.
    c. is naturally loud.
    d. usually angry.

66.   Statistics show that teenage mothers in the United States often have unhealthy babies. These babies often weigh less than normal. They also are generally less intelligent than babies of older mothers. Doctors have wondered about the reasons for these statistics. Two researchers in California may have found the answer: a poor diet. They have found that when female rats do not get enough healthy food, the baby rats are less healthy. The researchers believe that this is probably true of human beings, too. In fact, American teenage girls

a. generally eat lots of healthy food.
b. generally eat a lot.
c. often do not have healthy eating habits.
d. often are afraid of rats.

67.   Scientists believe that the first Americans came from northeast Asia. These people were probably hunters from what is now northern China, Japan, or Siberia. Many thousands of years ago, they crossed over from Asia to what is now Alaska. From there, they spread all through North and South America. The evidence for this theory lies in a discovery made in Chile in 1936. Anthropologists found the teeth of some very early Indians. These teeth proved to be very similar to the teeth of

a. Americans today.
b. people today in northern Asia.
c. Europeans today.
d. monkeys.

68.   We all know that monkeys are smart animals, but sometimes their intelligence is surprising. A psychologist once wanted to see just how smart a monkey was. He hung a banana high up in a monkey's cage. He put in several large boxes and a stick. He wanted to see if the monkey could use the boxes and the stick to get the banana. The monkey looked at the banana, the boxes, and the stick. Then it took the psychologist's hand and led him to where the banana was hanging. It jumped up onto his shoulders and

a. looked at the banana.
b. reached the banana from there.
c. jumped down onto one of the boxes.
d. hit him with the stick.

69.   Rubber is made from latex, a white liquid found in certain plants. Most of the world's supply of rubber comes from the Para rubber tree. This tree originally came from the Amazon Valley in Brazil. The Indians of that area used the latex from the rubber tree to make statues, cups and shoes. When latex was discovered by Europeans, they soon found many uses for it. For example, Charles Mackintosh, in England, invented a way to make waterproof cloth with latex. His method is no longer used, but even today, many people

a. call a raincoat an "overcoat."
b. don't like to use latex raincoats.
c. call a raincoat a "mackintosh."
d. like to plant rubber trees.

70.   Wool is one of the oldest kinds of material used for clothing. We do not know exactly when people started to use wool to make clothing. However, we do know that people were wearing wool clothes very early in man's history. People used the wool not only from sheep, but also from other animals. For example, in the desert they used the wool from camels. In the mountains of India they used the wool from cashmere goats. And in mountains of South America, they used the wool from the llama. All these kinds of wool have one thing in common. They protect the body from outside changes in temperature. This way, wool keeps

a. the body warm in summer and cool in winter.
b. insects away from the body.
c. the body cool in summer and warm in winter.
d. the body from sweating too much.

71.   Money has not always been made of metal or paper. In many parts of the world people have used other materials. Precious stones, valuable cloth (silk), and rare spices (saffron) have all been used as money at times. But people have also given special value to other kinds of objects. For example, in Ethiopia, blocks of salt have been used as money. In Malaysia, people have used large bronze drums. In India and in North America, special kinds of shells have been used. In fact, anything can become money if it

a. has very little value.
b. is shiny and small.
c. is accepted by everyone as money.
d. is worth at least one dollar.

72.   Today, farmers in most of the industrialized countries grow cash crops. This means that they usually grow large amounts of only a few crops, such as soy, wheat, or corn. They sell these crops and use the money to buy what they need for their families and their farms. In the past, farming was quite different. Most farmers used to grow lots of different kinds of crops. They sometimes sold some of the crops when there was extra. However,

a. most of the crops were kept to feed the farmer's family.
b. they preferred to sell all of the crops for cash.
c. people in the city needed food, too.
d. they didn't grow soy in those days.

73.   Textbooks for children in elementary school often give a false picture of women. They almost always show women as mothers and housewives. The women are seen in the home, usually doing very simple tasks. In reality, in many countries, the majority of younger women work outside the home. They may take care of children and do housework, but that is only part of their lives. Their situation is nothing like the situations shown in the school books. In fact, these books

a. do not help girls prepare for their future.
b. give girls a good idea of their future.
c. show women in many complex situations.
d. don't show enough housewives.

74.   Supermarket managers have all kinds of tricks to encourage people to spend more money. Their aim is to make customers go more slowly through the supermarket. They place colorful displays in surprising places to catch the customers' attention. They also make the corridors near the cash registers more narrow. Then customers with large shopping carts will get stuck or have to slow down. In some supermarkets, the floor is even slightly uphill for people going towards the exits. Managers hope that when customers slow down, they will

a. get angry and go home.
b. buy a few extra items.
c. fill their cart too full.
d. decide not to buy anything more.

75.   The guppy is a small fish that people often keep in bowls or tanks in their homes. In their bowls, guppies have never caused any harm to anyone. But, in the wild, the story is different. When some guppy owners in Nevada grew tired of their fish, they threw them in a lake. Since then, the guppies have multiplied and chased away the native fish. Now at least one species of fish—the white river spring fish—is almost extinct. Thus, even a little fish like the guppy

a. can live in lakes.
b. like to live in laces and rivers.
c. sometimes improves the ecology of lakes and rivers.
d. can cause changes in the ecology of lakes and rivers.

76.   Imagine what it would be like to wake up and find yourself in a metal box. This is what happened to a man in South Africa who had been in a car accident. The doctors thought he was dead, so he was put in the metal box. He remained there, uncon-scious, for two days. Then, he woke up and shouted for help. The people who heard him were at first somewhat frightened. But then they realized that he was alive and they let him out of the box. He was happy to be alive and free. However, his happi-ness did not last long. His girlfriend refused to see him because she did not believe that he was really alive. She said

a. he was a ghost who came back from the dead to frighten her.
b. she wanted to marry him immediately.
c. he should go back into the box.
d. he was not the same as he used to be.

77.   "One man's medicine is another man's poison." This expression can be true in a very literal sense. The Luo people from Kenya often cook and eat the leaves of a plant called black nightshade. This plant serves as an effective treatment for many stomach problems. The Luo eat it regularly from childhood and do not suffer any negative effects from it. However, when one American researcher ate just a small amount, she felt quite ill afterwards. In fact, the plant contains

a. a great deal of sugar.
b. a substance called solanine that can be poisonous.
c. a bitter-tasting substance.
d. many substances that benefit the digestive system.

78.   Sociologists and psychologists have argued for centuries about how a person's character is formed. The argument has long been known as "Nature versus Nurture," for the two main opposing theories. The first theory says that character is formed genetically before birth. According to this theory, nature—through genetics—determines what a person will be like. The other theory says, on the contrary, that a person's character is formed after birth. According to this theory, the most important factors are

   a. natural and genetic.
   b. scientific.
   c. theoretical.
   d. cultural and environmental.

79.   The problem of pollution has turned up on every continent on Earth—even Antarctica. Winter Quarters Bay, on Antarctica, is the site of an important scientific station. This bay, in fact, is as polluted as many city harbors. The reason is that for a long time people at the station dumped garbage into the bay. Now, however, that has stopped. An international agreement has limited the dumping of garbage in Antarctica. According to the agreement, scientific communities in Antarctica must

   a. dump all their garbage into the bay.
   b. take all their garbage away from Antarctica.
   c. close down all the stations.
   d. stop all scientific experiments.

80.   Four out of five people suffer from back pain at some time in their working lives. In the United States, it is the most expensive health problem in the workplace. In all, it costs people up to $60 billion in medical expenses and lost working time. Back pain is bad for business as well—it is the cause of 40% of all lost work days. That means a total of about 93 million sick days a year in the United States. Doctors now believe that exercise is the best treatment for back pain. For this reason, some companies

   a. do not let their employees exercise too much.
   b. send their employees to specialized doctors.
   c. tell their employees to rest more.
   d. have started special exercise programs for employees.

81.   Lichen are one of the few kinds of life that can survive in the mountains of Antarctica. These tiny plants live in small holes in the rocks. Outside, the extreme cold and strong winds do not allow any life at all. Inside the holes, these lichen manage to find enough water and warmth to keep alive. However, much of the time they are frozen. This fact means that the lichen function very, very slowly, and live a very long time. Scientists believe that a lichen may remain alive for thousands of years. If this is true, the lichen may

   a. be among the oldest forms of life on earth.
   b. die in only a few years.
   c. not survive another Antarctic winter.
   d. be one of the newest forms of life on earth.

82.   Edward Kennedy Ellington—known as "Duke"—was perhaps the best-known and loved jazz musician of all time. By the time of his death in 1974 he had written nearly 2,000 pieces of music. Many of them have become the classics of jazz. His famous Ellington Orchestra had its beginnings in Washington in 1922 and performed for almost 50 years. In spite of his fame, however, Ellington did not look for special attention for himself. His private life was not so important to him. Music was really his first love. He never let

a. music get in the way of his personal relationships.
b. personal relationships get in the way of his music making.
c. himself get too involved in his music.
d. too many people know about his music.

83.   The Celts were never an empire or a nation, just groups of tribes. They came out of central Europe in about 1,000 B.C. By 300 B.C., they had spread over all of Europe, from Turkey, to Spain, to the British Isles. They were conquered in the end by the Romans and by various Germanic tribes. However, many Celtic legends are still alive today. The best known of these is about King Arthur of the Round Table. There is some evidence that Arthur may really have been a Celtic leader in the early sixth century. Even if he never lived, however, his story involves

a. many typically British elements.
b. some typically Roman elements.
c. some traditionally European elements.
d. many typically Celtic elements.

84.   For the Japanese, a bath is not just a way to get clean. It is also a way to relax and recover from a stressful day. In Japan, in fact, people like to take very long, hot baths. While they are in the bathtub, they like to listen to music or read books. For this reason, a Japanese company has begun selling special "bath" books. These books

a. are made entirely of paper.
b. have plastic pages.
c. do not break when they fall.
d. are printed in English.

85.   Tourism continues to be a growing industry. Every year more and more people take trips to another part of the world for pleasure. This growth does not seem to be affected by the fact that local conflicts continue in many areas. The tourist industry also does not seem to suffer during periods of economic difficulty. People may spend less money on other things in these periods, but they continue to spend money on travel. In recent years, in fact,

a. tourism has declined by an average of 16%.
b. people have spent 16% more money on English courses.
c. tourism has grown by about 16%.
d. people have preferred to stay home.

86.   Every year, rich countries become richer and poor countries become poorer. In 1750, the richest country was about five times richer than the poorest country. Today, the richest country (Switzerland) is about 400 times richer than the poorest country (Mozambique). This greater difference is due largely to the growth of technology. The poorer countries are not able to keep up with the changing technology of the industrialized countries. With every new technological development, poor countries are likely to

    a. make more progress.
    b. be even poorer than they are today.
    c. catch up with the rich countries.
    d. become more like Switzerland.

87.   Monticello, the home of Thomas Jefferson, is much admired today for its wonderful views of the Virginia countryside. It is located on the top of a high hill—"monticello" means "little mountain" in Italian. In Jefferson's time, however, people thought he was a little crazy to build a house on a hilltop. In those days, people did not care so much about views. They cared more about comfort, so they usually built their houses

    a. on top of mountains.
    b. at the seaside.
    c. out of brick.
    d. on sheltered lowlands.

88.   After the "desktop," the "laptop," and the "notebook" computers, what will come next? The answer, according to the experts, is the "personal communicator." This is a little machine that serves many purposes. It can make "cellular" (wireless) telephone calls and send messages by fax or modem. It can also work with data, do word processing or play games, like other computers. For the traveling businessman, the personal communicator could replace

    a. both the telephone and the computer.
    b. the office secretary.
    c. most of his work.
    d. the typewriter and the car.

89.   Anthropologists used to believe that romantic love was invented by Europeans in the Middles Ages. By romantic love, they mean an intense attraction and longing to be with the loved person. Some anthropologists believed that this kind of love spread from the west to other cultures only recently. Others thought that it may have existed in some other cultures, but only among the rich and privileged. Now, however, most anthropologists agree that romantic love has probably always existed among humans. It is not surprising, then, that stories of romance, like Romeo and Juliet,

    a. exist only in the West.
    b. exist only in Italy.
    c. are unusual outside of the West.
    d. are found in many cultures around the world.

90.	Almost every language has a topic that is especially rich in vocabulary and idiomatic expressions. For example, the Eskimos have many different words to describe snow. The Irish, on the other hand, have many different ways to describe a green landscape. The English have many special words to talk about the flavors of different teas. The French and Italian languages are rich in vocabulary to describe wines. We can conclude that the development of a language is

a. influenced by the weather.
b. influenced by the environment and the culture.
c. not influenced by anything.
d. independent of cultural factors.

91.	What is the world's largest living creature? It may be a fungus that scientists have discovered in the state of Wisconsin. This fungus is huge—it spreads over about 37 acres and is still growing. This may seem like a science fiction nightmare. However, in fact, the fungus lives underground in the woods and does not disturb its environment. It also grows very slowly, having taken 1,500 years to reach its present size. The scientists used to think that this fungus was made up of many different fungi. Now, with DNA testing, they have definite proof that it is really

a. just one individual fungus.
b. separate fungi living close together.
c. dead material.
d. a science fiction nightmare.

92.	After Columbus traveled to the Americas, the Europeans began to import many kinds of products from the New World. Some of the products are well known, such as coffee, cocoa, tobacco, tomatoes, corn, potatoes, pumpkins, beans, and strawberries. But some of the products are little known today. For two centuries, one of the most important New World exports was the cochineal. This small red insect was used for making red cloth. It is still used for this purpose today and some insects are still exported from the Americas. However, with the invention of chemical colorants, the demand for the cochineal has

a. regained its commercial importance.
b. become extinct.
c. lost its commercial importance.
d. lost its brilliant red coloring.

93.	At Ashkelon, in Israel, archaeologists have found a very large dog cemetery. The cemetery dates from the fifth century B.C., when that area was part of the Persian Empire. So far, about 1,000 dog graves have been found in the cemetery. Archaeologists are not certain about the reason for so many graves. However, they believe that dogs must have been very important for the people there. In fact, all of the dogs died of natural causes and were buried very carefully. Perhaps, these people

a. gave dogs special powers in their religion.
b. ate dog meat.
c. wanted to get rid of all their dogs.
d. didn't like cats.

94.   Robots are entering into all kinds of activities. They've even taken up hunting in some places. Most states of the United States have very strict laws to limit the hunting of deer (a large mammal). Some hunters, however, do not obey the laws and try to kill too many deer. So, the forest services have developed a robot that looks and acts just like a deer. This robot-deer is left in the woods near a road where people will see it. It looks and acts just like a real deer. But if a hunter tries to shoot it, the police come out from the woods and check his hunting license. The hunter may have wanted to get a deer, but, instead the

a. police have gotten the deer.
b. deer has gotten the hunter.
c. hunter has gotten a large mammal.
d. deer has gotten the police.

95.   In many parts of England, hedges are an important part of the countryside. (A hedge is a kind of fence made of bushes or trees.) An English botanist, Max Hooper, studied the English hedges and found an interesting fact. The older the hedge, the more species of bushes and trees it contained. His conclusions became known as "Hooper's Rule." According to this rule, a hedge usually starts with one species and gains a species with each century. Using this rule, people have studied hedges in England and discovered that many of them are very old. Quite a few of them have more than ten species. This means that they

a. may be 1,000 years old
b. may be only 100 years old.
c. will be made of bushes and trees.
d. must be English.

96.   As more women have careers and important jobs, a new kind of family problem is becoming more common. What happens when a woman is offered a better job in another city? If she accepts the offer, that means her husband has to leave his job, too. He may have trouble finding another job in the same city. Or, the job he finds may not be as good as his old one. In the past, women often had to face this problem when their husbands found new jobs. But now it is more and more common for men. Many men do not accept the situation easily. A man often feels uncomfortable

a. getting a job that is better than his wife's job.
b. looking for the same kind of job as his wife.
c. following his wife to a new city and looking for a job.
d. looking for a job for his wife.

97.   Many people are afraid of going to the dentist. There are a number of reasons for this fear. One reason is that the patient cannot see what the dentist is doing. Another reason is that the patient (who is lying back) may feel very helpless. Social factors may also increase a person's fear. People may be influenced by the general belief that dentists are scary. And finally, many people

a. like seeing the dentist's shiny instruments.
b. do not like to brush their teeth very often.
c. are afraid of going to the doctor as well.
d. do not like the idea of instruments in their mouths.

98.   Immigration in the United States has been increasing rapidly. Each year about 600,000 new legal immigrants settle in this country. If all the illegal immigrants were counted, that number would be even higher. Today's immigrants are different from the immigrants of the early 20th century, who were mostly white and European. The more recent immigrants are mostly black, Hispanic, or Asian. However, they do have one thing in common: a desire to work and do well in their new homeland. For this reason, many people feel that the government should not shut its doors to immigrants. The immigrants have helped the country in the past, they say. Now, the United States

a. needs better laws to keep out immigrants.
b. could benefit from them again.
c. does not need people from other countries.
d. could benefit only from the younger immigrants.

99.   Texas is famous for its cattle farms, but another kind of farm is growing much faster: ostrich farms. Ten years ago, ostrich farms were rare, but there are now over 2,000 in the United States, many of them in Texas. It's easy to see why so many farmers are interested in ostriches these days. A pair of young adult ostriches are worth around $40,000. An ostrich egg may be worth up to $1,500. Since a female ostrich may lay up to 80 eggs a year,

a. farmers may not be able to make much profit.
b. ostrich farming is not a very profitable business.
c. farmers may prefer to raise cattle.
d. farmers can make a lot of profit quickly.

100.   The use of electric automobiles in the future will help reduce air pollution. This was the conclusion of a recent study by experts of a large area in the northeastern United States. The area is highly urban and includes the cities of New York and Boston. At present, the air quality is often very poor. However, the increased use of electric cars could improve the situation. By the year 2015, there will be about 3.3 million electric cars on the road in the Northeast. According to the study, this will mean

a. 20–50% less pollution.
b. 20–50% more pollution.
c. a gradual increase in the number of cars on the road.
d. a gradual reduction of air quality in the northeast.

Part Four

Reading Faster

Why read faster?

There are two important reasons for learning to read faster:

- You can read more in less time.

- You can improve your comprehension.

When you read slowly, you read one word at a time. The words seem separated like the words below. Is it easier or harder to understand?

What	really	happens	when	we	read?	Some
people	think	we	read	one	word	at	a	time.
They	think	we	read	a	word,	understand	it
and	then	move	on	to	the	next	word.

It is harder to understand because the separate words become separate pieces of information that you must remember. By the time you get to the end of a sentence you may have forgotten the beginning!

When you read faster, you understand better because you focus on ideas by reading groups of words that are connected.

How to read faster: four steps

Skip over unknown words

In order to read more quickly good readers usually skip over words they do not know. They also skip over many other words that are not important for the general meaning.

In fact, you can get the important ideas from a text even with many words missing.

Example a: In this passage, every eighth word is missing. Do not try to guess the missing words. Read the passage and answer the comprehension questions below.

Dear Joan,

I'm sorry not to have written sooner. I have been very busy since I _____ back from vacation. There has been so _____ to do at work lately! Almost every _____ I have to stay late. I've even _____ going in to the office on Saturdays, _____.

I've had no time to relax at _____ either. Every free moment has been taken _____ by work on the house. The roof _____ in very bad condition after the _____. But if I'd known how busy I'd be _____ work, I might have waited.

Anyway, it's _____ finished now. So at last I can _____ you to come over some weekend with _____ family. We could all take a walk _____ Mt. Grey.

Judy sends her love. We _____ to see you all soon.

Love,
George

1. Why has George not written sooner?

2. What has he been doing in his free time?

3. What does George suggest to Joan?

Example b: In this passage, every fifth word is missing. Again, do not try to guess the missing words. Read the passage and answer the questions below.

Grace Simmons is only 14, and she speaks no French, but she is famous in Paris. She has become a _____ model for a well-known _____ designer. Grace is from _____, Michigan. Her father is _____ car salesman and her _____ is a teacher. Grace _____ very unhappy as a _____ young girl because she _____ was very tall — almost _____ feet. The other children _____ fun of her all _____ time and she had _____ no friends. Then, when _____ was 11, her mother took _____ her to a modeling _____. There were other tall _____ at the school, so _____ finally felt normal. When _____ was younger, she had _____ been teased for her _____. With a Korean mother and a _____ American father, her looks _____, in fact, quite extraordinary. _____ as a fashion model, _____ looks have brought her _____ fame and money.

1. Why was Grace unhappy as a child?

2. When did her life change for the better?

3. How did she become rich and famous?

How many of the questions in Examples *a* and *b* were you able to answer? You probably could answer all of them. You did not need to read every word in order to understand!

Reading sprints

Sprints are often used by runners who want to improve their running speed. Reading sprints help you to break old habits and improve your reading speed.

Your teacher will time you, or you can time yourself. Use your pleasure reading book for these exercises.

Title of book: _____

1. Find out how many pages you can read normally in five minutes. _____

2. From where you just finished reading, count that number of pages ahead. (For example, if you normally read one and a half pages in five minutes, count ahead one and a half pages.) Mark the place in the margin with a pencil.

3. Try to read those pages in only *four* minutes. If you do not succeed the first time, keep trying until you do (with new pages each time). You will need to force your eyes to move faster along the page.

4. Now try to read that same number pages in *three* minutes. Count the number of pages again, and mark the page.

5. Finally, try to read the same number of pages in *two* minutes. You may be able to catch only a few words from the text. This does not matter. The important thing is to make your eyes move quickly and get *something* from the text.

6. Now you are ready to read "normally" again. Read for five minutes—without pushing yourself, but without relaxing too much either!

How many pages did you read? _____

How does that compare with your first five-minute reading?

Repeat these reading sprints regularly. They will help you build up speed in reading. As reading faster becomes easier, you will find that your comprehension improves as well.

Check your reading habits

Certain bad habits may be slowing you down.

a. Do you try to pronounce each word as you read? Pronunciation is not necessary for comprehension. In fact, if you try to say the words, even silently, you will probably understand less.

b. Do you usually move your lips while you read silently? If you do, you will never be able to read faster than 200 words per minute, the fastest speed at which English can be spoken.

c. Do you follow the words in the text with your finger or a pencil while you read? This is another habit that can slow you down. It also limits the way you read because you cannot skip around. Pointing at the words forces your eyes to follow the lines of text too closely. *Your eyes should follow your thoughts, not your finger!*

d. Do you translate into your native language as you read in English? Do you often write translations of words in the English text? This will slow down your reading speed and it will interfere with your ability to think in English.

Practice reading faster by timing yourself

Another way to increase your reading speed is to practice reading against the clock. Many students find that they have a reading rate between 50 and 200 words per minute. Reading at less than 200 words per minute means that you are almost certainly reading word by word and having trouble understanding.

When you read against the clock, be sure to record the exact time you start and finish reading the passage. Practice timing yourself with the example on the next page.

➤ *Example: Write your starting time on the line. Preview the passage and then read it all the way through to the end. Try to push yourself to read a little faster than usual.*

The Frozen Man

Write your starting time _____

On a September day in 1991, two Germans were climbing the mountains between Austria and Italy. High up on a mountain pass, they found the body of a man lying on the ice. At that height (3,200 meters), the ice is usually permanent. But 1991 had been an especially warm year. The mountain ice had melted more than usual and so the body had come to the surface.

It was lying face downward. The skeleton was in perfect condition, except for a large wound in the head. There was still skin on the bones and the remains of some clothes. The hands were still holding the wooden handle of an ax. On the feet there were very simple leather and cloth boots. Nearby was a pair of gloves made of tree bark and a holder for arrows.

Who was this man? How and when had he died? Everybody had a different answer to these questions. The mountain climbers who had found the body said it seemed thousands of years old. But others thought that it might be from this century. Perhaps it was the body of a soldier who died in World War I. In fact, several World War I soldiers had already been found in that area of the mountains. On the other hand, a Swiss woman believed it might be her father. He had died in those mountains 20 years before and his body had never been found.

When Italian and Austrian scientists heard about the discovery they rushed to the mountaintop. The body couldn't possibly be the Swiss woman's father, they said. The boots, the gloves, and the ax were clearly from further back in the past. For the same reason, they said it couldn't be a World War I soldier. It had to be at least several centuries old, they said, maybe even five centuries. It could have been one of the soldiers in the army of Frederick, Duke of Austria.

Before they could be sure about this guess, however, the scientists needed more data. They needed to bring the body down the mountain so they could study it in their laboratories. The question was, whom did it belong to? It was lying almost exactly on the border between Italy and Austria. Naturally, both countries wanted the frozen man for their laboratories and their museums. For two days, the body lay there in the mountains while diplomats argued. Finally, they decided that it lay on Austrian ground. By that time the body was partly unfrozen and somewhat damaged.

When the Austrian scientists examined the body more closely, they changed their minds. They did not know yet how he had died, but they did know when: in about 2,700 B.C. This was a very important discovery, they said. It would teach them a great deal about this very distant period of European history. From the clothes and tools they could learn about how men lived in those times.

Write the time you finished reading _____

Subtract your starting time −_____

Your reading time is _____

➤ *Answer the questions on the following page.*

➤ *Do not look back at the passage. Circle the best answer.*

1. This passage is about
   a. a soldier who died in World War I.
   b. mountaintop discoveries.
   c. how men lived in the distant past.
   d. a frozen body found in the mountains.

2. The body was found by
   a. some Austrian scientists.
   b. a Swiss woman.
   c. two German mountain climbers.
   d. soldiers in the army of Frederick of Austria.

3. The body was in good condition because
   a. it had always been frozen.
   b. the scientists took good care of it.
   c. the air was very dry.
   d. it had just fallen there.

4. When the body was first found
   a. everyone thought it must be 20 years old.
   b. everyone had a different theory about it.
   c. no one had any idea about where it came from.
   d. scientists were sure it was thousands of years old.

5. When the scientists saw the body, they said it
   a. might be five centuries old.
   b. must be from this century.
   c. was probably the Swiss woman's father.
   d. probably was a soldier from World War I.

6. The body lay on the mountain for two days because
   a. the Swiss woman didn't want anyone to touch it.
   b. no one could find it.
   c. the Austrian and Italian governments were fighting over it.
   d. neither the Austrians nor the Italians wanted it.

7. After examining the body, the scientists said
   a. the frozen man had died in war.
   b. it was partly unfrozen.
   c. the frozen man was almost 5,000 years old.
   d. they did not know the cause of his death.

8. We can learn about how people lived in the distant past from
   a. their feet.
   b. their clothes and tools.
   c. their museums.
   d. the mountains.

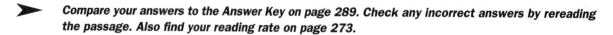

➤ *Compare your answers to the Answer Key on page 289. Check any incorrect answers by rereading the passage. Also find your reading rate on page 273.*

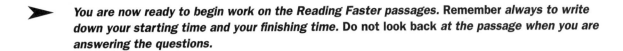

➤ **You are now ready to begin work on the *Reading Faster* passages. Remember *always to write down your starting time and your finishing time*. Do not look back *at the passage when you are answering the questions*.**

Guidelines for Faster Reading

1. Push yourself to read a little faster than you normally do.

2. Answer the questions *without* looking back at the text.

3. Check your answers in the Answer Key on page 289. If you have some incorrect answers, look back at the text to find out why.

4. Check your reading rate on page 273.

5. Record your reading rate and comprehension score (the number of correct answers) on the chart on page 274.

6. After you have read four or five chapters, note any changes in your reading or comprehension rate. Your aim should be to gradually increase your rate, while keeping your comprehension at about 80%.

   • If your rate stays the same, that means you need to push yourself more.

   • If you miss more than three questions, you might be pushing yourself too much. Try to slow down a little and concentrate better.

The Hawaiian Islands

1. The Hawaiian Islands

Starting time _____

If you would like to go to a beautiful, faraway place, you should go to the Hawaiian Islands. Located in the middle of the Pacific Ocean, these islands are far from any other land. They are, in fact, the farthest from land of any islands on earth—about 2,400 miles from San Francisco, 3,830 miles from Tokyo, and 5,540 miles from Hong Kong.

There are eight Hawaiian Islands. In order of size, they are Hawaii (the "Big Island"), Maui, Oahu, Kauai, Molokai, Lanai, Niihau, and Kahoolawe. In 1959, the islands together became Hawaii, the 50th state of the United States.

While they differ from one another in some ways, the islands share many of the same features. They all have a tropical climate, first of all. The average daytime temperature is about 78 degrees Fahrenheit in the winter and 85 degrees Fahrenheit in the summer. However, it is never uncomfortably hot. The nighttime temperature is always cooler and there is generally a little wind. Rain falls often, but usually not for long. People in Hawaii say that it rains every day somewhere on the islands.

The islands also are similar in their natural beauty. They all have volcanic mountains and waterfalls, rain forests and beautiful beaches. The warm, clear water around the islands is filled with many kinds of sea creatures. There are giant sea turtles, whales, and dolphins as well as lots of tropical fish. The forests are full of beautiful birds and flowers. Many of them cannot be found anywhere else in the world.

The Hawaiian Islands, in fact, have an interesting natural history. Until modern times, birds and insects were the only kinds of animals living on the islands, with just a few exceptions. The exceptions were the monk seal (a sea mammal) and a kind of bat (a flying mammal). There were no other mammals until people arrived in about 500 A.D. They brought some animals, such as pigs, for food. Other animals, such as mice, probably traveled to the islands hidden in their boats.

Each of the islands also has features that are special. For example, the Big Island, Hawaii, is the only island with active volcanoes. Both Mauna Loa and Kilauea on Hawaii occasionally erupt, pouring out hot lava and smoke. The island of Oahu is the site of the modern capital of Hawaii, Honolulu. This island also has one of the world's most famous beaches, Waikiki Beach, especially popular with surfers.

And finally, the island of Maui is important to Hawaiians for its role in the history of the islands. In 1800, Kamehameha the Great became the king of the islands. He established his capital on Maui, where it remained until early in the 20th century.

Today, with its tropical climate and natural beauty, Hawaii is a major tourist attraction. People come from all over the world to view the volcanoes, the seacoast and the rain forests. They come to sunbathe or surf at the beaches, or they come just to relax in the warm, sweet air.

Finishing time _____   Reading time _____

➤ *Do not look back at the passage.*

1. This passage is about
   a. some of the main features of the Hawaiian Islands.
   b. the climate of the Hawaiian Islands.
   c. the remoteness of the Hawaiian Islands.
   d. volcanoes in Hawaii.

2. The Hawaiian Islands are called remote because they are
   a. always warm.
   b. very beautiful.
   c. in the middle of the Pacific Ocean.
   d. far away from any land.

3. The Hawaiian Islands are closest to
   a. Hong Kong.
   b. Japan.
   c. Oahu.
   d. San Francisco.

4. The temperature in the islands is
   a. warm all year round.
   b. cold in the winter.
   c. warmer at night.
   d. very cold at night.

5. The features that you can find on all of the Hawaiian Islands are
   a. active volcanoes.
   b. good restaurants.
   c. beautiful scenery and a warm climate.
   d. good hotels and restaurants.

6. Many kinds of birds and flowers on the islands
   a. can be found all over the Pacific.
   b. are like birds and flowers in the United States.
   c. cannot be found anywhere else.
   d. came to the islands with the first people.

7. You can infer from this passage that, apart from Hawaii, the other islands
   a. do not have volcanoes.
   b. have volcanoes, but they are inactive.
   c. do not have beaches.
   d. have no mammals.

8. The island of Maui is especially known for its
   a. beaches.
   b. active volcanoes.
   c. history.
   d. tropical fish.

2. Kauai—a Tropical Paradise   Starting time _____

Of all the Hawaiian Islands, Kauai may be the best example of a tropical paradise. In fact, when some film directors were looking for a place to film the movie "South Pacific," they chose Kauai. Since then, millions of people around the world have seen that Hollywood classic. So now Kauai, with its beautiful landscapes, is their idea of the perfect tropical island.

All the islands, including Kauai, have been affected by development in recent years. The tourist industry, agriculture, and spreading cities have destroyed much of the natural beauty. But on Kauai, there are also large areas that have remained untouched by development—so far, at least.

Thick green rain forests cover many square miles of Kauai. In other areas, there are great swamps—wet places of rain, mist, water plants, and mud. Near the beaches that circle the island, there are palm trees and flowering bushes. Everywhere, the air is warm and moist, with a hint of perfume from all the flowers. This air makes your skin feel soft and smooth. In fact, after some time on Kauai, you will feel healthier all over. There is little pollution here, and no stress.

The beaches of Kauai are a large part of its beauty. They all have lovely, clean white sand. At some beaches, the waves can be large and dangerous. At others, the water is so calm that even small children can play in it safely. Many kinds of brightly colored fish usually swim close to the shore. If you put on a mask and air tube (snorkel), you can swim among them.

But Kauai's scenery also offers some dramatic contrasts. Along one shore of the island, in an area called Napali, there are steep cliffs. No roads can be built in this area, so the only way to visit is by foot. Hiking here is a real adventure, since the trails are narrow and steep. Along these trails, you can get a close look at rare and beautiful plants and birds. Each turn in the trail brings a breathtaking view. For the visitor, the scene may seem unreal: the green vegetation, the white beaches below, and the wide blue ocean may seem too colorful to be real.

Kauai has its mountains, too. The tallest of these, Mount Waialeale, catches the clouds and collects rain. This mountainside is called the "wettest spot on earth." About 460 inches of rain fall on it every year. Streams and rivers rush down the mountain to the sea. It is not surprising that Kauai is full of wonderful gardens that bloom all year round.

A few miles from Mount Waialeale, a very different landscape can be seen: the Waimea Canyon. This canyon is often called the "Grand Canyon of the Pacific." That is because its tall cliffs resemble those of the Grand Canyon in the western United States. The rocks and earth in the Waimea Canyon are reddish brown. All around is the rich green of the trees and bushes. It is an unforgettable scene.

Finishing time _____   Reading time _____

➤ *Do not look back at the passage.*

1. This passage is about
   a. the features of the Waimea Canyon.
   b. what makes Kauai a tropical paradise.
   c. hiking on the Napali cliffs.
   d. the beaches of Kauai.

2. Kauai is like a paradise because
   a. "South Pacific" was filmed there.
   b. it has a warm climate and beautiful scenery.
   c. it has tall cliffs.
   d. it rains a lot there.

3. Unlike some of the other islands, Kauai has
   a. large undeveloped areas.
   b. many gardens.
   c. many birds.
   d. trees near the beaches.

4. You can infer from this passage that
   a. all of the beaches in Kauai are dangerous.
   b. the beaches cannot be reached by car.
   c. children do not like to go swimming because of all the fish.
   d. snorkeling is probably a popular sport on Kauai.

5. Kauai is a good place for hiking because
   a. there are many scenic trails.
   b. you can drive to every interesting place.
   c. it is very cool all year round.
   d. the swamps are so full of mud.

6. Mount Waialeale is called the wettest spot on earth because it
   a. is very tall.
   b. has many gardens.
   c. collects lots of rain.
   d. has many rivers and streams.

7. You can infer from this passage that Kauai's climate is
   a. uncomfortable for tourists.
   b. very dry.
   c. cooler than the other islands.
   d. good for growing flowers.

8. The Waimea Canyon is called the "Grand Canyon of the Pacific" because it
   a. is the only canyon in the Pacific.
   b. has reddish-brown rocks.
   c. looks like the Grand Canyon in the western United States.
   d. is so large.

3. Natural Disasters

The Hawaiian Islands are a tropical paradise most of the time. But even there, nature can sometimes show its more violent side. The islands have been hit by numerous natural disasters in the recent past. These disasters have caused deaths and great damage.

Through all of Hawaii's history, volcanoes have played an important part. The islands were formed by the eruption of volcanoes under the ocean. On the big island of Hawaii, the volcanoes continue to erupt. During an eruption, hot lava pours out of the top of a volcano and down the side. The red, hot lava covers everything in its path. The air is filled with smoke and horrible-smelling gas that is sometimes poisonous. Once, in 1790, poisonous gas blew down into a populated valley and killed 80 people. In 1950, a volcano on Hawaii erupted and lava poured out for 23 days. The lava covered 35 miles and closed off the main coastal road.

Native Hawaiians believe that volcanoes are a natural part of life. In their traditional religion, volcanoes are ruled by the goddess, Pele. When Pele is angry, the volcanoes erupt. Before an eruption she takes a human form. If you meet her and are kind to her, you will not be hurt by the lava. Today, Hawaiians have forgotten most of the ancient gods, but not Pele. They continue to honor her and her volcanoes.

Another kind of natural disaster that has hit Hawaii is the tidal wave, or tsunami. Unlike volcanoes, tsunamis come from far away under the ocean. When an earthquake occurs underwater, it creates huge waves. If these waves hit land, they destroy everything along the coast. Two terrible tsunamis have hit the big island of Hawaii in modern times. One enormous wave washed away a whole school with the children and their teacher. Another killed 61 people.

These days, all of the Hawaiian Islands have special signals to warn of tsunamis. When the signal sounds, everyone knows it is time to run. They must try to get as far from the seashore as possible. Anyone who stays near the coast will be washed away, along with cars, trees, and houses.

Hurricanes have also caused much trouble for Hawaiians recently. When a hurricane passes over an island, the wind may be very strong, over 80 miles an hour. It can blow away windows, roofs, and even whole buildings. The shore line may be changed, as the large waves wash over beaches and break up cliffs.

In the past, people in Hawaii did not worry about these storms. They rarely occurred in that area. Scientists believed that the water around the islands was too warm for hurricanes. However, that has changed, for some reason. Dangerous hurricanes have hit the island of Kauai twice in the past ten years. In 1982, Hurricane Iwa caused $200 million dollars worth of damage. The people of the island rebuilt their homes. New hotels and vacation resorts were built. And then, in 1992, they were hit by Hurricane Iniki, which caused even more damage!

➤ *Do not look back at the passage.*

1. This passage is about
    a. three types of natural disasters in Hawaii.
    b. Hawaii's volcanoes.
    c. the damage caused by natural disasters.
    d. Hawaii's natural history.

2. Volcanoes were the cause of
    a. the formation of the Hawaiian Islands.
    b. the warm climate of the islands.
    c. many tsunamis in the Pacific Ocean.
    d. Hawaii's recent hurricanes.

3. During a volcanic eruption
    a. the goddess Pele is angry.
    b. the air is full of hot smoke and terrible smells.
    c. houses and cars are safe from the lava.
    d. only small areas of the island are in danger.

4. You can infer from this that most Hawaiians today
    a. follow their traditional religion.
    b. do not follow their traditional religion.
    c. do not understand volcanoes.
    d. do not worry about storms.

5. Tsunamis are caused by
    a. volcanic eruptions.
    b. strong winds far out at sea.
    c. rain storms in the Pacific Ocean.
    d. underwater earthquakes.

6. If you hear a tsunami signal, you should
    a. close all your windows.
    b. stay away from trees.
    c. go down to the beach.
    d. hurry away from the seashore.

7. You can infer from this passage that hurricanes
    a. have caused the most damage on Kauai.
    b. are very common on all of the islands.
    c. are caused by warm ocean water.
    d. can be predicted.

8. Volcanoes, tsunamis, and hurricanes
    a. can all be prevented by careful planning.
    b. are caused by the forces of nature.
    c. are controlled by Hawaiian gods of nature.
    d. have caused little damage in Hawaii.

4. Water Sports in Hawaii   Starting time _____

If you enjoy water sports, Hawaii is the place for you! You can go swimming all year round in the warm water. You can go sport fishing from the shore or from a boat. If you like boats, you can go sailing, canoeing, or windsurfing. Or, you can also try some other water sports that are especially popular in Hawaii: surfing, snorkeling and scuba diving.

Surfing is a sport which started in Hawaii many years ago. The Hawaiians called it "he'enalu," which means "to slide on a wave." Long before the arrival of the Europeans, the Hawaiians would ride on the waves on long, narrow wooden boards. When the first Europeans came to the islands, they were amazed by these surfing Hawaiians. Since that time, surfing has become a very popular sport on the California coast and in Australia, among other places.

If you want to try surfing, you need, first of all, to be a good swimmer. You also have to have an excellent sense of balance. You must swim out from the beach with your surfboard under your arm. When you get to where the waves begin to break, you wait for a calm moment. Then you try to stand up on the board. The wave will begin to rise under you. You must try to steer the board with your feet so you stay on top of the wave. The important thing is to keep your balance and not fall down. If you can manage this, you will have an exciting ride all the way in to the shore.

Scuba diving and snorkeling are two ways to get a close look at the beauty lying below the surface of the ocean. The waters off the Hawaiian Islands are clean, clear, and warm. They contain hundreds of kinds of colorful fish. The undersea world is made even more colorful by the coral reefs of red, gold, white, and light purple. Among these reefs there may be larger fish or sea turtles.

Scuba diving allows you to see the most interesting undersea sights. "SCUBA" means "Self-Contained Underwater Breathing Apparatus," that is, equipment for breathing and swimming around far under water. In Hawaii, you can take special courses to learn how to scuba dive. After the courses, you can get a certificate that will allow you to dive alone. Since it can be dangerous, proper instruction and great care are always necessary when you are scuba diving.

If you are less adventurous, you might try snorkeling instead of scuba diving. Less equipment is needed, just a face mask, a breathing tube (snorkel), and flippers for your feet. It only takes a few minutes to learn how to snorkel. Although you cannot dive deep into the water, you can swim with your face below the surface. Breathing through the tube, you float on the surface and keep yourself moving with your flippers. Even from the surface like this, there will be plenty of color and beauty to see.

Finishing time _____   Reading time _____

➤ *Do not look back at the passage.*

1. This passage is about
   a. water sports around the world.
   b. surfing.
   c. tourist activities in Hawaii.
   d. water sports in Hawaii.

2. You can infer from this passage that
   a. water sports are all expensive.
   b. you need to take a course for all water sports.
   c. everyone can find a way to enjoy sports on the water.
   d. swimming in Hawaii can be dangerous.

3. You can go deep under water when you are
   a. snorkeling.
   b. scuba diving.
   c. swimming.
   d. surfing.

4. Surfing
   a. began as a sport in 1943.
   b. was invented by the native Hawaiians.
   c. requires expensive equipment.
   d. is very dangerous.

5. If you want to try surfing, you
   a. need to be a good swimmer.
   b. should not go out into deep water.
   c. need to wait for a windy day.
   d. should go to Australia.

6. The water around the Hawaiian Islands is
   a. often quite cold.
   b. full of colorful things to see.
   c. usually very dark.
   d. full of dangerous fish.

7. Scuba diving
   a. is an ancient Hawaiian water sport.
   b. requires special equipment and training.
   c. is the only way to see the fish underwater.
   d. requires good balance.

8. Snorkeling
   a. requires more expensive equipment than scuba diving.
   b. can be dangerous.
   c. is an easy way to see the underwater life.
   d. was invented in ancient times.

5. The Mystery Islands

Of the eight Hawaiian Islands, Niihau and Kahoolawe are the smallest. These islands are quite unlike the others—they do not have hotels or resorts for tourists. Both islands, for different reasons, have had no tourists at all for many years.

Niihau is located just 17 miles off the west coast of the island of Kauai. It is very small—18 miles long and six miles wide. Niihau is owned by one family, the Robinsons, who bought the island in the 1860s from King Kamehameha IV of Hawaii. They started a large cattle and sheep ranch on the island that still operates today. The Robinsons do not allow any uninvited visitors on the island and so it is often called "The Forbidden Island."

About 230 people live on Niihau—95 percent of them Hawaiian and 5 percent Japanese. Most of the people live and work on the ranch, where there are no telephones, electricity, or television. The people use two-way radios to communicate and they use horses for transportation. There is an elementary school, but the children must go to Kauai to high school. The official language of the island is Hawaiian.

Among this small population, Hawaiian traditions are still strong, stronger than anywhere else. While, on the other islands, Hawaiians have adopted a different, modern lifestyle, life on Niihau has changed little. For this reason, some people want to keep the island the same. But others feel that this is not right. Life is difficult on Niihau, and the people there have few choices about their lives. Many Hawaiians feel that it is not right for one family to own and rule over a whole island.

Kahoolawe, the other "mystery island," does not have anyone living on it today. The smallest of the Hawaiian Islands, it is just 11 miles long and six miles wide. It is located seven miles south of the island of Maui.

Kahoolawe has not always been so empty. In past centuries, Hawaiians lived there and used the island for religious ceremonies. Then, in 1918, a Scotsman rented the island to start a cattle and sheep ranch. Before long, however, he and everyone else had to leave. The United States Navy took over the island as a practice ground for bombing and explosives. Navy planes bombed the island regularly.

Hawaiians were not happy about this situation. They wanted to return to Kahoolawe, to use it for their religious ceremonies. An organization called "Ohana" worked with the government to make this happen. Now, the island has been returned to the Hawaiian people. It will not be bombed anymore, and all of the old bombs will be removed. It will be, again, a place for special Hawaiian religious and cultural activities.

For Hawaiians, both Niihau and Kahoolawe raise important questions. Is it right for others to use their islands, giving them no choices at all? Who should decide about how to use these islands? And to whom should they really belong?

➤ *Do not look back at the passage.*

1. This passage is about

    a. the people living on Niihau and Kahoolawe.

    b. the location of Niihau and Kahoolawe.

    c. how the islands of Niihau and Kahoolawe are used.

    d. what the Hawaiians believe.

2. Niihau and Kahoolawe are

    a. very close together.

    b. very similar to the other islands.

    c. overcrowded.

    d. not visited by tourists.

3. On the island of Niihau there

    a. are lots of children.

    b. is a cattle ranch.

    c. is a United States Navy base.

    d. is an organization called Ohana.

4. Niihau's people are mostly

    a. Japanese.

    b. Scottish.

    c. Hawaiian.

    d. Robinsons.

5. You can infer from this passage that

    a. on the other islands, life has changed a lot for Hawaiians.

    b. Hawaiian life is just the same as always.

    c. Hawaiians like to live with no electricity.

    d. all the islands are owned by one family.

6. Until recently, the island of Kahoolawe was used mostly for

    a. cattle ranching.

    b. religious ceremonies.

    c. testing bombs and explosives.

    d. a vacation home.

7. You can infer from this passage that

    a. native Hawaiians made the decisions about Kahoolawe.

    b. a Scottish farmer made the decisions about Kahoolawe.

    c. an organization called Ohana made the decisions about Kahoolawe.

    d. the U.S. Navy made the decisions about Kahoolawe.

8. Hawaiians started an organization called Ohana to

    a. get electricity on all the islands.

    b. be able to return to Kahoolawe.

    c. stop the Robinsons' cattle and sheep ranch.

    d. welcome tourists to Niihau and Kahoolawe.

6. Hawaiian Traditions

Hawaiian culture was once rich in colorful traditions. Though some of them have been forgotten, two important traditions are very much alive today. One of these is the "lei" (a necklace made of flowers) and the other is the "hula" (a Hawaiian dance). According to local history, leis were first given to Hawaiians by the goddess of mercy and protection. She traveled to all the islands and destroyed the evil spirits. Leis were worn by Hawaiian chiefs at peace conferences. They are still important to the Hawaiian people, and are still symbolic of peace and friendship. Hawaiians wear leis at weddings, funerals, and at important ceremonies. A Hawaiian host will almost always give a lei to non-Hawaiian visitors. When the guest arrives, the lei is placed around his or her neck, with the traditional greeting, "Aloha."

Handmade by older women, leis are created from the many kinds of fresh flowers found on the islands. The flowers are sewn together to form a large circle. It takes many flowers to make a lei and the effect is richly colorful. Since the flowers must be fresh, the leis cannot be made in advance. In Hawaii, you can find women selling leis in every shopping center and at the airports. Each island has its typical lei, with a different kind of flower. May l is "Lei Day" on all the islands.

Leis are often worn by Hawaiians when they dance the hula. According to Hawaiian tradition, the goddess Laka taught the people how to dance the hula. They say that she set up a temple for teaching the hula on the Napali coast in Kauai. At first it was part of a religious ceremony and was danced only by the men. But later, women began to dance the hula, too. Now it is danced mostly by women.

Many Hawaiians have learned how to dance the hula. But the best hula dancers have taken classes for years and worked hard to learn the special movements. It is not easy to do the hula, though it may seem so simple and graceful when done well. The hula dancer must learn to control every part of her body, even her face. Then, she uses her hands and hips and feet to tell a story.

Music played on Hawaiian instruments accompanies the dancing. These instruments are made of bamboo, wood, and gourds (large vegetables that have been dried and hollowed out). The musicians also perform a kind of soft singing with the music. The music, singing, and dancing together form a Hawaiian-style opera. In this sense, hula dancing is typical of the extensive use of nonverbal expression in Hawaiian culture.

When Europeans came to Hawaii in the early 1800s, they did not like the hula. They thought such dancing went against proper religious beliefs. Therefore, they discouraged the hula and it almost disappeared from Hawaii. However, in the late 1800s King Kalakaua formed a special dance group and saved this important tradition.

Finishing time _____   Reading time _____

➤ *Do not look back at the passage.*

1. This passage is about
    a. a special kind of dance.
    b. two special Hawaiian traditions.
    c. peace and nonverbal expression.
    d. the use of flowers in Hawaiian tradition.

2. Leis and hula dancing are
    a. expressions of the Hawaiian way of life.
    b. ways to make money for Hawaiians.
    c. only seen at religious ceremonies.
    d. no longer part of the Hawaiian way of life.

3. You can infer that, according to Hawaiian tradition, a guest is
    a. considered an important person.
    b. not given any special treatment.
    c. discouraged from arriving.
    d. treated like one of the family.

4. Leis are
    a. made of plastic flowers.
    b. always made by hand.
    c. made by machine on some islands.
    d. always made by graceful girls.

5. Hula dancing is
    a. part of a religious ceremony.
    b. done only by young women.
    c. found only on the island of Kauai.
    d. a way of telling a story.

6. Hula dancers are usually accompanied by
    a. men dancers.
    b. music and soft singing.
    c. loud music.
    d. lots of singers.

7. According to Hawaiian tradition, leis and hula dancing were
    a. both started by goddesses.
    b. both discouraged by the Europeans.
    c. started mainly for the tourists.
    d. both started by Hawaiian chiefs.

8. You can infer from this passage that many Hawaiians
    a. still care about their traditions.
    b. are not interested in their traditions.
    c. only are interested in making money.
    d. do not know very much about their traditions.

7. *How the Islands Were Formed*   Starting time _____

The formation of the Hawaiian Islands was very different from the formation of the continents. Geologists (scientists who study the earth) believe that the islands appeared separately and more recently. According to the geological evidence, they were formed by volcanoes only about 30 million years ago.

These volcanoes began when some cracks appeared on the bottom of the Pacific Ocean. Deep under the earth's surface, the rocks are very hot, so hot that they are in a liquid form called lava. This lava can sometimes come up through openings on the surface of the earth. The piles of lava slowly build up and become mountains. When the openings are on the ocean floor, the mountains are at first underwater. They may eventually become tall enough to rise above the water and form islands. This is how the Hawaiian Archipelago was created. This archipelago, or collection of islands, consists of 132 points of land. The larger points of land of the archipelago are the Hawaiian Islands.

According to geologists, the islands in the Hawaiian Archipelago are still changing, like living things. The oldest islands, such as the Kure Atoll, are slowly disappearing under the sea. Over thousands of years, they have gradually been worn down by storms and the ocean waves. Now nothing is left but a semi-circle of coral reef (rock-like forms made by tiny sea animals).

Other, younger islands, however, are still growing. The Big Island of Hawaii has two active volcanoes which are still adding new lava to the island. There are also new islands in the archipelago in the process of formation. Geologists have found an underwater volcano about 30 miles south of the island of Hawaii. Now about 3,000 feet below the surface of the ocean, it will probably rise above the water. Someday, this volcano could become another Hawaiian island.

The islands at first were bare rock and empty of all life. They remained this way for millions of years. The first kinds of plant life were probably carried there as seeds by the wind or by the ocean. Plants grew well in the rich, volcanic dirt and birds were attracted to the islands. Birds may then have brought more seeds from faraway places, and so introduced other new plants.

All this took a very long time. Scientists believe that at the most, one new plant arrived every 20,000 years! But slowly the plants and the birds on the islands became more numerous and more varied. They also gradually evolved, changing to adapt themselves to their conditions. That is why the islands are home to so many plants and birds that can be found nowhere else.

The plants on the islands also attracted insects, which may have been blown there by storms. With just a few exceptions, plants, birds, and insects were the only forms of life. Then, about 1,500 years ago, the first humans arrived, bringing other animals with them. It was the beginning of an era of change for the Hawaiian Islands.

Finishing time _____   Reading time _____

➤ *Do not look back at the passage.*

1. This passage is about
   a. geologists at work.
   b. underwater volcanic eruptions in the Pacific Ocean.
   c. the age of the Hawaiian Archipelago.
   d. the formation of the Hawaiian Islands.

2. The Hawaiian Islands
   a. are older than the continents.
   b. are younger than the continents.
   c. have more birds than the continents.
   d. have more volcanoes than the continents.

3. Lava is very hot melted rock found
   a. under the sea.
   b. deep under the surface of the earth.
   c. on coral reefs.
   d. only on the top of volcanic mountains.

4. When lava comes through cracks in the earth's surface
   a. islands are formed.
   b. the ocean becomes warmer.
   c. mountains of lava are formed.
   d. coral reefs are formed.

5. The Hawaiian Islands are like living things because
   a. plants grow there so easily.
   b. they grow, change, and disappear.
   c. many coral reefs are forming there.
   d. the islands are made of hot lava.

6. You can infer from this passage that
   a. some day all the islands could disappear.
   b. there will always be new islands.
   c. the Big Island of Hawaii may get a new volcano.
   d. the first trees were planted by geologists.

7. The Big Island of Hawaii will probably
   a. become an archipelago.
   b. get more volcanoes.
   c. become larger.
   d. be the next island to disappear.

8. The first plants in Hawaii
   a. were brought there by the geologists.
   b. were carried to the islands by the wind and the sea.
   c. grew out of the hot lava.
   d. came from another archipelago.

8. The First Hawaiians

The first people to settle in the Hawaiian Islands were the Polynesians. They came from the Marquesa Islands, many thousands of miles to the southeast. In about 500 A.D., the Polynesians on the Marquesa Islands were facing many problems. They had lost a war with other Polynesians. On their islands there were too many people and not enough food. So some of them decided they wanted to start a new life somewhere else.

The Polynesians had learned songs and poems about a wonderful place far to the north. We do not know how this knowledge became a part of their culture. Maybe they had guessed it from the birds that flew to the north and never returned. Or perhaps they had seen bits of wood arrive with the north winds. We do know that the Polynesians were excellent sailors. They had no instruments to help them. Instead, they used the sun, the stars, the ocean currents, and the wind to guide them. They managed to travel to many distant places in the Pacific Ocean.

The people from the Marquesa Islands filled their boats for a long journey. They used large double canoes, about 80-100 feet long. In these canoes, they put food, water, goats, pigs, chickens, and plants. They carried everything they needed for their way of life, even statues of their gods. Many of the canoes were probably lost at sea. But a few did find their way to the Hawaiian Islands.

These early settlers were a very fierce and warlike people. They practiced cannibalism (eating people). However, in Hawaii they lost their violent ways and lived peacefully. Over the next few centuries, more Polynesians joined them in Hawaii. The many different tribes lived together quietly for about 500 years. For a period of several hundred years they had no contact with other people.

Then, in about 1200 A.D., a new group of people arrived from Tahiti. These people introduced a very different way of life. Their religion was full of strict rules and angry gods. Anyone who broke the rules could be put to death. They might be killed and sometimes even eaten by other people. However, the newcomers, too, became less violent after a while. They did continue to fight among themselves, but they no longer practiced cannibalism.

No one knows what happened to the first settlers on the island. They may have mixed in with the invaders. Or they may have died or moved to other islands. For the next 500 years, the people on the islands again had no contact with anyone from the outside world. Each island had its own king and chiefs, and for many centuries no single ruler was successful in controlling all the islands.

Then, in 1800, a king—Kamehameha—managed for the first time to gain power over all of the Hawaiian Islands. But this event now seems of little importance in the history of the islands. Another event was much more important in the long run: in 1778 Captain James Cook's ships landed in Hawaii. With the arrival of the Europeans, Hawaii was changed forever.

➤ *Do not look back at the passage.*

1. This passage is about
   a. the Polynesian people.
   b. the Marquesa Islands.
   c. how people sailed to Hawaii.
   d. early settlers in Hawaii.

2. In order to find the way to Hawaii, the Polynesians
   a. took statues of their gods.
   b. used the sun and the stars.
   c. watched the birds.
   d. fought a war with Tahiti.

3. The Polynesians from Marquesa came to Hawaii with
   a. lots of food and supplies.
   b. Tahitian gods.
   c. a peaceful spirit.
   d. Captain James Cook.

4. You can infer from this passage that
   a. sailing to Hawaii was difficult and dangerous.
   b. all of the Marquesans arrived safely in Hawaii.
   c. the Marquesans were better warriors than the Tahitians.
   d. the Marquesans faced many problems in Hawaii.

5. When the first Marquesans arrived in Hawaii, they probably found
   a. many Polynesians.
   b. a rich, fertile land.
   c. the first settlers.
   d. a new god.

6. The Tahitians who arrived in 1200 A.D.
   a. lived in peace with the people already in Hawaii.
   b. became the rulers of the Hawaiian Islands.
   c. had no gods.
   d. believed that all people were equal.

7. The original Marquesan settlers in Hawaii
   a. are still living in Honolulu.
   b. were killed by Captain Cook.
   c. have disappeared.
   d. became the rulers of the Tahitians.

8. The first person to control all of the islands was
   a. King Kamehameha I.
   b. a Polynesian leader.
   c. Captain James Cook.
   d. a European.

9. Newcomers to Hawaii

The arrival of Captain James Cook brought Hawaii in contact with the rest of the world. Cook, an English seaman, was exploring the Pacific Ocean. In January, 1778, he sailed into the port of Kealakekua on the island of Hawaii. The Hawaiians welcomed him as if he were a god. In fact, he had sailed into the harbor on a special day. It was the very day the Hawaiians believed that their god, Lono, would come to them!

However, the islanders soon began to have doubts about these newcomers. Cook and his sailors offended the Hawaiians and demanded goods and supplies. They also passed on many diseases to the Hawaiian people. The islanders were happy to see them sail away. Unfortunately, the Englishmen had to turn back because of a terrible storm. This time the Hawaiians gave them a different kind of welcome and they killed Captain Cook. A battle broke out after this, in which four Englishmen and many Hawaiians died. The first contact with Europeans was a disaster. From then on, the history of the native Hawaiians is a sad story of suffering and disasters.

News of the Hawaiian Islands quickly reached England and the United States. By 1819, two new groups of foreigners had arrived in Hawaii. Some of these foreigners came to hunt whales in the nearby waters, and others wanted to teach the Hawaiians about Christianity. More foreigners soon came to Hawaii to start trading companies and sugar or pineapple plantations. All of these foreigners cared little about the native Hawaiians, their language, or culture. Many did their best to eliminate the people and their traditions.

At first, King Kamehameha I tried to limit the activities of the foreigners, but he did not have much power. The kings and queens who followed him had even less power. The islands became more and more under the control of foreigners. Some Hawaiians stopped speaking their language and forgot their traditions.

Among the foreigners, the Americans were the most numerous and the wealthiest. They owned most of the land, the businesses, and the banks. These Americans wanted Hawaii to become part of the United States. Many Hawaiians did not want this to happen, but they were powerless. In 1893, the United States government took over the islands from Queen Liliuokalani.

By this time, the population of the islands had changed a great deal. Aside from the Americans and Europeans, many other people had come to Hawaii from different parts of the world. In the mid-nineteenth century, workers were needed for the large sugar and pineapple plantations. The first workers to come were Chinese. Later, other workers came from many other parts of the world: Japan, Samoa, the Philippines, Portugal, and Puerto Rico. Some came alone for short periods, but others brought their families and stayed.

Today, there are many ethnic groups on the islands. Sadly, the people with the fewest numbers, the least power, and the least property are the original Hawaiians.

Finishing time _____   Reading time _____

➤ *Do not look back at the passage.*

1. This passage is about

    a. Hawaii's history since the 1700s.
    b. how Captain Cook came to Hawaii.
    c. how Hawaii became part of the United States.
    d. the last queen of the islands.

2. When Captain James Cook first sailed into port in Hawaii, he

    a. was attacked by the religious leaders of Hawaii.
    b. was mistaken for a god.
    c. wanted to learn the Hawaiian language.
    d. wanted Hawaiians to think that he was a god.

3. The Hawaiians were glad to see Cook sail away because he

    a. had treated them very well.
    b. reminded them of a god.
    c. had treated them very badly.
    d. didn't speak their language.

4. You can infer from this passage that the early foreigners

    a. were afraid of the islanders.
    b. were more powerful than the islanders.
    c. never needed to fight the islanders.
    d. had to fight many battles against the islanders.

5. The kings and queens of Hawaii

    a. wanted to start their own businesses.
    b. began to forget their language and religion.
    c. weren't able to keep control of the islands.
    d. wanted to become part of the United States.

6. People from China and other countries came to Hawaii mainly to

    a. attend the new churches.
    b. start new businesses and banks.
    c. learn about the Hawaiian culture.
    d. work on the sugar and pineapple plantations.

7. You can infer from this passage that

    a. the newcomers were very interested in Hawaiian religion.
    b. the American businessmen in Hawaii were not interested in the Hawaiian people.
    c. many Hawaiian people wanted to be under the U.S. government.
    d. most Hawaiians did not want to keep their religion.

8. Now, over 200 years after Captain Cook, the Hawaiian Islands have

    a. become more Hawaiian.
    b. fewer people than when he arrived.
    c. the same special culture and religion.
    d. become a mixture of many cultures.

10. The Ethnic Rainbow of Hawaii Today   Starting time _____

In present-day Hawaii, there are at least twelve different ethnic groups. None of these is large enough to form a majority of the population. The largest groups are the Japanese, the Europeans, the Chinese, the Filipinos, the part-Hawaiians, and the people from mixed families.

No other state in the United States has such a mixed population. However, in many other states the ethnic groups are growing. Soon those states may be like Hawaii, with many cultural groups living together. Hawaii is thus a good example of how people from different ethnic groups can get along.

In Hawaii, in fact, the lack of an ethnic majority means that people from different ethnic groups must work together. One result is that everyone has more opportunities to meet people of other ethnic groups and to learn about their culture. With this experience, people can learn to respect each other's ideas and ways of life. Children can grow up to be more tolerant as adults, more willing to accept differences. This tolerance can have obvious benefits for society as a whole. In the long run, it can mean less social tension, and probably less poverty and violence.

One way to measure the level of tolerance in Hawaii is by the percentage of mixed marriages. In fact, over 45 percent of the marriages in Hawaii are between people from different ethnic groups. Children from mixed marriages are called "hapas." The children from these marriages may marry people from yet other ethnic groups. Their children may have quite a complex ethnic mixture in their blood. Here are some real examples of the many possible cultural mixtures: Irish, Portuguese, and Hawaiian; Japanese and Portuguese; Japanese, German-Jewish, Spanish, and East Indian.

The special mixture of cultures that is Hawaii also gives the individual more opportunities for different cultural experiences. Hawaiians, in general, take good advantage of these opportunities. Each ethnic group keeps its traditions—its style of cooking, its costumes and music. But many people also participate in some way in the traditions of other groups. Frequent ethnic festivals give everyone a chance to learn about the traditions of other groups. These events are usually well-attended, and not just by the ethnic group in question.

Many different ethnic foods are available everywhere. Restaurants serve dishes from all corners of the earth. In every supermarket, you can find a wide variety of food specialties: noodles from the Philippines, fish from Portugal, special snacks from Japan, and vegetables from China. And, of course, the traditional Hawaiian dish called "poi" is in every shop, too.

As some Hawaiians like to say, Hawaiian society is like a rainbow. Each ethnic group brings its color to the rainbow, because each group has something important and beautiful to offer. But what is really special is the way the people are living side by side, creating a beautiful whole.

Finishing time _____   Reading time _____

➤ **Do not look back at the passage.**

1. This passage is about
    a. mixed marriages.
    b. Hawaii's majority culture.
    c. rainbows in Hawaii.
    d. the mixture of cultures in Hawaii.

2. Hawaiian society is unusual because
    a. there are few mixed marriages.
    b. all Hawaiians have the same beliefs.
    c. it is a mixed society.
    d. there are many Japanese families.

3. In Hawaii there is no majority culture, so
    a. problems are never solved.
    b. people don't get along.
    c. different groups must work together.
    d. people are afraid of other cultures.

4. One advantage of a mixed society is that
    a. people have many choices.
    b. people do not have to make many choices.
    c. ethnic groups do not have to mix.
    d. people have "hapas."

5. Mixed marriages in Hawaii
    a. are not accepted by most Hawaiians.
    b. make up almost half the marriages.
    c. cause prejudice and unhappiness.
    d. are not permitted.

6. Hawaiians use the word "hapa" for
    a. a person who marries someone from another ethnic group.
    b. someone who is part-Hawaiian.
    c. the child of a mixed marriage.
    d. any child who is born in Hawaii.

7. You can infer that everyone who lives in Hawaii
    a. eats the same kind of food.
    b. marries someone from another ethnic group.
    c. is uninterested in ethnic traditions.
    d. learns something about native Hawaiian traditions.

8. Some Hawaiians say that the ethnic groups in Hawaii
    a. are all becoming the same.
    b. are like a colorful rainbow.
    c. will never get along.
    d. are unimportant.

Maria Montessori

1. Childhood

When Maria Montessori was born in Italy in 1870, her future seemed certain. Women did not have careers in those days, nor did they attend college. People generally believed that women were not very intelligent and not capable of complex thought. So Maria, it seemed, had little choice. Like her mother and most women of her day, she would become a mother and a housewife.

She did, in fact, become a mother, but otherwise her life took a very different course. She became a doctor—the first woman doctor in Italy. With her brilliant medical studies and research, she proved that women could indeed think and work as well as men. Later, she became internationally famous as the inventor of the Montessori method of teaching. To this day, Montessori schools around the world follow her method.

She was born in Chiaravalle, near Ancona, Italy. Her father, Alessandro Montessori, was a government official in the state-run tobacco industry. In his youth, he had fought for the liberation and unification of Italy. He was well-educated and wanted the best for his daughter. However, he was also conservative, and did not approve of her unusual choices. Only later, when she became famous, did he change his mind and become proud of her.

Maria's mother, however, never had any doubts about her daughter. She supported all of Maria's decisions and helped her through many difficult times. Her own life was ordinary enough, but she wanted her daughter's life to be different. It was she who gave Maria the optimism and the ideals necessary for success. She also taught Maria not to be afraid of hard work. Even as a small girl, Maria always had her share of housework to do. And finally, Maria's mother gave her a sense of responsibility towards others. This was an important factor in her later work as a doctor and as an educator.

The Montessori family moved several times when Maria was young. When she was five, they went to live in Rome and there she started primary school. Only an average student at that time, Maria did not seem very ambitious. Nor did she sympathize with the competitive behavior of some of her classmates. When she won a prize in the first grade, it was for good behavior. In second grade, she won another prize for sewing and needlework. So far, her interests and achievements were the same as those of any other girl of her time.

However, something in Maria's character stood out among the other children. She was often the leader in their games. Self-confident and strong-willed, she came to believe that her life was somehow going to be different. At the age of ten, when she became dangerously ill, that belief in herself was already strong. She told her mother she couldn't die because she had too much to do in life.

➤ *Do not look back at the passage.*

1. This passage is about

    a. Maria Montessori's parents.

    b. girls in the nineteenth century.

    c. Maria Montessori's background and childhood.

    d. Maria Montessori's education.

2. We can infer from this passage that before Maria,

    a. many Italian women had studied medicine.

    b. Italian women didn't go to doctors.

    c. Italian women often became lawyers.

    d. no Italian women had ever studied medicine.

3. Maria Montessori

    a. was like most other women of her time.

    b. was very ordinary.

    c. became a mother and a housewife.

    d. was not like most other women of her time.

4. Maria's father

    a. worked as a government official.

    b. ran a tobacco company.

    c. was a doctor.

    d. was a soldier.

5. The most important influence on Maria's development was probably her

    a. teacher.

    b. mother.

    c. father.

    d. illness.

6. Maria's mother believed in

    a. hard work and helping others.

    b. leaving the work for others.

    c. giving others hard work to do.

    d. helping her husband at work.

7. In primary school Maria was

    a. a very brilliant student.

    b. a most unusual girl.

    c. not a very brilliant student.

    d. a terrible student.

8. As a child Maria felt that

    a. her life was going to be short.

    b. she was going to be different from others.

    c. she was going to be just like others.

    d. her life was going to be very long.

2. Going Her Own Way

When she was twelve, Maria made her first important decision about the course of her life. She decided that she wanted to continue her education. Most girls from middle-class families chose to stay home after primary school. Some attended private Catholic "finishing" schools. There they learned a little about music, art, needlework, and how to make polite conversation. However, this was not the sort of education that interested Maria—or her mother. By this time, she had begun to take her studies more seriously. She read constantly and brought her books everywhere. One time she even brought her math book to the theater and tried to study in the dark.

Maria knew that she wanted to go on learning in a serious way. That meant attending the public high schools, something that very few girls did. In Italy at the time, there were two types of high schools: the "classical" schools and the "technical" schools. In the classical schools, the students followed a very traditional program of studies. The courses included Latin and Greek language and literature, and Italian literature and history. The girls who continued studying after primary school usually chose these schools.

Maria, however, wanted to attend a technical school. The technical schools were a little more modern than the classical schools. The courses they offered included modern languages, mathematics, some science and commercial subjects. Most people—including Maria's father—believed that girls would never be able to understand these subjects. Furthermore, they did not think it was proper for girls to study them.

Maria did not care if it was proper or not. Math and science were the subjects that interested her most. But before she could sign up for the technical school, she had to win her father's approval. She finally did, with her mother's help. For many years after, though, there was tension in the family. Maria's father continued to oppose her plans, while her mother helped her.

In 1883, at age 13, Maria entered the "Regia Scuola Tecnica Michelangelo Buonarroti" in Rome. Her experience at this school is difficult for us to imagine. Though the courses included modern subjects, the teaching methods were very traditional. Learning consisted of memorizing long lists of facts and repeating them back to the teacher. Teachers believed in strict discipline in the classroom and they sometimes used severe punishments.

It took a strong character to survive these methods. Everyone predicted that Maria would fail, but instead, she succeeded brilliantly. She proved, with her high marks in math and science, that girls, too, could think about complex subjects. For a while Maria wanted to be an engineer, like many of her male school companions. But by the time she finished school, she had changed her mind. She had become very interested in biology, and she wanted to study medicine. It didn't matter to her that no woman in Italy had ever studied medicine before.

Reading Faster

➤ *Do not look back at the passage.*

1. This passage is about
   a. Maria's high school years.
   b. technical schools in Italy.
   c. high school courses.
   d. Maria's favorite courses.

2. Maria wanted to attend
   a. a private "finishing school."
   b. a school which gave art and music lessons.
   c. a technical high school.
   d. the theater.

3. In those days most Italian girls
   a. went to classical schools.
   b. went to finishing schools.
   c. did not go to high school.
   d. had two choices about high schools.

4. You can infer from this passage that
   a. girls usually attended private primary schools.
   b. only boys usually attended technical schools.
   c. girls did not like going to school.
   d. classical schools were harder than technical schools.

5. Maria's father probably
   a. had very modern views about women.
   b. had very traditional views about women.
   c. had no opinion about women.
   d. thought women could not learn Latin.

6. High school teachers in Italy in those days were
   a. very modern.
   b. very intelligent.
   c. quite scientific.
   d. quite strict.

7. Many of Maria's school companions wanted to be
   a. engineers.
   b. teachers.
   c. biologists.
   d. technicians.

8. In her high school years Maria showed that she was
   a. afraid of criticism.
   b. eager to please her father.
   c. serious about learning.
   d. not interested in science.

3. Starting at the University

Starting time _____

The first step towards becoming a doctor was easy for Maria. In a short time, she had completed the pre-medical program at the University of Rome and passed her exams. Then she was ready to begin studying at the University's department of clinical medicine. However, the university was not ready for her. There had never been a woman in the department and the professors did not want one.

No one knows how Maria managed to convince the university to accept her. She spoke with the head of the medical faculty, Professor Baccelli, who was also an important politician. He wanted to reform the Italian school system and the university, but he did not want women to study medicine. So he was no help. There were reports that she also spoke with Pope Leo XIII and that he helped her. However, this story may not be true. It may only be one of the many legends that later surrounded Maria.

In any case, in 1892, Maria began to attend classes in clinical medicine. She was not received well by her fellow students. They laughed at her and made unpleasant comments to her about women doctors. The presence of a woman in their classes, especially an intelligent woman like Maria, clearly disturbed them. They did not like the fact that she received better grades than many of her male classmates. But they also did not like the way she took her studies so seriously. In fact, many medical students at that time cared only about improving their social position. They were not interested in learning about medicine or in working as doctors.

Maria, however, felt very differently about her studies. She was interested, first of all, in the subjects themselves. Then, too, she wanted to lead a useful life. She believed she could do this best as a doctor. With these beliefs to strengthen her, she paid no attention to the other students. If someone was rude to her at the university, she just stared back at him. In time, her fellow students came to respect her strong nerves as well as her ability.

Only once did Maria have any doubts about her career. That was when she began to attend anatomy classes. These classes came as a terrible shock to her. Women in those days were not used to looking at or talking about people's body parts. Both women and men, in fact, wore clothes that almost completely covered their bodies. Women, especially, were never supposed to talk about or even think about bodily functions.

So Maria was extremely embarrassed the first time she had to examine a naked body. She also hated the idea of working with dead bodies. When she went home after the first anatomy lesson, she felt so awful that she got sick to her stomach. She later wrote that she was ready at that point to quit studying medicine.

But she did not quit. The next day she went back. Somehow she managed to control her feelings and continue.

Finishing time _____   Reading time _____

➤ *Do not look back at the passage.*

1. This passage is about
   a. how Italians studied medicine.
   b. Maria's feelings about medicine.
   c. Maria's first experiences at the university.
   d. how Maria got accepted to the university.

2. Some people thought that Pope Leo XIII
   a. helped Maria with her studies.
   b. wrote newspaper articles about Maria.
   c. wanted to reform the university system.
   d. helped Maria get accepted into medical school.

3. Many of Maria's fellow students
   a. liked having a woman in their classes.
   b. did not like having a woman in their classes.
   c. were interested in a woman like Maria.
   d. wanted Maria to become a doctor.

4. As a student, Maria
   a. performed less well than her fellow students.
   b. got the same grades as her fellow students.
   c. performed better than many of her fellow students.
   d. got lower grades than most of her fellow students.

5. You can infer from this passage that doctors in Italy
   a. had a high social status.
   b. were laughed at by the public.
   c. had a low social status.
   d. were often very religious.

6. Maria
   a. didn't take her studies very seriously.
   b. was too upset to study seriously.
   c. took her studies very seriously.
   d. was only interested in her social status.

7. At first Maria found the anatomy classes very
   a. interesting.
   b. upsetting.
   c. easy.
   d. amusing.

8. From this passage it seems that Maria
   a. often doubted her decision to become a doctor.
   b. never doubted her decision to become a doctor.
   c. was very uncertain about her decision to become a doctor.
   d. rarely doubted her decision to become a doctor.

4. Success at the University   Starting time _____

As a woman student at the university, Maria had to follow many special rules. Young women could never be alone in public in Italy. That meant she always had to find someone to walk with her to classes. She was not supposed to have very close contact with the male students. So she had to wait to enter the lecture hall until they were all in their seats. And finally, she couldn't work on the dead bodies in the anatomy lab together with male students. Instead she had separate sessions alone in the evenings.

As the only woman, Maria was inevitably very visible. Before long, however, she began to attract a different kind of attention. Her professors began to be impressed by her seriousness and her ability. At the end of her second year she won a large scholarship, the Rolli Prize. The scholarship gave Maria financial independence. This was important because her father had threatened to cut off all financial support. He still opposed her choice of careers, though her mother continued to support her.

After her first success, Maria went on to others. The next year she won a tough competition for a position as an assistant in a hospital in Rome. Then, in her fourth and final year, she gave a lecture that was received with great applause. All the audience stood up to congratulate her. Among the people who attended the lecture was her father. He had decided to go only at the last minute, and he, too, was impressed by Maria. That was the beginning of a change in his attitude towards his daughter's career.

Maria's final assignment at the university was to write a thesis on an original topic. She completed her thesis—on a psychiatric subject—in the spring of 1896. After discussing it with the examiners, she was given her degree with high honors on July 10, 1886. Since Maria was the first woman graduate, a special diploma had to be written out for her. The traditional wording had to be changed so that it no longer referred only to the male sex.

The new doctor was much talked about in Rome. She couldn't go for a walk in a park without being noticed. People would stop her mother and ask about her extraordinary daughter. They were surprised to see that Maria was an attractive young woman, quite modest and feminine. They probably had expected an older, more severe kind of person. And they must have wondered how such a delicate-looking woman could work with naked, dead bodies. Or how she could have the courage to speak in public about such difficult scientific matters!

Maria was famous, but sometimes she wondered about this fame. Were people really interested in her ability and intelligence? Or were they simply curious because she was different? She was sure about one thing, however. It had taken a great deal of courage and effort to succeed.

Finishing time _____   Reading time _____

➤ **Do not look back at the passage.**

1. This passage is about
   a. the years Maria attended the university.
   b. universities in Italy.
   c. women medical students.
   d. how Maria was awarded high honors with her degree.

2. At the university Maria
   a. was free to do what she wanted.
   b. was treated like all the other students.
   c. had to work together with the other students.
   d. was much less free than the other students.

3. Maria won the Rolli Prize because
   a. she was a woman.
   b. of her ability.
   c. of her father.
   d. she needed money.

4. Maria's final lecture was
   a. much applauded.
   b. not applauded.
   c. poorly attended.
   d. about the economy.

5. Maria's father
   a. didn't care about her career.
   b. was always proud of his daughter.
   c. began to change his mind about her career.
   d. didn't want her to have a career.

6. Maria's diploma had to be rewritten because
   a. she had won high honors.
   b. she was a woman.
   c. it was too traditional.
   d. it didn't mention her family.

7. People in Rome probably thought a woman doctor
   a. should be especially attractive.
   b. would be much younger than Maria was.
   c. should be able to discuss scientific matters.
   d. would not be attractive.

8. You can infer from this passage that
   a. many Italian woman spoke in public.
   b. Italian women generally did not speak much in public.
   c. most Italian women liked to walk in public parks.
   d. Italian women liked to listen to public speaking.

5. The Young Doctor

Only two months after graduating, Maria was faced with a new and different kind of challenge. She was invited to be a delegate to the International Woman's Congress in Berlin. At the congress, she was a great success once again. She gave two speeches —about education for women and about the condition of working women in Italy. Both speeches were received with great enthusiasm. Newspaper reporters from all over Europe interviewed her and praised her in their articles. They described the young doctor from Italy as both intelligent and charming. They were amazed, too, that she had used no notes for her long speeches.

When she returned from Berlin, Maria settled down to serious work in Rome. She continued to work in several hospitals, including a women's hospital and a children's hospital. She also had some private patients. Some of these patients wrote letters of thanks afterwards which Maria's mother kept for many years. From these letters, it is clear that Maria was no ordinary doctor. She often stayed for hours with her patients, particularly those who could not afford nursing help. One time, for example, Maria arrived at the home of the young mother of very sick baby twins. She saw at once that the mother was desperately tired, so Maria sent her to bed. Then she bathed the babies, prepared their food and stayed with them all day. The mother believed that Maria's special care saved her children's lives.

Along with her hospital work, Maria continued to do research at a psychiatric clinic. She became more and more involved in this research, especially when it concerned children. She was particularly interested in the case of the so-called "idiot children." These children with severe developmental problems could not function at home or at school. No one knew what to do with them, so they were locked up in hospitals. There they were treated like little animals and they did nothing but eat and sleep.

Maria believed that it might be possible to do something for these children. She spent many hours watching them in the hospital. One thing she noticed, was that at feeding time, they often played with bits of food. She also noticed how terribly bare their rooms were. They had nothing to look at, nothing to touch or play with—until their food arrived. The fact that they played with bits of food was a positive sign, Maria thought. It showed that they could respond to something, that their minds were not completely closed off. Maybe what they needed was more opportunity to play, so they could use their minds more.

The question of the "idiot children" came to occupy Maria's thinking more and more. She refused to accept that they were unteachable, as other doctors said. Somehow, she felt, it must be possible to reach these children. With the right kind of teaching, she believed that she could help them become human again.

> *Do not look back at the passage.*

1. This passage is about
   a. Maria's research.
   b. the responsibilities of an Italian doctor.
   c. Maria's life in Rome.
   d. Maria's work after she finished her studies.

2. You can infer from this passage that
   a. most public speakers used notes for their speeches.
   b. Maria usually used notes for her speeches.
   c. most public speakers did not use notes for their speeches.
   d. Maria did not like to give interviews to reporters.

3. Maria worked
   a. only with private patients.
   b. at hospitals and with private patients.
   c. only in private hospitals.
   d. as a nurse in private homes.

4. When Maria went to visit a patient she
   a. sent them to the hospital.
   b. often stayed for dinner.
   c. often stayed to help nurse the patient.
   d. was too busy to stay long.

5. We can infer from this passage that Maria
   a. was much liked by her patients.
   b. did not have many patients.
   c. was not much liked by her patients.
   d. did not like to go to her patients.

6. Maria's research involved
   a. patients who had problems with children.
   b. children in hospitals.
   c. the feeding of children.
   d. some children with severe developmental problems.

7. The "idiot children" were sent to hospitals because
   a. they had no families.
   b. they were happier there.
   c. no one knew what to do with them.
   d. they could be studied better.

8. Maria believed that these children
   a. did not want to play.
   b. were hopeless cases.
   c. needed more opportunities to play.
   d. needed to be fed more.

6. Maria Becomes a School Director

Maria continued to work for several years in the hospitals and with private patients. In her free time, however, she began to study what was known about children with developmental problems. She was particularly interested in the work of a French doctor, Edouard Seguin. He had developed special methods for teaching these children and had started a school for them in Paris. There he taught them many skills that people had thought they would never be able to learn.

Dr. Seguin's ideas about teaching these children were very close to Maria's own ideas. She decided that she needed to know more about educational theory in general. So she read everything on the subject that she could find and she attended a course at the university.

As Maria began to have clearer ideas about the education of children with developmental problems, she expressed those ideas in writing. Her articles attracted much attention and she was invited to give speeches as well. In 1898, in Turin, she gave a speech at the National Teachers Congress. In this speech, she argued that Italy should have special schools for children with developmental problems. Children in these schools could become useful members of society. They would no longer be condemned to a life in hospitals, or on the streets as criminals.

Among the teachers and among the Italian people there was strong support for Maria's idea of special schools. An organization was started to raise money for such schools. Maria gave many speeches for this organization and became one of its directors. By that time she was widely recognized as an expert in children's mental problems. Her fame increased when she won an award in 1898 for her hospital work.

Then, in 1900, the organization had enough money and support to open a school in Rome. Maria was chosen to be its director. This was a great honor for such a young doctor. It was also an extraordinary achievement for a woman. But with her ideas, her experience and her strong personality, she was clearly the best candidate.

The school was called the Orthophrenic School for Teachers. It was an unusual institution in many ways. Its goal was to educate not only the children, but also teachers from the regular schools. They would then return to their classes better prepared to deal with problem children. At the end of its first year, the school gave a public demonstration. Among the visitors were many important doctors, professors, and politicians. Everyone was amazed at how much the children had learned in such a short time.

On August 31, 1900, Maria celebrated her thirtieth birthday. As a present, her father gave her an enormous book that he had put together. It contained 200 newspaper articles about Maria that had been published over the years. Now at least Maria would have no doubts about his love and support.

➤ *Do not look back at the passage.*

1. This passage is about

   a. an organization for children with developmental problems.

   b. Maria's beliefs about children with problems.

   c. how Maria became the director of a school.

   d. the Orthophrenic School for Teachers.

2. Maria was interested in Seguin because of his

   a. school.

   b. hospital work.

   c. theories about how to give speeches.

   d. ideas about teaching children.

3. The organization Maria worked for

   a. wanted special schools for problem children.

   b. had already started many special schools.

   c. organized courses about educational theory.

   d. was founded by Edouard Seguin.

4. You can infer that in Italy children with developmental problems were

   a. not useful members of society.

   b. not permitted in the streets.

   c. treated well in the schools.

   d. invited to a congress.

5. By 1900, Maria was well known

   a. as a politician.

   b. for her journalism.

   c. as a children's doctor.

   d. as a university professor.

6. You can infer from this passage that in Italy there

   a. weren't many young women directors of schools.

   b. were many young women directors of schools.

   c. weren't many young women teachers.

   d. were many young women who gave speeches.

7. The new school was unusual because it taught

   a. many new skills.

   b. retarded children to read.

   c. both children and teachers.

   d. teachers how to be useful.

8. Maria's father showed that he

   a. had many doubts about the new school.

   b. had many doubts about his daughter.

   c. was very proud of his daughter.

   d. was very proud of his book.

7. Big Changes
Starting time _____

While she was the director of the Orthophrenic School Maria worked closely with the children. At night she studied her notes and designed new materials for particular problems. There was one young girl, for example, who seemed unable to learn how to sew. Maria invented a weaving exercise so that her hands could practice the in-and-out movement of sewing. When the girl next tried sewing, she was far more successful.

Maria found that the children generally learned much more easily if they were prepared first with exercises. This seemed to be true for reading and writing as well. The regular Italian schools had always used repetition as a teaching method. Many children—both normal and with developmental problems—had learned little that way.

The new methods of Maria's school, however, gave quite different results. Some of the children even managed to pass the regular state elementary school examinations. This seemed like a miracle to many people. For Maria, however, this success brought new questions. She wondered if her methods would work as well in teaching normal children.

At this point in her career, Maria made a decision that surprised everyone. In 1900, she left the Orthophrenic school and went back to the university as a student of education. No one could imagine why she would want to leave her position at the school where she was well-respected. At the time, she simply said that she felt she must learn more about education. But this explanation was probably only part of the truth.

This period in Maria's life is surrounded by mystery, but one thing is sure. She had a romance with one of her fellow doctors, Dr. Giuseppe Montesano. He had worked in hospitals with Maria and then had become co-director of the Orthophrenic School. Maria and Giuseppe were together day after day, and eventually their relationship became more than professional. They were both young, after all, and Maria was a beautiful, lively woman.

Soon Maria was expecting a baby. It is hard to imagine how she hid her changing shape during this busy period. But somehow she did and her son Mario was born in 1898. For some reason she did not marry Montesano. They may have made an agreement never to get married to anyone. Dr. Montesano, however, did marry someone else in 1900. That may have been the real reason for Maria's decision to leave the school.

With Maria's love of children, it may seem surprising that she gave her son to another family to bring up. However, in those days it was shameful for an unmarried woman to have a child. Maria may not have cared about scandal, but her mother probably did. And if the public had known about her son, Maria's career would probably have ended. The fact that Maria did not bring up her son may have influenced her later life and work. Having missed the experience of caring for her son, she may have cared even more about helping other children.

Finishing time _____   Reading time _____

➤ **Do not look back at the passage.**

1. This passage is about
    a. Maria's romance with Montesano.
    b. how Maria taught retarded children.
    c. the end of Maria's career.
    d. important changes in Maria's life.

2. Maria got ideas for new materials by
    a. reading books.
    b. working with the children.
    c. doing sewing exercises.
    d. talking with other teachers.

3. Italian schools usually made children
    a. repeat tasks again and again.
    b. prepare for a task.
    c. do lots of sewing.
    d. read their notes every night.

4. Maria said she left the school so she
    a. would have more time to design materials.
    b. could study education.
    c. could have her baby.
    d. would be better respected.

5. You can infer from this passage that Italian children
    a. all passed the elementary school examinations.
    b. did a lot of homework.
    c. had to take examinations in elementary school.
    d. had normal intelligence.

6. Maria's decision to leave the school was surprising because she
    a. had a good job at the school.
    b. didn't like being a student.
    c. wanted to have a child.
    d. wasn't happy at the school.

7. Maria got to know Dr. Montesano
    a. as students together.
    b. at work.
    c. in his office.
    d. at home.

8. The fact that Maria had a child probably made her
    a. less interested in children generally.
    b. want to get married.
    c. interested in a university education.
    d. more interested in children generally.

8. The Children's House

After studying for a few years, Maria became a university professor in 1904. She taught educational theory and methods at the University of Rome. At the same time, she was also very involved in efforts to change the Italian school system. Her earlier experience had shown her how poorly the schools functioned for children with problems. Now she believed that they functioned poorly for normal children as well. And she thought she knew how to improve them.

Then, in 1906, a group of bankers decided to fix up some apartment buildings in a very poor area of Rome. In these buildings, they wanted to create nursery schools for the children who lived there. Since Maria was well known for her work with children, they asked her to become the director of these schools. Some of her friends thought that a doctor and university professor like Maria should not work in a nursery school. But Maria saw this as a perfect opportunity to try out some of her theories.

The first school was opened on January 6, 1907. It was called `La Casa dei Bambini,' the Children's House. The bankers had given Maria a large room and an assistant—and not much else. Friends and supporters gave her some small tables and chairs, a few toys, and paper and pencils. To that, she added the materials she had designed for the Orthophrenic School. Later she also brought in some plants and pictures, and even several small animals in cages.

On the first opening day in January, there were about 50 children from three to five years old. They were frightened and were crying miserably. When they got over their fear, some children were violent, while others refused to talk. Before long, though, as Maria introduced her activities, their behavior changed. The violent children calmed down and the silent ones began to communicate. They all became more sociable and cooperative, and were soon all enthusiastic about the school.

Maria noticed that they seemed to prefer her materials to the ordinary toys. She also found that they were not interested in rewards, but in the activities themselves. The way they gave all their attention to their tasks amazed her sometimes. Once, for example, a little girl was playing with a set of blocks of different shapes. She did not notice when Maria told the children to sing and march around the room. She did not even notice when her chair was picked up and set on a table. She just kept on fitting the blocks into the right-shaped holes. When she had done this 42 times, she suddenly stopped and smiled. She was done.

This was how children should learn, Maria believed. They should be free to choose their activities, to start and stop as they liked. The desire to learn was natural in children, she felt. The teacher's role was to provide materials and show the children how to use them. But then the teacher should stand aside and let the learning happen. The children were really their own best teachers.

Finishing time _____   Reading time _____

➤ *Do not look back at the passage.*

1. This passage is about
   - a. Maria's educational theories.
   - b. teaching small children.
   - c. using blocks for learning.
   - d. the opening of the Children's House.

2. Maria wanted to improve
   - a. the Italian universities.
   - b. the Roman apartment buildings.
   - c. the Italian schools.
   - d. her career situation.

3. Maria was chosen as director of the Children's House because she
   - a. knew a lot about teaching children.
   - b. was a professor and a doctor.
   - c. liked small children.
   - d. wanted to reform the educational system.

4. Some Italians thought that working in a nursery school was
   - a. suitable for a professor.
   - b. suitable for a woman.
   - c. unsuitable for a professor.
   - d. unsuitable for a woman.

5. You can infer from this passage that Maria thought a nursery school should
   - a. be very simple and bare.
   - b. always have music.
   - c. be comfortable and interesting.
   - d. have only her teaching materials in it.

6. At first the children were
   - a. happy and excited.
   - b. hungry and tired.
   - c. interested and busy.
   - d. unhappy and afraid.

7. You can infer from this passage that Italian nursery schools usually
   - a. let the children do what they wanted.
   - b. did not give the children much freedom.
   - c. had lots of toys.
   - d. did not reward the children.

8. Her experience at the Children's House taught Maria that children really
   - a. want to learn.
   - b. need teachers.
   - c. like to play with blocks.
   - d. want rewards.

9. *The Montessori Method Takes Shape*   Starting time _____

As time went by, Maria continued to try out new ideas at the Children's House. In order for the children to be free in their learning, she felt they needed to become more independent. She had noticed that they liked to get out the toys and books by themselves. She encouraged them to do this all the time, and she taught them to put things away, too.

The eagerness of the children to do things themselves led Maria to teach them many everyday tasks. They learned how to wash, dress, and eat by themselves. Soon they were helping to prepare and serve the noon meal at school and were cleaning up the classroom. These "exercises in practical life" became an important part of Maria's teaching method.

In April of 1907, a second Children's House was opened. This was organized like the first one. Here, too, the children started out unhappy and confused. But again, they soon changed. As news of the schools spread around Rome, visitors began to appear. They were all impressed. In those days, no one expected to see children so involved and happy, especially not children from poor families.

That first year, Maria did not try to teach reading or writing. She thought, as most people did, that children were not ready for those skills until they were six. The children, however, wanted to learn, and their mothers encouraged them. Many mothers could not read or write themselves. They saw, too, how easily the children learned with Maria, much more easily than at the regular schools.

So in the fall, Maria started to experiment with writing. She cut out large letters of paper and sandpaper. The children felt the shapes, learned to copy them and practiced the sounds for each letter. Gradually, they learned to put the letters together and combine sounds. Then one day, they suddenly were writing whole words.

Their excitement was extraordinary. They wanted to write all the time. They wrote everywhere — on the walls, the floor, and even on the loaves of bread. Not long after that the children began to read, too. For Christmas that year, two of the children wrote a letter to the bankers who had started the schools. Though only four years old, they wrote as well as eight-year-olds.

By this time, the Children's Houses were well known all over Italy. In 1908, another was opened in Milan and two more in Rome. Maria could not direct all these schools herself so she began to train other teachers. Her theories and the experience of these years began to take a more definite shape. To help in training teachers, she put all her ideas into a book, *The Montessori Method*, published in 1909.

This small book had an enormous influence on the teaching of children—and not just in Italy. In fact, schools around the world still follow many of Maria's ideas. Her belief that children basically want to learn was revolutionary at the time. By now, however, it is universally accepted.

Finishing time _____   Reading time _____

➤ *Do not look back at the passage.*

1. This passage is about
   a. how Maria taught reading and writing.
   b. how Maria developed her ideas about teaching.
   c. exercises in practical life.
   d. the Children's House.

2. Maria thought that children should
   a. be clean.
   b. get lots of exercise.
   c. be organized.
   d. be independent.

3. The "exercises in practical life" taught children how to
   a. do daily tasks.
   b. brush their hair.
   c. read and write.
   d. play with blocks.

4. You can infer from this passage that Italian children
   a. were not usually very clean.
   b. were not usually happy and quiet in schools.
   c. were usually much happier at school.
   d. usually learned how to serve their meals.

5. People generally thought that children
   a. were ready to read and write in nursery school.
   b. could not learn to read and write in school.
   c. could not learn to read and write until age six.
   d. were ready to read and write at home.

6. To teach the children to read and write, Maria
   a. used colored blocks.
   b. sent the children to school.
   c. asked the mothers to help.
   d. used large letter shapes.

7. When the children started to write they
   a. were confused.
   b. stopped talking.
   c. were very excited.
   d. wanted to eat bread.

8. Maria wrote a book
   a. to explain her teaching methods.
   b. to thank the bankers.
   c. about the children she had known.
   d. about how to teach reading and writing.

10. The Montessori Movement

Interest in the Montessori method grew in many parts of the world. By 1912, the Montessori method had become an official part of the school systems of Italy and Switzerland. The cities of Rome, London, Stockholm, and Johannesburg had adopted the method. There were Montessori schools in England, the United States, and many European countries, as well as India, China, Mexico, Korea, Japan, Syria, Australia, New Zealand, and Argentina.

For a few years, Maria continued to teach at the university and to work as a doctor. Then, in 1911, she decided to give up all other work so that she would have more time for organizing Montessori schools. She wished to train the teachers herself, and to keep firm control of the many new Montessori Societies. She did not want her materials and method to be used incorrectly.

In her work for the Montessori movement, Maria traveled constantly, giving lectures and training teachers. Her first trip to the United States in 1913 was an enormous success. In fact, in this period before World War I, Maria's ideas were extremely popular. Many articles and books appeared about her work. Educators were discussing her ideas everywhere. All kinds of people—teachers, politicians, priests, and princes—came to Rome to see Maria and observe her schools. Sometimes they had to wait for days because she was so busy. Now Maria had a group of followers. Some of these young women lived with her and helped her with her work.

Maria's personal life also changed in this period. In 1912, her mother died. For many years after that, Maria wore only black clothes. However, without her mother, she may have felt freer in some ways. In fact, soon after her mother's death, Maria took her son, Mario, back to live with her. She had visited him now and then during his childhood, but always as a mysterious stranger. Then, one day when he was fifteen, she came to his school. He guessed somehow that she was his mother, and he wanted to stay with her. From then on, he always used his mother's name and he remained close to her for the rest of her life. When he married and had four children, she became a very loving and caring grandmother to them.

Another major change for Maria was brought about by the international situation. In 1916, she left Italy and went with Mario to live in Spain. Her main reason was that she did not want him to serve in the Italian army during the war. She remained in Spain until 1936, when the events of the Spanish Civil War forced her to leave. From there, she moved to Holland with her family. Then in 1939, she traveled to India and remained trapped there for seven years during World War II. Afterwards, she returned to Holland, where she died in 1952 at the age of 82.

Her ideas, though, are still very much alive today. And they continue to make a difference in the lives of countless children.

➤ *Do not look back at the passage.*

1. This passage is about
   a. Maria's son, Mario.
   b. how Maria traveled around a lot.
   c. Maria's later life.
   d. an international movement.

2. Italy and Switzerland
   a. used the Montessori method in their schools.
   b. sent teachers to Rome.
   c. had many schools.
   d. invited Montessori to teach her method.

3. Maria gave up her academic and medical work so that
   a. her son could live with her.
   b. she could travel more often.
   c. she could spend all her time on the movement.
   d. her followers could spend more time with her.

4. Maria thought it was important
   a. for her followers to be women.
   b. to train Montessori teachers herself.
   c. to speak many languages.
   d. to teach her grandchildren herself.

5. You can infer from this passage that
   a. many Americans were enthusiastic about Maria's ideas.
   b. few Americans showed any interested in Maria's ideas.
   c. Maria was not very interested in American education.
   d. there were no Montessori societies in the United States.

6. After her mother died, Maria
   a. didn't want to live in Italy.
   b. changed her name.
   c. brought her son home.
   d. stopped working on her method.

7. During his childhood, Mario
   a. never knew who his mother was.
   b. always knew Maria was his mother.
   c. didn't want to stay with his mother.
   d. wore only black clothes.

8. Maria had to move several times because of
   a. her health.
   b. her work.
   c. wars.
   d. the weather.

Global Issues

1. Global Thinking in the 21st Century   Starting time _____

At the end of the 20th century, the world is changing in important ways. Until recently, nations acted independently. Each country did its business and tried to solve its problems alone. But now, the economy is worldwide and communications technologies have connected people all over the globe. Many problems are global, too, and can no longer be solved by individual nations.

Environmental destruction is one of these problems. As the world's population has grown and technology has developed, the environment has suffered. Some nations have begun to try to stop the pollution and the environmental destruction. But the environment is global—the atmosphere, the oceans, and many forms of life are all connected. Thus, the solutions require global thinking.

The problem of ocean pollution is a good example. All the oceans of the world are connected. Pollution does not stay where it begins. It spreads out from every river and every harbor and affects bodies of water everywhere.

For centuries, people have used the oceans as a dumping place. Many cities take tons of garbage out to sea and dump it there. The quantity of garbage that ends up in the water is incredible. Five million plastic containers are thrown into the world's oceans every day! Aside from plastics, many other dangerous substances are dumped in oceans. These include human waste and chemicals used in agriculture. And every year, oil tankers accidentally spill millions of gallons of oil into the sea.

Some people believe that the oceans are so large that chemicals and waste will disappear. However, many things, such as chemicals and plastics, stay in the water and create problems. They eventually float to shore and are eaten by tiny sea creatures. Then the larger animals that eat the tiny creatures are poisoned and die. Harbors and coasts around the world have become unsafe for humans or animals. The world's fish populations are rapidly shrinking.

Another global pollution problem concerns the atmosphere. Until recently, chlorfluorocarbons (CFCs) were used around the world in manufacturing refrigerators. Scientists discovered that these CFCs were destroying the ozone layer in the atmosphere. The ozone layer helps protect the earth from the sun's rays. Without this layer, most forms of life on earth—including humans—probably would not be able to live.

CFCs will soon be completely banned in the United States and in most developed countries. But many other countries still use CFCs in manufacturing. Among these countries are some of the most populous on earth, such as India and China. These countries need to change their refrigerator factories to non-CFC processes. But they may not be able to make this change alone. They will need help from the industrialized countries. This is what global thinking means—working together for solutions.

Finishing time _____   Reading time _____

➤ *Do not look back at the passage.*

1. This passage is about
   a. air pollution.
   b. old ways of thinking.
   c. global thinking.
   d. refrigerator factories in China.

2. You may infer from this passage that in the past
   a. problems were more local.
   b. nations were more interested in the environment.
   c. the economy was more global.
   d. individual nations did not have as many problems.

3. Until now, most nations followed the principal that
   a. all countries should share their problems.
   b. all nations were enemies.
   c. each nation should take care of its own problems.
   d. what happens in China affects everyone.

4. According to this passage, many environmental problems
   a. are caused by global thinking.
   b. are caused by old ways of thinking.
   c. are caused by the United States and Japan.
   d. cannot be solved by local laws.

5. The solution to ocean pollution requires global thinking because
   a. no one cares about the ocean.
   b. the oceans are so large.
   c. all the world's oceans are connected.
   d. more oil is needed in the developing countries.

6. Increasing global population and the development of technology
   a. will solve the problem of ocean pollution.
   b. have made the pollution problem worse.
   c. is a result of global thinking.
   d. have resulted in more business opportunities.

7. From this article, we can infer that, in manufacturing refrigerators,
   a. CFCs must be used all around the world.
   b. only China uses CFCs.
   c. other chemicals can be used in place of CFCs.
   d. only CFCs are available in China.

8. Nations must learn to think globally because
   a. communication technologies will solve our problems
   b. large businesses will spread around the world
   c. changes in the world require stronger nations.
   d. that is the only way to solve global problems.

2. The Population Explosion   Starting time _____

The population of the earth is growing fast. In 1950, it was 2.5 billion. By 1992, it had jumped to 5.5 billion. By the year 2050, it will probably reach 10 billion. The worldwide trend is clearly towards rapid population growth. However, it is not happening in all parts of the world.

The population of industrialized countries has almost stopped growing. But in less-developed countries, it continues to grow at a very fast rate. Every year, about 97 million people are added to the world population. About 90 percent of these are in less-developed countries.

The reason for this difference in population growth lies in the birth rate. (The birth rate is the average number of children per woman of child-bearing age.) Population increases or decreases according to the birth rate. When the birth rate is over 2.0, the population grows. When it is less than 2.0, the population decreases.

In industrialized countries, a very low birth rate has caused population growth to slow down or stop altogether. Italy has the lowest birth rate in the world—only 1.3. In most European countries and in Japan, the birth rate is under 2.0. The birth rate in the United States is just over 2.0.

While birth rates have been declining in these countries, life expectancy has been increasing. (Life expectancy is the average length of a person's life.) In almost all the industrialized countries, life expectancy is now well over 70 years of age. This means that the percentage of older people in the population is increasing. In Italy, for example, one quarter of all Italians will be over 65 years old by the year 2015.

In less-developed countries, the situation is completely different. The birth rate in many places is extremely high. It is over 7.0 in many African countries and as high as 8.3 in Rwanda. At the same time, life expectancy in these countries is very low. For example, the life expectancy of an Ethiopian is less than 40 years. The population, on average, is very young, which means a high percentage of women of child-bearing age. Thus, even if birth rates decline, the population will continue to increase for many years.

Rapid population growth also partly explains why less-developed countries remain much poorer than industrialized countries. There is already an enormous difference in wealth. The average annual income per person in industrialized countries is about $16,500. In less-developed countries, it is only about $750. As the population increases, so do the problems. Crowding on the land means that water, food, and firewood become ever more difficult to find. Hunger and disease kill millions, especially children. And, as a result, people flood to the cities, or to other countries to look for a better life.

Thus, the population explosion is another global problem that needs a global solution.

Finishing time _____   Reading time _____

➤ **Do not look back at the passage.**

1. This passage is about
   a. population growth in less-developed countries.
   b. birth rates around the world.
   c. population growth in different parts of the world.
   d. life expectancy in industrialized countries.

2. Population growth is
   a. fastest in less-developed countries.
   b. slowest in less-developed countries.
   c. happening everywhere at the same rate.
   d. slowing down around the world.

3. Population generally grows fastest when
   a. life expectancy increases.
   b. the birth rate increases.
   c. average income increases.
   d. the birth rate declines.

4. The birth rate in industrialized countries is
   a. about 1.3.
   b. generally high.
   c. rapidly increasing.
   d. around 2.0 or less.

5. We can infer from this passage that life expectancy in Italy
   a. is lower than in Japan.
   b. is under 70 years.
   c. is over 70 years.
   d. will decline in a few years.

6. In some less-developed countries, the birth rate is
   a. as high as 8.0.
   b. generally around 2.0.
   c. slowly decreasing.
   d. lower than in the industrialized countries.

7. The population in less-developed countries is very young because of a
   a. high life expectancy and low birth rate.
   b. low life expectancy and high birth rate.
   c. low average annual income.
   d. high percentage of women of child-bearing age.

8. Many less-developed countries stay poor because of
   a. their low annual income.
   b. the crowded cities.
   c. hunger and disease.
   d. the rapidly increasing population.

3. Why So Many Children?

The rapid population growth in less-developed countries is a result of high birth rates. Women in these countries have many children on average. Why do they have such large families, when feeding and caring for them can be a problem? The answer may often be that they have no choice. Many factors make it difficult for women to limit the size of their families.

Economics undoubtedly plays an important role. In poor countries, a large family is necessary for economic survival. More children mean more hands for work. They also mean someone to take care of the parents in old age. In industrialized countries, on the other hand, children do not increase family income. Instead, they are an expense. Furthermore, people in these countries usually do not depend on their children in their old age.

However, economics cannot entirely explain birth rates. Saudi Arabia, for example, has one of the highest per-capita incomes in the world, but it also has a very high birth rate (7.0). Mexico and Indonesia also do not follow the general rule. Though they are poor countries, they have reduced their population growth by 53 percent and 25 percent in recent years.

Clearly, other factors are involved. These factors may relate to the economic situation, but not necessarily. Population experts now believe that the most important of these factors is the condition of women. A high birth rate almost always goes together with lack of education and low status for women.

This would explain the high birth rate of Saudi Arabia. Traditional Arab culture gives women little education or independence and few possibilities outside the home. It also explains the decline in birth rates in Mexico, Thailand, and Indonesia. Their governments took measures to improve education for women and opportunities for them outside the home.

Another key factor in the birth rate is the availability of birth control. Women may want to limit their families, but have no way to do so. In Ireland, for example, birth control is illegal. Not surprisingly, Ireland has the highest birth rate in Europe. Where governments have made birth control easily available, on the other hand, birth rates have gone down. This is the case in Singapore, Sri Lanka, and India, as well as in Indonesia, Thailand, and Mexico. In these countries women have also been provided with health care and help in planning their families.

Yet another factor to influence birth rate is infant mortality. (Infant mortality is the percentage of babies who die in their first year.) In industrialized countries, infant mortality is around 1.5 percent. In less-developed countries, however, it can be 20 percent or more. Fearing the loss of some children, women are encouraged to have more.

Thus, an effective program to reduce population growth must work in many areas. But above all it must be aimed at women and their needs. Only then does it have any chance of success.

Finishing time _____   Reading time _____

➤ *Do not look back at the passage.*

1. This passage is about
   a. women in less-developed countries.
   b. how economics can influence the birth rate.
   c. population growth.
   d. the main factors that influence birth rate.

2. In poor countries,
   a. the birth rate is usually high.
   b. the birth rate is usually low.
   c. the pro-capita income is usually high.
   d. children are an expense for the family.

3. In industrialized countries, children
   a. are necessary for economic survival.
   b. help to care for their parents in old age.
   c. do not usually depend on their parents.
   d. are an expense for the family.

4. According to this passage, Saudi Arabia is a
   a. rich country with a low birth rate.
   b. poor country with a high birth rate.
   c. rich country with a high birth rate.
   d. poor country with a low birth rate.

5. We can infer from this passage that women generally prefer to
   a. have smaller families.
   b. work at home.
   c. have no children.
   d. have large families.

6. One reason for the high birth rate in Ireland is that
   a. birth control is easily available.
   b. many women work outside the home.
   c. birth control is not easily available.
   d. infant mortality is high.

7. A high infant mortality usually goes together with
   a. easily available birth control.
   b. traditional cultures.
   c. education for women.
   d. a high birth rate.

8. Governments are successful in slowing down population growth when
   a. infant mortality is eliminated.
   b. they focus on the needs of women.
   c. parents are provided with old age pensions.
   d. they help women to take care of their families.

4. Cutting Down the Forests

Starting time _____

There is nothing new about people cutting down trees. In ancient times, Greece, Italy, and Great Britain were covered with forests. Over the centuries those forests were gradually cut back, until now almost nothing is left.

Today, however, trees are being cut down far more rapidly. Each year, about 42 million acres of forest are cut down. That is more than equal to the area of the whole of Great Britain. While there are important reasons for cutting down trees, there are also dangerous consequences for life on earth.

A major cause of the present destruction is the worldwide demand for wood. In industrialized countries, people are using more and more wood for paper, furniture, and houses. There is not enough wood in these countries to satisfy the demand. Wood companies, therefore, have begun taking wood from the forests of Asia, Africa, South America, and even Siberia.

Wood is also in great demand as firewood in developing countries. In many areas, people depend on wood to cook their food. As the population grows, the need for wood grows, too. But when too many trees are cut at once, forests are destroyed. A future source of wood is destroyed as well. When some trees in a forest are left standing, the forest can grow back. But only if it is not cut again for at least 100 years. In reality, it usually has no chance to grow back. Small farmers who are desperate for land move in. They cut down the rest of the trees and burn them. In this way, many millions of acres of forest are destroyed every year. Unfortunately, the forest soil is not good for growing food. Thus, these poor farmers remain as poor and desperate as before. They have also lost the resources of the forest.

However, the desperate and poor people are not the only ones to cut and burn forests. In Brazil and Central America, large landowners want to raise lots of cattle for export. They put too many cattle on too little land. When that land has been ruined, they burn parts of the forests. Then they move the cattle into the forest land. This way both land and forest are destroyed.

The destruction of forests affects first the people who used to live there. However, it also has other effects far away. For example, on the mountainsides, trees help to absorb heavy rains. When the trees are cut down, the rain pours all at once into the rivers and there are terrible floods downstream. This has happened to the Ganges, the Mekong, and other major rivers in Asia.

But finally, the loss of forests may have an effect on the climate of our planet. Together with increasing pollution, it could cause temperatures to rise and the climate to change around the world. No one knows exactly what effects this would have on our lives. For many people, however, the effects would probably be destructive.

Finishing time _____   Reading time _____

➤ *Do not look back at the passage.*

1. This passage is about
   a. the tropical forests.
   b. how landowners cut down trees in Brazil.
   c. the destruction of forests.
   d. why people are cutting down so many trees.

2. Greece, Italy, and Great Britain
   a. are all covered by forests.
   b. never had any forests.
   c. have growing populations.
   d. used to be covered by forests.

3. These days, forests are being cut down in
   a. Asia, Africa, and South America.
   b. Australia, New Zealand, and Tanzania.
   c. Greece, Italy, and Great Britain.
   d. the industrialized countries.

4. The demand for wood in industrialized countries
   a. is helping to save the forests.
   b. is one cause of the forests' destruction.
   c. is easily satisfied by the United States.
   d. has declined in recent years.

5. We can infer from this passage that poor people generally
   a. do not like living in the forests.
   b. make a lot of money from the forests.
   c. do not benefit from cutting down the forests.
   d. want the forest to grow back again.

6. Large landowners in Brazil and Central America
   a. use the forests for hunting.
   b. worry about the effects of cutting down the forests.
   c. use a lot of wood to build their houses.
   d. destroy forests to raise beef cattle.

7. When trees are cut down on mountainsides,
   a. the wood is usually of poor quality.
   b. they grow back quickly.
   c. there are floods downriver.
   d. cattle come in to eat the grass.

8. The cutting down of forests
   a. could improve the climate.
   b. could cause heavy rains.
   c. has no effect on people in cities.
   d. could affect the climate.

5. From Farmland to Desert

Starting time _____

It doesn't take long to turn farmland into desert. American farmers found this out in the 1930s. They planted wheat in large areas of grassland in the south central United States. For a few years there was plenty of rain and lots of wheat. Then the rains stopped, as they often do in this dry region. The wheat dried up and the top soil turned to dust. Before long, it had all blown away in great dust storms. The area became known as the "Dust Bowl."

What happened in the Dust Bowl is a perfect example of erosion caused by modern farming methods. (Erosion is the loss of top soil.) Top soil blows away more easily when it is no longer protected by grasses or trees. In ten years or less, several feet of good soil can disappear. And once it is gone, there is no way to get it back quickly. It may take from one hundred to a thousand years for new top soil to form.

Unfortunately, it seems that farmers have not learned from the example of the Dust Bowl. In the United States alone, five billion tons of top soil are lost every year. Farmers continue to use the same destructive methods. They plant the same crops and use tons of chemical fertilizers.

The situation in other parts of the world is even more serious. The total loss of top soil worldwide is 24 billion tons a year. Areas of the earth with a dry climate (about one third of the planet) are hit worst. In these areas, about 12 million hectares of land are lost to agriculture per year because of erosion.

In developing countries, this often leads to hunger and death. The recent history of one part of Africa, the Sahel, is a good example. In the 1960s and 1970s much good farmland was taken over for export crops, such as sugar and cotton. Many people moved into the drier interior areas to grow their food. During that period, there was more rain than usual. Food and cattle production increased and so did the population.

Before long, there were too many people in these areas. The land began to suffer the effects. It was no longer protected by trees, which had been cut down for firewood. The grass and bushes were gone, eaten by the cattle, sheep, and other animals. Animal manure was used for burning instead of for fertilizing the soil.

Then came a long period of no rain. The ruined top soil quickly blew away. The Sahara Desert advanced in some areas as much as 100 kilometers. In other areas, the semi-desert land became completely unproductive. Now millions of people have no way to make a living. Many have died of hunger, while others have moved to the already crowded cities.

The events in the Sahel were an important lesson for government officials and farmers around the world. But again, the lesson has been ignored. More and more people are hungry on our planet, but farmland continues to be ruined.

Finishing time _____   Reading time _____

➤ *Do not look back at the passage.*

1. This passage is about
   a. the "Dust Bowl."
   b. how farmers can ruin the land.
   c. the problem of erosion around the world.
   d. the loss of top soil in the African Sahel.

2. The "Dust Bowl"
   a. is a naturally dusty area.
   b. used to be desert.
   c. was always green farmland.
   d. used to be grassland.

3. The dust storms
   a. started after farmers planted wheat.
   b. were always present in that area.
   c. stopped when it rained.
   d. brought lots of good top soil.

4. We can infer from this passage that chemical fertilizers
   a. help keep the top soil.
   b. help destroy the soil.
   c. do not have any effect on the soil.
   d. are not used much by American farmers.

5. The problem of erosion is worst in
   a. the central United States.
   b. the desert.
   c. Africa.
   d. the dry regions of the world.

6. We can infer from this passage that one important factor in the Sahel disaster was the
   a. international demand for export crops.
   b. expansion of the Sahara Desert.
   c. worldwide change in climate.
   d. lack of good top soil in Africa.

7. The top soil in the Sahel was ruined by
   a. the planting of export crops.
   b. the effects of too many people and animals.
   c. too much manure from cattle and sheep.
   d. too much rain for too many years.

8. Many people in the Sahel died of hunger because
   a. there were too many sheep and cattle.
   b. there were terrible dust storms.
   c. there were no trees for firewood.
   d. the land was no longer any good for farming.

6. The "Green Revolution"   Starting time _____

From 1950 to 1980, the so-called "Green Revolution" swept the world. World food production doubled with the introduction of a new approach to agriculture. It involved the large-scale cultivation of new types of grain (wheat, corn, and rice), and the extensive use of chemicals and farm machinery.

These features were the cause of the early, enormous success of this "revolution." However, the "Green Revolution" methods no longer appear to be so successful. Though the population continues to grow, food production has failed to keep up with it.

There are a number of reasons for this. One reason lies in the expense of the new farming methods. The new kinds of grain produce much more than traditional grains, but only under certain conditions. In order to get maximum production, farmers must use large amounts of expensive chemical fertilizers. They also need to use expensive chemical insecticides since the new grains are more easily damaged by insects. Expensive watering systems are also necessary for these grains, especially in drier areas. Many farmers cannot afford to buy all the chemicals and equipment.

Erosion is another reason for the lower grain production. The large-scale farming of a single crop creates the perfect conditions for erosion. In dry areas, especially, the loss of top soil has lowered the productivity of the land. In these areas, also, grain production has been limited by the lack of water. The new types of grain, in fact, require much more water than the grains people used to grow.

Yet another reason for lower production lies in the nature of the chemicals that farmers have used. Though these fertilizers and pesticides raise production levels at first, they must be used in increasing amounts after that. Many farmers cannot afford to buy more, and so production decreases. These chemicals have other effects that are expensive in the long run. They flow into the ground water, causing pollution and health problems. As people learn about these problems, they put pressure on farmers to further limit their use of chemicals.

Finally, the Green Revolution has brought about social and political conflict that has interfered with food production. The problem lies in the cost of the new agricultural methods. Only the larger landowners can afford to make the necessary investments for maximum production of the new grains. With their profits, the large landowners then buy land from the smaller farmers. This way, the large landowners become ever richer and the number of landless poor people increases. Social tensions naturally increase in this situation.

Clearly, it is time to question the methods of the Green Revolution. Governments and farmers need to look at the overall picture and long-term effects. They need to find new methods that will better meet the needs of the world's hungry people and will also be less destructive.

Finishing time _____   Reading time _____

Reading Faster

➤ *Do not look back at the passage.*

1. This passage is about
    a. how the Green Revolution increased grain production.
    b. the environmental effects of the Green Revolution.
    c. some negative aspects of the Green Revolution.
    d. the success of the Green Revolution.

2. The production of grain worldwide has
    a. not kept up with the world population.
    b. increased faster than the population has increased.
    c. more than doubled in recent years.
    d. decreased by half in recent years.

3. The new types of grain are
    a. easier to cultivate than the traditional kinds.
    b. more expensive to cultivate than the traditional kinds.
    c. cheaper to cultivate than the traditional kinds.
    d. better tasting than the traditional kinds.

4. Erosion is often the result of
    a. traditional methods of farming.
    b. the costliness of farm equipment.
    c. the use of too much water in farming.
    d. single crop farming on a large scale.

5. Chemical fertilizers and insecticides
    a. rarely have any effect on people.
    b. can cause large-scale erosion.
    c. are both expensive and damaging.
    d. are not always necessary with the new types of grain.

6. In some regions, the new farming methods have
    a. increased the differences between rich and poor.
    b. increased the size of the middle class.
    c. encouraged small farmers to produce more.
    d. increased the profits of both rich and poor.

7. We can infer from this passage that traditional farming methods were probably
    a. more expensive.
    b. less damaging to people and the environment.
    c. preferred by the large landowners.
    d. the cause of many social problems.

8. The Green Revolution methods are
    a. the most productive that we know.
    b. damaging only to farmers.
    c. often unproductive and destructive.
    d. the only way to solve the problem of world hunger.

7. Disappearing Species

Two hundred years ago, passenger pigeons were the most numerous birds in the world. A flock of passenger pigeons might include over two million birds. When they flew overhead, they darkened the sky for hundreds of miles. Today, not a single one of these birds exists. Incredible as it may seem, all those millions of birds were hunted down for food, feathers, and sport.

The story of the passenger pigeon is just one of many sad stories about animals that have disappeared. At least 461 species of birds and mammals have become extinct in the past 400 years. Many more species—about 555 mammals and 1,073 birds—are now at risk of extinction. Among reptiles, fish, and invertebrates, at least 2,961 are at risk. And among plant species the number at risk reaches 25,000.

The cause of this terrible destruction is always the same: humankind. Sometimes people have killed off species directly by hunting them, as with the passenger pigeon. In other cases, people have caused extinction indirectly, as with the dodo bird of Mauritius (an island in the Indian Ocean). Though brutally hunted by the first European settlers, some dodos managed to survive in the interior forests. However, these were soon eliminated by the cats, dogs, pigs, and rats the Europeans brought with them.

The most frequent cause of extinction, however, is the human destruction of the environment. On the Hawaiian Islands, for instance, European and American settlers cut down the forests for farmland. This killed off many of Hawaii's unique species of birds and plants. Even more dramatic, today, is the situation in the Amazon rain forest. Here, each square mile of the forest contains thousands of plant and animal species. These species depend on each other and on their special environment. When the trees are cut down, the environment changes or is destroyed altogether. And many species disappear forever.

Scientists are very concerned about the many species that are disappearing around the world. The loss of our fellow creatures is a loss for us as well. Not only do we lose the chance to learn more about ourselves and our environment. We also lose valuable economic or scientific resources. Many wild plants, such as the wild tomato and the wild sunflower, are useful in genetically improving food crops. Other plants or animals are useful in medical research. In this way, medicines have been found to help fight leukemia, cancer, and many other diseases.

Aside from the uses that research has already discovered, there may be countless more. Who knows what we are losing in the forests that are being cut down? Every year, as more plants and animals disappear, we lose opportunities for science and medicine. That means opportunities to improve our lives. The loss of species also means a narrower range of genetic possibilities in the world. Scientists do not know what that will mean, but they are worried.

Finishing time _____   Reading time _____

➤ *Do not look back at the passage.*

1. This passage is about
   a. many kinds of plants and animals.
   b. the extinction of plants and animals.
   c. how Europeans destroyed species on Mauritius.
   d. how hunting causes animals to become extinct.

2. The passenger pigeon became extinct because
   a. there were too many of them.
   b. people destroyed its environment.
   c. there was not enough food for it.
   d. people killed them all.

3. In the past 400 years,
   a. only a few kinds of animals have become extinct.
   b. millions of animals have become extinct.
   c. over 461 species of birds and mammals have become extinct.
   d. no new kinds of birds or animals have become extinct.

4. The importation of animals by humans may cause
   a. some native species to become extinct.
   b. those animals to die.
   c. some native species to increase in number.
   d. hunters to kill native species.

5. The Hawaiian Islands are a good example of how
   a. cutting down forests causes extinction.
   b. people have taken care to save plants and animals.
   c. native plants and animals can be killed by imported species.
   d. islands make good farmland.

6. When people cut down large areas of rain forest they
   a. are likely to kill the Dodo birds.
   b. help many species of plants and animals.
   c. discover useful species of plants and animals.
   d. eliminate many species of plants and animals.

7. We can infer from this passage that people
   a. have often been concerned about the survival of species.
   b. have rarely been concerned about saving species.
   c. have eliminated species whenever possible.
   d. do not like wild animals very much.

8. Scientists believe that many species
   a. are useless for humans.
   b. are genetically unable to survive.
   c. could be useful to humans.
   d. are useful only after they are extinct.

8. Farming for the Future

Every year, more people face poverty and hunger and more of the earth's resources are ruined. The problems are enormous, but many experts believe that the situation is not hopeless. The solution will require big changes in how we think about agriculture, food, and our planet.

First of all, farmers everywhere need to develop methods that are less destructive to the environment. The change from single crop farming to a mixed crop system would be one important step. The planting of various crops improves the soil and helps prevent erosion. Erosion could further be prevented by planting trees to protect the fields from the wind. Another way farmers could improve their soil is to stop deep plowing. In fact, only a light plowing is necessary, or sometimes no plowing at all.

If the soil were treated better, farmers would not need to use chemical fertilizers. They could use natural animal and vegetable products instead. With mixed crops, farmers would also not need as much or any chemical insecticides. They could use other biological methods of controlling insects and disease.

Farmers could also help save some of the earth's precious supplies of water and petroleum. To save water, they could plant less "thirsty" crops, instead of the standard types of wheat or corn. They could also use watering systems that are much less wasteful. To save petroleum, farmers could make use of bio-gas generators for energy. These generators could be fueled by the vegetable and animal wastes of the farms. In less-developed countries, bio-gas generators could reduce the need for firewood and so help save forests, as well.

In less-developed countries, the small farmers need help. They need to learn more about crops that are better suited to the local conditions. They need to learn how to limit erosion and make the best use of their resources. But these farmers will never be successful without land for themselves and economic aid. This should be the aim of governments and international agencies. The present policies of encouraging industry and cash crops are only making the situation worse.

The industrialized countries could use their economic resources to help bring about these changes. They also could make some changes in their own policies. At present, much food is wasted in these countries for political reasons. In Europe alone mountains of fruit and dairy products are thrown away every year. Eating habits, too, could be changed in these countries. For example, people often eat foods from distant places instead of local foods. The transportation of the imported foods adds to the global pollution problem. People in the industrialized countries also eat a lot of meat, especially beef. In fact, a large percentage of the grain grown in these countries is used for feeding cattle. If people in these countries ate less meat, there would be more grain to feed the hungry people of the world.

➤ *Do not look back at the passage.*

1. This passage is about

    a. biological methods of farming.

    b. how we can change the way food is produced worldwide.

    c. how millions of people are facing hunger and poverty.

    d. farming around the world.

2. We can infer from this passage that single crop farming

    a. is destructive to the environment.

    b. is good for the environment.

    c. is cheaper for the farmer.

    d. does not cause erosion.

3. Deep plowing of the soil

    a. prevents erosion.

    b. improves the soil.

    c. causes erosion.

    d. helps the plants grow.

4. Mixed crop farming

    a. reduces erosion and the need for insecticides.

    b. increases erosion and the need for insecticides.

    c. eliminates erosion and the need for insecticides.

    d. does not affect erosion and the need for insecticides.

5. We can infer from this passage that farmers at present

    a. use very little water on average.

    b. are now very careful about their water use.

    c. always use too much water.

    d. often waste a lot of water.

6. Bio-gas generators on farms would

    a. mean an increase in the use of other fuels.

    b. encourage farmers to raise cash crops.

    c. reduce the need for other fuels.

    d. help farmers raise cattle.

7. The governments of less-developed countries

    a. should encourage the growing of cash crops.

    b. need to encourage people to eat less beef.

    c. should increase the size of farms.

    d. need to help small farmers.

8. People in industrialized countries could help by

    a. eating more meat.

    b. raising more cattle.

    c. reducing the amount of beef they eat.

    d. reducing the amount of grain they eat.

9. *Where Do All Those Tires Go?* Starting time _____

Around the world, billions of tires from trucks and cars are replaced every year. In the United States, about 260 million used truck and auto tires are thrown away every year. Where do the old tires go? Quite often, they go into large dumps where they remain for many years.

The mountains of worn-out tires in these dumps present a number of health and environmental dangers. First, they attract mosquitoes and rats, which then spread disease among humans. The tires can also catch on fire, and these fires are very difficult to put out. They may burn from a few days to a few months. While the tires burn, they release cancer-causing gases into the air. These gases spread over nearby towns and cause health problems for people who live there.

After a tire dump fire is put out, pieces of burned tires remain on the ground. When it rains, chemicals from the burned parts wash into the soil and into the ground water. This pollutes the soil and the drinking water in the area.

Aside from these problems, the tire dumps represent a terrible waste of resources. So, in order to avoid the problems and the waste, people are looking for ways to reuse or recycle tires. Recycling is common for other materials, such as paper, glass, and aluminum. Now tires are also being recycled in a number of creative ways.

One solution is to burn the tires to create energy. An energy company with plants in Connecticut and California burns tires to produce steam for generating electricity. When the tires are burned properly, the fire does not pollute the air. Every day, workers check to make sure that no dangerous gases are allowed out of the energy plant's chimneys. A total of about 15 million tires are burned every year in the company's two plants. This produces enough electricity to supply about 42,000 houses.

Another solution is to find a new use for the tires. Tires are now being used to make various products, from doormats to fishing supplies. Several shoe companies have started using tires to make the soles of tennis shoes. This is not a new idea, in fact. During the Great Depression, shoes with tire soles were very common in the United States.

The state of Maine has found yet another use for old tires. The climate in Maine is very cold, and in the winter the ground freezes solid. Large bumps are formed in the roads, and then in the spring, the bumps may turn into holes. Roads must be rebuilt often, at great expense to the state. To prevent this, road workers have started to use old tires broken into small pieces. These tire pieces are spread in a thick layer underneath the surface of a new road. The tires then act as a blanket, keeping the ground below the road from freezing. This way the road surface remains smooth.

Up to now, only a small percentage of used tires are being recycled in the United States. But there are plans and new ideas about ways to reuse more of the tires that end up in tire dumps.

Finishing time _____ Reading time _____

➤   *Do not look back at the passage.*

1. This passage is mainly about the
   a. effects of burning tires.
   b. dangers of tire dumps.
   c. problem of what to do with old tires.
   d. ways old tires can be recycled.

2. A fire at a tire dump is
   a. a good source of electricity.
   b. a good way to get rid of old tires.
   c. a source of dangerous pollution.
   d. quickly put out.

3. When tires are burned at the energy plants,
   a. air pollution is a big problem.
   b. air pollution is not a problem.
   c. only a few tires are burned.
   d. workers are exposed to dangerous gases.

4. You may infer from this passage that
   a. the number of tire dumps will greatly increase.
   b. very few uses can be found for old tires.
   c. only western countries can recycle tires.
   d. tire recycling methods could be used anywhere.

5. Recycling tires is
   a. a way of saving resources.
   b. a very complicated process.
   c. dangerous to human health.
   d. a major source of water and soil pollution.

6. Using recycled tires to make everyday products is
   a. a new idea.
   b. a cause of pollution.
   c. not a new idea.
   d. not possible.

7. When workers use tires to build roads they
   a. spread a layer of tire pieces first.
   b. fill all the holes with tire pieces.
   c. often work in freezing weather.
   d. check carefully to be sure that no dangerous gases are formed.

8. Using old tires for building roads in the state of Maine can result in
   a. warmer roads.
   b. more expense to the state.
   c. less expense to the state.
   d. bumps and holes in some roads.

10. Global Warming   Starting time _____

National borders have no meaning for the atmosphere. This was demonstrated to the world by the Chernobyl nuclear plant disaster and again by the eruption of Mt. Pinatubo. Whatever enters the atmosphere in one country soon travels around the world. And so, scientists are now worried about the global effects of air pollution. Research shows, in fact, that the earth's atmosphere is changing in ways that could be destructive to life. Pollution could be a major cause of this.

One of the pollutants that is causing the greatest concern is carbon dioxide. It is released into the air when coal or petroleum is burned. Carbon dioxide has always been a part of our atmosphere, the product of certain natural processes. However, in recent decades, the amount of carbon dioxide in the atmosphere has greatly increased. This is the result of an enormous increase in the amount of coal and petroleum burned for fuel.

At the same time, the earth's ability to absorb carbon dioxide has greatly decreased. Absorption of carbon dioxide occurs mainly in areas of thick forest. Those areas are rapidly disappearing as more and more forests are cut down.

The result of the increase of carbon dioxide in the atmosphere is the so-called "greenhouse effect." The carbon dioxide acts like a glass screen, making the sun's heat more intense. There are already signs of global warming, say many scientists. Over the next century, average temperatures could rise by as much as four degrees centigrade.

Such a temperature change could be disastrous. Vast areas, such as the whole central United States, could become too hot and dry for agriculture. Because of the melting of polar ice, the water level of the oceans would rise and many low coastal areas would disappear. For example, large parts of the Netherlands, Bangladesh, and the state of Florida would be under water.

In most of the industrialized countries, there are now laws that limit carbon dioxide released into the air. However, in many other countries, such as India and China, there are no such laws. These countries plan, in fact, to double or triple the amount of coal they burn. They cannot afford to change to other kinds of fuel that pollute the air less. And so, they will be releasing even more carbon dioxide into the air.

Thus, laws passed in the industrialized countries will have little effect on the worldwide situation. Our planet is likely to continue to warm up unless the less-developed countries make some changes, too.

A global disaster can only be avoided by a global solution. The industrialized nations need to "think globally." They need to look beyond their own borders at the needs of the earth as a whole. They must put some of their wealth and technology to work in poorer countries. This may be the only way to clean up our atmosphere and prevent disastrous changes.

Finishing time _____   Reading time _____

➤ *Do not look back at the passage.*

1. This passage is about
    a. carbon dioxide in the atmosphere.
    b. how some countries pollute the air.
    c. how air pollution is a global problem.
    d. the effects of global warming.

2. The Chernobyl disaster showed that
    a. the atmosphere has not changed.
    b. pollutants in the air can travel far.
    c. scientists do not understand air pollution.
    d. air pollution is mainly a local problem.

3. Carbon dioxide
    a. is produced by the burning of coal and petroleum.
    b. is produced by forests.
    c. was produced by the Chernobyl disaster.
    d. is no longer produced by natural processes.

4. Air pollution from burning fuels has caused
    a. a decrease in carbon dioxide levels.
    b. no change in carbon dioxide levels.
    c. a dramatic increase in carbon dioxide levels.
    d. a small increase in carbon dioxide levels.

5. The "greenhouse effect" will
    a. lead to a cooler climate worldwide.
    b. lead to a warmer climate worldwide.
    c. cause the earth's forests to disappear.
    d. increase the levels of carbon dioxide.

6. One effect of global warming could be
    a. the melting of the polar ice.
    b. the shrinking of the earth's oceans.
    c. the need for less coal and petroleum.
    d. an increase in air pollution.

7. At present, India and China plan to
    a. limit the amount of coal they will burn.
    b. stop burning coal for fuel.
    c. greatly increase the amount of coal they will burn.
    d. pass laws limiting carbon dioxide pollution.

8. Global warming can be stopped only if
    a. the United States passes better laws about pollution.
    b. all nations work together on a global solution.
    c. India and China start using more coal.
    d. average worldwide temperatures rise four degrees.

Reading Rate Table

All of the passages are about 500 words long.

Reading Time (Min.:sec.)	Rate (Words Per Minute)
:30 sec.	1,000 wpm
:35	857
:40	750
:45	668
:50	597
:55	545
1:00	500
1:05	463
1:10	429
1:15	400
1:20	375
1:25	353
1:30	333
1:35	316
1:40	300
1:45	286
1:50	273
1:55	261
2:00	250
2:05	240
2:10	231
2:15	222
2:20	215
2:25	207
2:30	200
2:35	194
2:40	188
2:45	182
2:50	176
2:55	172
3:00	166
3:15	154
3:30	143
3:45	135
4:00	125
4:15	117
4:30	111
4:45	105
5:00	100

Mark the box corresponding to your reading rate. Write the number of correct answers at the top of this chart.

passage	Hawaii										Maria Montessori										Global Issues									
	1	2	3	4	5	6	7	8	9	10	1	2	3	4	5	6	7	8	9	10	1	2	3	4	5	6	7	8	9	10
number correct																														
1000																														
857																														
750																														
668																														
597																														
545																														
500																														
463																														
429																														
400																														
375																														
353																														
333																														
316																														
300																														
286																														
273																														
261																														
250																														
240																														
231																														
222																														
215																														
207																														
200																														
194																														
188																														
182																														
176																														
172																														
166																														
154																														
143																														
135																														
125																														
117																														
111																														
105																														
100																														

Reading Rate (Words Per Minute)

Date

Answer Key

Part Two: Reading Comprehension Skills

Unit 1: Scanning, page 15

Exercise 1
1. 4
2. Part 4
3. 10
4. Main Ideas
5. 68
6. Part One
7. Part Four
8. 100

Exercise 2
1. Escort Wagon
2. Taurus GL, Explorers, Escort Wagons, Crown Victorias, Tempos, Taurus SHOS
3. 50
4. no
5. all except the F150 Super Cabs
6. Taurus SHOS
7. Ranger XLT
8. Tempo
9. 3
10. Branford

Exercise 3
A. 1. 3
   2. $1.99
   3. 8 oz.
   4. 8
   5. Stop and Go
B. 1. They are both the same.
   2. yes
   3. Ad 2
   4. Tony's Pizza
   5. 2
   6. Seneca Juice
   7. 6
   8. Totino's Pizza
   9. 5 lb.
   10. yes
   6. yes
   7. 6
   8. Ad 1
   9. Cole's
   10. Ad 2 (16)

Exercise 4
1. Element, Symbol, Atomic number, Atomic weight
2. Fe
3. 50
4. lead
5. 1.0080
6. Chlorine
7. Si
8. Gold
9. Lawrencium
10. Mendelevium, Einsteinium

Exercise 5
1. TBS
2. from 6:00 to 11:30
3. In Cold Blood
4. 7:30
5. 6
6. True Confessions
7. Copacabana
8. 15, 16
9. the named channels
10. 27

Exercise 6
1. John Grisham and Michael Crichton
2. The Line of Fire
3. Sara Peretsky
4. 28 weeks
5. The Doomsday Conspiracy
6. Andrew Morton
7. $10.00
8. the role of oil in world history
9. Stephen R. Covey
10. Ballantine

Exercise 7
1. Connecticut, Maine, Massachusetts, New Hampshire, Rhode Island, and Vermont
2. you do
3. McIntosh
4. sometimes
5. at most two hours
6. go for pony rides, ride on a hay wagon, watch a horse show, visit cows and sheep, take a hike, have a picnic
7. Only as many as you need
8. Put them in the refrigerator
9. Freeze them
10. Write to the Department of Agriculture

Exercise 8
1. 1988
2. John Waihee
3. A model multicultural community
4. Dan Boylan
5. the Japanese
6. 211, 478
7. 47, 787
8. 0.5%
9. 191,553
10. No

Exercise 9

1. November 7, 1867
2. Sklodowska
3. Warsaw, Poland
4. Warsaw and Paris
5. Pierre Curie
6. Radioactivity
7. Over than 4 years
8. 1903
9. Herbert Hoover
10. *Traité de radioactivité*

Exercise 10

1. Arthur C. Clarke
2. Score
3. Dwight D. Eisenhower
4. United States, England, and the Soviet Union
5. Telstar I
6. Up to 6,000 miles (9,600 km)
7. 5
8. April 6, 1965
9. Early Bird (Intelsat I)
10. Intelsat 5

Unit 2: Previewing and Predicting, page 34

Exercises 1-3

Answers will vary.

Exercise 4

A. Beatrice S. Mikulecky and Linda Jeffries
   1996, 300 pages
   Yes, there is an Introduction.
   4 parts
   Table of contents, illustrations, charts
B. Answers will vary.

Exercise 5

1. In a newspaper
2. In Sao Paulo
3. A two-year-old girl
4. She fell out of a fifth floor window.
5. Alfonso works near where Carmelita lives. He and his father and brother caught Carmelita when she fell.

Exercise 6

1. Why women generally live longer than men.
2. Women's hormones have a positive effect on the heart and help prevent infections.
3. Female genes slow down aging. Male genes age more quickly. Women generally smoke and drink less. They suffer from stress less, and they are in better physical condition.

4. Some of the cultural reasons for women's longer life are changing, but not the biological reasons. Thus, women will still live longer.
5. Answers will vary.

Exercise 7

1. c	2. b	3. a	4. c	5. c
6. a	7. b	8. b	9. a	10. b

Exercise 8

1. b	2. b	3. c	4. b	5. a
6. a	7. a	8. a	9. c	10. a

Unit 3: Vocabulary Knowledge for Effective Reading, page 49

In these exercises, the answers may vary. The important thing is that students have good reasons for their answers.

Exercise 1

1. very hungry
2. something to wear on your feet when you are swimming
3. to close just one eye
4. unhealthy looking
5. earth walls that are built near rivers and seas to keep the water off the land
6. very bright and colorful

Exercise 2

1. the quality of a sound (its frequency)
2. small, torn off pieces
3. a form used to make similar shapes
4. the part of a roof where it meets the walls of a house
5. very important
6. an outdoor or enclosed room with a separate roof, that is attached to a house

Exercise 3

1. bend down towards the ground
2. storm
3. to flow very fast and suddenly
4. rough, not easy or smooth
5. a child who misbehaves, but in a charming way
6. very wet and full of water

Exercise 4

1. adjective, weak
2. noun, noise
3. verb, smelled
4. adverb, quickly and in many directions
5. verb, work hard
6. noun, messy or difficult situation

Exercise 5
1. adverb, with disapproval
2. adjective, continuing
3. verb, complain
4. noun, ruined buildings
5. noun, lump
6. adjective, careless

Exercise 6
1. a special kind of city taxi that people share
2. a visa
3. a city transportation ticket or pass
4. a map
5. a mini-bus or taxi that takes people to several different places

Exercise 7
1. a garbage dump
2. a fish farm
3. recycle

Exercise 8
1. a large ocean bird (albatross)
2. fly
3. a river

Exercise 9
1. computer
2. 1. they—unwanted computers
   2. it—the problem
   3. They—the computer industry and government
   4. They—computers
3. 1. they—old computers
   2. These—the parts
   3. they—the parts
   4. them—the parts

Exercise 10
1. 1. it—a pedicab
   2. he—a businessman
   3. them—pedicabs
   4. they—pedicabs
   5. them—pedicabs
   6. they—people (passengers)
2. 1. They—drivers
   2. He—the owner
   3. them—drivers
   4. he—the typical driver
   5. He—the driver
   6. he—the driver
   7. he—one driver
   8. He—one driver
   9. he—one driver
3. 1. them—pedicabs
   2. He—the owner
   3. they—pedicabs

4. They—baseball fans
5. them—pedicabs
6. he—the owner
7. he—the owner
8. they—pedicabs
9. them—pedicabs

Exercise 11
1. this small eastern-European nation
2. Tallinn
3. choral concerts
4. the event
5. the medieval building
6. university
7. strongholds
8. cottages
9. Society of Estonian Nudists
10. their favorite beverage

Exercise 12
1. oaks, maples
   trees
   forests
2. biology class
   physiology department
   medical school
   university
3. loan department
   State Street Bank
   bank
   financial institution
4. personal computers, fax machines
   office equipment
   modern technology
5. malaria, cholera, tuberculosis
   infectious diseases
   diseases
6. Hungarian, Estonian, Finnish
   Finno-Ugric language family
   languages
7. Port-au-Prince
   Haiti
   Carribbean
   western hemisphere
8. Sistine Chapel
   Michelangelo
   Italian Renaissance
   history of western art
9. baseball, skiing, football
   sports
   outdoor activities
10. Big Mac with fries
    lunch
    meal

Exercise 13

1. R
   Lassie was a famous actor in the movies and on TV. Stories about this brown and white <u>collie</u> were first written in books. Millions of children have learned to love the beautiful <u>dog</u>. She may have been an <u>animal</u>, but to her fans, she was as smart as any living <u>creature</u>.

2. R
   Mt. McKinley is one of the world's most beautiful sights. Many people believe that if you want to climb a real <u>mountain</u>, this is the one! Its <u>summit</u> is the tallest in North America, rising 6,197.6 meters above sea level. The snow-capped <u>peak</u> was first climbed in 1913.

3. Jackie went canoeing on the Saco River in Maine last weekend. Although she had never paddled such a boat (R) before, she learned very fast. When the <u>craft</u> went through some rough, rocky places in the river, she kept it afloat. After an hour, Jackie brought the <u>vessel</u> safely to shore, proud of her new-found talent.

4. R
   Steve has been playing the oboe for many years. He first started to learn to play this <u>woodwind</u> <u>instrument</u> when he was in college. Now he performs in the <u>woodwind</u> <u>section</u> of the Denver Symphony <u>Orchestra</u>. He is proud to be a part of such a great musical <u>organization</u>.

5. R
   a. Many people enjoy the paintings of Rembrandt. <u>Masterpieces</u> by this Dutchman are found in many of the world's museums. Some of the master's best <u>works</u> can be seen in New York's famous Metropolitan Museum. There, museum visitors can fully appreciate the <u>work</u> of this 17th century genius.

   b. Many people enjoy the paintings of Rembrandt (R). Masterpieces by this <u>Dutchman</u> are found in many of the world's museums. Some of the <u>master's</u> best works can be seen in New York's famous Metropolitan Museum. There, museum visitors can fully appreciate the work of this <u>17th</u> <u>century</u> <u>genius</u>.

Exercise 14

1. sports
2. planets
3. infectious diseases
4. electronic appliances
5. planting a tree
6. making a peanut butter and jelly sandwich
7. Newton's three laws of motion
8. places for religious services
9. parts of speech
10. snorkeling

Exercise 15

3	It—	Antarctica
	that	opposite to the Arctic
6	this difference—	between the Arctic's and the Antarctic's geography
8	it—	the climate
12	both poles—	North and South
16	It—	the record temperature of –127 F.
17	this climatic difference—	between the Arctic and Antarctic
	two regions—	Arctic and Antarctic
23	These animals—	foxes, bear, reindeer and lemmings
26	the area—	Antarctica
31	this great volume of ice—	the ice at South Pole
32	this—	the melting of ice at South Pole

Exercise 16

3	these—	dangerous dumping practices
	some of which—	dangerous dumping practices
5	these—	hazardous chemical wastes
6	such chemicals—	heavy metals and by-products of technology
9	they—	wastes
11	this—	the leaking of waste materials
12	it—	the local soil
13	it—	the soil
15	the latter effect—	reach water tables deep in the earth
17	there—	the river bed
	they—	wastes

Unit 4: Topics, page 68

Exercise 1
1. water sports
2. basketball game
3. car equipment
4. sea creatures
5. string quartet
6. flowers
7. nuts

Exercise 2
1. reference book
2. African languages
3. cities
4. camping
5. move
6. medicine
7. garden

8. Hawaiian Islands
9. medical subjects
10. Reading for Pleasure

8. France
9. office
10. restaurant

Note: For the following exercises, students may use slightly different words to name the topics.

Exercise 3
1. U.S. Presidents
2. piano
3. stringed instruments
4. computer
5. people who make a movie
6. English royalty
7. supermarket employees
8. European languages
9. tropical fruits
10. early astronomers

Exercise 4
1. metals
2. forms of land on earth
3. sailboat
4. tools for wood-working
5. kinds of cloth
6. small household appliances
7. the world's tallest mountains
8. parts of a car engine
9. continents
10. kinds of music

Exercise 5
1. planets (Earth, Pluto)
2. dairy products (ice cream, sour cream, etc.)
3. celestial objects (moon, sun, stars, etc.)
4. weather (sunny, windy, dry, etc.)
5. Canadian cities (Montreal, Ottawa, Calgary, etc.)
6. trees that lose their leaves in the fall (oak, ash, etc.)
7. geometric shapes (rectangle, sphere, etc.)
8. footwear (shoes, tennis shoes, boots, etc.)
9. French impressionist artists (Manet, Van Gogh, etc.)
10. sources of energy (solar, food, coal)

Exercise 6
Answers will vary.

Exercise 7
1. American rivers
2. Classical composers
3. rock musicians
4. American cars
5. cars from outside the U.S.
6. countries of eastern Europe
7. British Isles
8. types of cars

Exercise 8
1. objects for drinking
2. adjectives for describing a nice-looking person or object
3. buildings for religious services
4. contagious diseases
5. sports played with a ball
6. sections of a newspaper
7. large islands
8. parts of a shoe
9. mountain ranges
10. major world religions

Exercise 9
1. external parts of the body/sweeteners
2. vegetables that grow under ground/vegetables that grow above ground
3. parts of a bicycle/breeds of dogs
4. fruits/cooking oils or fats
5. bones in the human body/internal organs in the body

Exercise 10
1. British poets (Frost)
2. adjectives (swimming)
3. dances (dogtrot)
4. animals raised by farmers (mice)
5. names of jobs that both men and women can be called (actor)
6. singers (piano)
7. trees which lose their leaves in the fall (pine)
8. beach equipment (gloves)
9. objects for keeping the sun out of the window (screens)
10. kinds of homes (kitchen)

Unit 5: Topics of Paragraphs, page 78

Example
a. no   b. yes

Exercise 1
1. yes   2. no   3. no   4. yes
   Iceland   Two aspects
                                                  of Istanbul

Exercise 2
1. a. too specific
   b. too general
   c. topic
2. a. topic
   b. too general
   c. too specific
3. a. too general
   b. too specific
   c. topic

Exercise 3
1. a. topic
   b. too specific
   c. too general
2. a. too general
   b. topic
   c. too specific
3. a. too specific
   b. too general
   c. topic

Exercise 4
1. What to do if you get a blow-out
2. The importance of checking your tires
3. Some special measures to care for tires

Exercise 5
1. The increasing number of single fathers in the United States

2. Changes in fathers' roles shown in advertising
3. Alcoholic fathers and birth defects

Exercise 6

1. The Los Angeles Lakers basketball team (Most basketball teams are based in large cities.)
2. The Boston Celtics basketball team (Boston fans also support a baseball team, an ice hockey team, and a football team.)
3. Basketball as big business (Television advertising is now aimed at specific markets such as ethnic groups or the elderly.)

Exercise 7

1. How cigarette smoke affects the children of smokers (Many people smoke in order to feel more relaxed in social situations.)
2. Why many young children die in poor countries (Milk is a very important source of vitamins and minerals.)
3. How homes can be dangerous to young children (Before the days of detergents, people used to make soap from animal fat.)

Exercise 8

1. c   2. a   3. e   4. b

Exercise 9

1. Violent storms cause damage and deaths all over the world, but sometimes people make the consequences worse.
2. There are a number of ways to make life more comfortable in the heat.
3. Scientists believe that the earth's climate may be warming up.

Unit 6: Main Ideas, page 89

Exercise 1

1. The "idea box" is a useful concept in management.
2. The study showed that American managers are generally not happy with their working schedules.
3. There are many advantages to working at home, including more flexible hours and better productivity.

Exercise 2

1. Topic: New services for older customers
   Topic Sentence: That means that many businesses in those countries must adjust to older customers.
   Main Idea: c
2. Topic: Causes of depression in elderly people
   Topic Sentence: In industrialized countries today, many elderly people suffer from depression.
   Main Idea: a

Exercise 3

1. b.   2. a   3. c

Exercise 4

1. A new kind of jogging shoe has lights on them for night safety.
2. Quieting machines reduce noise at work and at home.
3. A new laser potato peeler reduces waste in factories.

Exercise 5

1. Topic: The giant panda
   Main Idea: The giant panda is slowly dying out in China.
2. Topic: A newborn panda
   Main Idea: A newborn panda is small and helpless for over a year.
3. Topic: A mother panda
   Main Idea: A mother panda is very loving to its young.

Exercise 6

1. Topic: Large buildings with unhealthy air
   Main Idea: Large buildings with unhealthy air can cause illness for people who work in them.
2. Topic: Infections from pet reptiles
   Main Idea: Infections from pet reptiles can spread to their owners.
3. Topic: Browned or blackened meat
   Main Idea: Browned or blackened meat can result in cancer if you eat it often.

Exercise 7

1. Topic: Hand-drawn maps of the worlds
   Main Idea: Hand-drawn maps of the world often do not show accurate sizes of the continents.
2. Topic: The size of Europe and Africa on most hand-drawn maps
   Main Idea: On hand-drawn maps of the world, Europe and Africa are often drawn the wrong size.
3. Topic: Errors on maps of Africa
   Main Idea: Errors on maps of Africa often were due to ignorance about the African continent.

Exercise 8

1. Topic: The oil spilled by the Exxon Valdez tank ship
   Main Idea: The oil spilled by the Exxon Valdez tank ship resulted in an expensive and difficult clean-up job.
2. Topic: Some consequences of the oil spill
   Main Idea: Some consequences of the oil spill are not immediately apparent.
3. Topic: The effects of the oil spill
   Main Idea: The effects of the oil spill include long term problems for many animals.

Unit 7: Patterns of Organization, page 99

Exercise 1

1. S	2. CC	3. L	4. CE	5. S
6. CE	7. CC	8. L	9. S	10. CE

Listing Example: Scientists have found several new fuels to replace gasoline for automobiles.

One of these	methanol
Another	natural gas
A third	electricity

Exercise 2

1. E-mail has many advantages over the telephone and regular mail service.

The main	messages can be sent very fast
Another	it is inexpensive and convenient
Lastly	you can send a message to many people at once

2. E-mail is increasingly popular for several reasons.

First	some people do not like to use the telephone
Second	it is good for sending suggestions and requests
Also	all e-mail messages look the same
Furthermore	e-mail messages are uniform and do not show the sender's characteristics
In addition	e-mail messages do not show the sender's feelings

3. One executive explains why he doesn't use e-mail.

The main reason	He doesn't have time to learn to use the new system
Aside from that	e-mail is impersonal
In addition	e-mail is too fast and easy
too	lots of information about the sender is lost with e-mail

Exercise 3

1. Monticello, home of Thomas Jefferson, is famous for several reasons.

first of all	it belonged to a President
also	a fine example of early 19th century American architecture
furthermore	the design combines graceful style with American concern for comfort

2. Homes are full of both obvious and less obvious dangerous things which should be kept away from small children.

for example	stairs and sharp corners of a table
another	fire and matches
for example	poisoning from medicine
the same	alcohol and cigarettes
Finally	soaps and chemicals for cleaning

3. People can make home life more comfortable in the heat.

First of all	keep home cool, close curtains
also	keep yourself cool, wear cotton clothing
finally	try to stay calm and relaxed, rest after meals

Exercise 4

Answers will vary. Check your work to make sure that you used listing signal words for each example in your paragraph.

Sequence Examples

a. Chronological

Franklin D. Roosevelt served his country for most of his life.

January 30, 1882	born
1903	studied at Harvard
1905	married Eleanor
After	had served in the N.Y. State Senate
1921	worked in Washington
at that time	became ill with polio
1928	ran for governor of New York
1933	elected president
April 12, 1945	died

b. Steps in a Process

Making orange juice concentrate from fresh oranges is done entirely by machine.

First	oranges dumped on moving belt
Next	oranges are rolled into juicing machines
Then	rinds are thrown out
At the same time	juice goes through small holes
Next	finisher removes tiny seeds and objects
Last	most of water is removed from juice

Exercise 5

1. There are many things to do to prepare for a trip to another country.

First	decide where you want to go
Next	look at maps and books
Then	find out what kind of documents you'll need
In the meantime	learn about the language of the country
Finally	make a packing list

2. In the last seventy-five years, passenger planes have carried increasing numbers of passengers at faster and faster speeds.

1919	passenger service began in Europe
1927	U.S. air travel began
1950	planes could carry 100 passengers
1989	U.S. airlines carried 452 million passengers
1990s	modern jetliners carry more than 300 passengers in a plane

3. The process of traveling by plane is much the same no matter where you travel.

at least an hour before the flight	arrive at airport
right away	check in with agent
Then	go to the gate
As you walk there	make last-minute purchases
When at the gate	security examines bags and people
Finally	your flight is ready to depart

Exercise 6

1. Kareem Abdul-Jabbar had a long and very successful career as a professional basketball player.

1946	born in New York
in the late 1960s	studied at UCLA
At that time	led the basketball team to three championships
during his college years	converted to Muslim faith, changed his name
1969	began professional career on Milwaukee Bucks
1975	joined Los Angeles Lakers
1989	retired with several records and awards

2. Although Maya Angelou had many difficult experiences while growing up, she became a successful and famous author.

1929	born in California
when she was 3	parents separated
Then	she and her brother lived with grandmother
Later on	she lived with mother and grandmother
When she was 8 years old	mother's boyfriend hurt her
often	badly treated due to racial prejudice
In her childhood	learned of love from grandmother and brother
As she grew older	loved literature
After junior high school	went to live with her mother
1945	graduated from high school and had a son
In later years	included all her experiences in her writing
1993	wrote and read official poem for presidential inauguration

3. Spike Lee is young but he is already a famous film director.

1957	born in Atlanta
when he was two	moved to Brooklyn, New York
as a youngster	Spike became interested in movies
After college graduation	studied film-making at NYU
Soon after that	made "She's Gotta Have It"
Since that movie	made five more successful movies
latest achievement	teach at Harvard

Exercise 7

1. When a blow-out occurs, it can be very dangerous if you do not know a few important procedures.

the first thing	hold the steering wheel tightly
next step	get off the road carefully
after	move to the side of road
Then	turn on your flashing lights

2. A newborn panda is small and helpless for over a year.

newborn	tiny, helpless
5 months old	begin to walk
at least a year	only food is mother's milk
by the time they are a year old	weigh 55 pounds
Around that time	eat bamboo
18 months old	may weigh over 100 pounds

Exercise 8

Correct order: 6, 7, 1, 3, 10, 9, 2, 5, 4, 8

Comparison-Contrast Examples

a. The subway systems of Paris and New York are similar, but there are also some striking differences.

Both	depend on vast subway systems
both	cities (New York City and Paris)
Another likeness	very noisy
further similarity	large area/little expense for commuter
However	big differences
While	New York's stations are often ugly, some of Paris' are quite beautiful
On the other hand	Paris's trains are clean and reliable/New York's are quite dirty and unreliable

b. In Ukraine and Japan, people like to eat a similar food.

in common	an aspect of their cooking
like it	pastries with meat
both	eat it with sauce

c. When the first baby arrives in a household, everything changes.

While before	alarm clock
now	baby wakes mom
Formerly	parents watched television or read
but not now	they admire their infant
In contrast	life is more carefully planned
While they used to	go out whenever they wanted to
any more	must arrange a baby-sitter
Unlike	neat apartment
difference	topic of conversation is always baby

Exercise 9

1. New vending machines provide much better-tasting and more interesting foods than the machines of the past.

Both	
Like	a quick and convenient way to buy food
But	new machines improved
However	old machines swallowed coins/new machines use plastic cards
In contrast	old machines gave tasteless food/new machines sell delicious meals

2. New laptop computers are smaller, lighter, and easier to use than the old portables.

Differences	
Unlike	old portables were heavy/laptops weigh 5 pounds
	old portables were large/laptops are small
	old portables had small screen, memory/new laptops have larger screen, more memory

3. Electric cars are similar in use and appearance to gasoline-powered cars, but they are silent.

Both	
similar	both provide private transportation
	interior, wheels and brakes are alike
On the other hand	major difference
Unlike	electric vehicle is totally silent
In contrast	electric vehicle has no sound of ignition

Exercise 10

1. In some ways, college life is very similar to high school life.

Similarities	
In both places	you must be a responsible student
Similarly	you can make friends
also resembles	many student activities

2. The University of Bologna is different from most North American universities.

Differences

major difference	very old—founded in the tenth century/American universities are newer
different	located in the heart of the city/American universities are often outside city center
Unlike	no trees or open spaces

3. Russian foreign language schools are similar to regular public schools, but they have some special features.

Both

similar	students do not pay
also similar	subjects
However	school subjects are taught in a foreign language
unlike	students are selected
greatest difference	language abilities
In contrast	students learn to express themselves fluently in a foreign language

Exercise 11

1. The similarities between the elephant and the whale may show a shared history.

Similarities

similar	shape of head
also	swimming ability
like	use of sound to show anger and to communicate
like	female whales and elephants both help at time of birth of young

2. Houses in hot countries have many features that are different from houses in cold countries.

Differences

different	hot countries—thick walls and small windows
	cold countries—think walls and large windows
Another difference	hot countries—outdoor living area
	cold countries—no such areas

Exercise 12

Paragraphs will differ. Be sure that you have used the signal words of comparison or contrast in your paragraph.

Exercise 13

A. 1. AIDS< HIV
   2. epidemics < bacteria
   3. coughs < colds and flu
   4. improperly stored food > food poisoning
   5. slow infant development < poor nutrition
   6. skin cancer < too much exposure to the sun
   7. swimming in pools > ear infection
   8. heart trouble < high fat content in diet
   9. lung cancer < cigarette smoking
   10. skiing > broken leg

B. There are many correct ways to write these sentences. These answers are examples of correct answers.
   1. HIV leads to AIDS.
   2. Epidemics can be caused by bacteria.
   3. Coughs can result from colds and flu.
   4. Improperly stored food can lead to food poisoning.
   5. Slow infant development can be the result of poor nutrition.
   6. Skin cancer is caused by too much exposure to the sun.
   7. Swimming in pools can result in ear infection.
   8. Heart trouble can be caused by a diet high in fat.
   9. Lung cancer is a consequence of cigarette smoking.
   10. Skiing can cause broken legs.

Exercise 14

1. C (Coal-burning factories) > E (acid rain)
2. C (Stricter anti-pollution laws) > E (higher prices)
3. E (The death of lakes and streams) < C (acid rain)
4. E (Forests have become diseased) < C (acid rain)
5. C (Coal burning) > E (higher levels of sulfur dioxide)
6. E (Higher infant death rates) < C (sulfur dioxide pollution)
7. C (Coal burning) > E (exterior walls of buildings to decay)
8. C (Anti-pollution laws > E (miners to lose their jobs)
9. C (Special equipment in coal furnaces > E (reduce pollution)
10. E (Decreased pollution from carbon fuels) < C (use of solar energy)

Multiple Causes or Effects Examples

Example a
Cause: Hurricane Iniki
Effects: telephone lines were out of order
airport was closed
homes were damages
hotels were washed away
tourists' holidays were ruined
people lost their jobs

Example b
Effect: The Frozen Yogurt Company closed its shop
Causes: poor economy
fewer customers
higher prices
higher bills and rent

Exercise 15
There may be some differences in these answers. Students who can give a good reason for an answer may count it as correct.

A. Cause 1: Learning a new language
Effects: a, b, e, f, g, h
Cause 2: Living in a new city
Effects: a, b, c, d, f, i
B. Effect 1: Many animals have become extinct
Causes: a, b, e, h
Effect 2: Many cities are overcrowded
Causes: d, f, g

Exercise 16
1. There are several explanations for the increase in number of ear infections in children.
Cause(s): increased use of day care
Effect(s): more ear infections

2. An untreated ear infection can lead to several serious consequences.
Cause(s): Untreated ear infection
Effect(s): cause general illness
damage to hearing ability
delay proper language development

3. The greater numbers of ear infections could result from social and economic factors.
Cause(s):
parents aware of importance of treatment
doctors have more time to find the infections
doctors might want to make more money
Effect(s): bring children in more often

Exercise 17
1. When people move from place to place, new diseases may be spread.

Cause(s): people move from one city or country to another
Effect(s): spread new germs
catch new germs

2. Supplies of heating oil can have several effects.
Cause(s): changes in heating systems
Effect(s): lower temperature in heating system >
growth of germ > illness and death

3. Pollution of the oceans can also result in the spread of disease.
Cause(s): pollution of oceans from human waste and chemical fertilizers
Effect(s): growth of algae>growth of cholera germs in algae > algae sticks to ships > germs are carried around the world

Exercise 18
1. Many children die before the age of one in some poor countries.
Cause(s): lack of medical care
poor quality of food
dirty drinking water which carries diseases
Effect(s): children die before age one

2. People who work in large office buildings get sick because of the poor quality of the air in the buildings.
Cause(s): windows that don't open
chemicals from furniture, rugs, and machines
cigarette smoke
Effect(s): poor air quality > people get sick more often than normal

3. The Valdez oil spill also caused long term problems for many animals.
Cause(s): oil spill
Effect(s): death of many animals
illness and fewer young among the harbor seals

Exercise 19
1. CE	2. S	3. CC	4. CE	5. L
6. CE	7. S	8. CE	9. CC	10. S

Exercise 20
1. CE	2. CC	3. L	4. S	5. CE
6. S	7. CE	8. CC	9. L	10. CC

Exercise 21
1. Sentence c   Pattern CC

2. Sentence a   Pattern S
3. Sentence d   Pattern CE
4. Sentence b   Pattern L

Exercise 22
1. Sentence c   Pattern S
2. Sentence e   Pattern CC
3. Sentence b   Pattern L
4. Sentence a   Pattern CE

Exercise 23
1. Sentence c   Pattern L
2. Sentence e   Pattern S
3. Sentence d   Pattern CC
4. Sentence b   Pattern CE

Exercise 24
1. Sequence
2. In about 500 A.D.; over the next few centuries; for about 500 years; Then, in about 1200; For the next 500 years; Then, in 1800; in 1778
3. Par. 1. Cause/Effect
   Par. 3. Listing
   Par. 5. Listing
   Par. 7. Contrast

Unit 8: Skimming, page 132

Exercises 1-4
Answers will vary.

Exercise 5
A. 1. They are lost
   2. They are very worried
   3. Answers will vary
B. 1. The boys were found
   2. They knew they would be rescued, but they were cold
   3. No, it took the whole night
   4. Very happy and thankful

Exercise 6
1. Eastward. It is worse because the body naturally suffers more when the day is shortened than when it is lengthened.
2. Exhaustion before starting a trip, lack of sleep, and disturbing your internal biological clock
3. Rest before the flight, eat and rest in the plane according to the new time, follow the new time when you arrive, avoid alcohol and drugs you don't usually use
4. Not yet.

Exercise 7
1. Answers will vary. Give reasons for your answer.

2. A ruined environment, the lack of food and water, the extinction of many species, wars
3. Cut human reproduction in half, so there will be fewer people added to the world's population.

Exercise 8
1. the second one
2. the second one
3. Answers will vary. Support your answers.
4. Eleanor had to be much more involved in her husband's work.

Exercise 9
1. the second one
2. the first one
3. Answers will vary. Support your answers.
4. No
5. Answers will vary.

Unit 9: Making Inferences, page 150

Example: a baby bird
Note: In all of the exercises in this unit, the "correct answer" is not important. What is important is that the students have reasons or evidence to support the answers that they give.

Exercise 1
Norway (the land of the midnight sun)
Arnie and Sarah (probably her husband and daughter)

Exercise 2
Notice is from the principal of a school
A parents' meeting

Exercise 3
1. Outside a theater after a performance
2. They are waiting for one of the performers (male) to come out
3. The performer
4. Probably women, but answers could vary

Exercise 4
1. In an apartment building
2. Neighbors. B is probably younger than A
3. The loud music and the rules about noise
4. Answers will vary.

Exercise 5
1. In a coffee shop
2. Ordering a cup of coffee
3. Answers will vary.

Exercise 6
1. At work in an office

2. Co-workers
3. B's vacation trip
4. B is a woman (she has a husband), can't tell about A.

Exercise 7
1. At a gas station
2. Buying gas and paying for it
3. Answers will vary.

Exercise 8
1. In a shop for gifts, clothing or jewelry
2. A gift B is buying for his wife
3. The gift, something small and colorful
4. About 60 years old or more

Exercise 9
1. Father, mother, son, and daughter
2. In the family's home (There may be more specific inferences)
3. The children have eaten dinner.
   The father has come home from work.
   The mother had served dinner and gone upstairs.
   The mother has done something she feels guilty about. (There may be more inferences here)
4. The father
5. Many possible ideas here.

Exercise 10
1. The narrator, Liz and Ben Prescott
2. At the Prescott's house
3. Mr. Prescott died. The narrator has spent the day with her mother.
4. Answers will vary.

Exercise 11
1. Stella and Blanche are sisters or close friends. Stanley is Stella's husband.
2. In Stella's bedroom
3. The night before, Stella's husband got violent. He broke the radio and made a mess of the living room.
4. Can't tell.
5. Blanche and Stella may have a misunderstanding or a fight. (Other ideas are possible.)

Exercise 12
1. Nancy is Bridget's mother.
2. In Nancy's room
3. Bridget does not live with her mother. Many years ago, her mother left her father because he did not love her. She then fell in love with another man, Jay. She wanted to have Bridget living with her, but couldn't get her away from

her ex-husband. Bridget has grown up far away, resentful of the fact that her mother left.
4. Answers will vary.

Exercise 13
1. Watching television
2. Doing the laundry (washing clothes in a washing machine)

Exercise 14
1. Bus or truck driver
2. Mail carrier
3. Car salesman

Exercise 15
1. There is a natural drop in body temperature that tends to make you sleepy in the afternoon.
2. There are several advantages to taking a nap in the middle of the day.
3. To get the most rest, a nap should not be too late or too long.

Exercise 16
1. The reviewer thinks the book is well-written and enjoyable to read.
2. The reviewer thinks the book is very boring and not worth reading.

Unit 10: Summarizing, page 167

Exercise 1
Note: Answers may vary.
1. Michiko made a cake.
2. Liz came home.
3. Serge left the house.
4. The Chens were robbed.
5. Natasha has a variety of books.
6. Yoko bought many things with her credit card.
7. You can do many things along the Charles in the summertime.
8. Bill planted a garden.
9. The islanders prepared for the storm.
10. Sue got ready to study.

Exercise 2
1. Malls have certain common features.
2. Malls in rich neighborhoods are much nicer than malls in poor neighborhoods.
3. Malls can have negative effects on local business and on the environment.

Exercise 3
1. In 1984, NASA chose Christa MacAuliffe, a school teacher, to be an astronaut.

2. Christa went through a long and difficult training program.
3. The Challenger crashed.

Exercise 4

Shopping malls are similar, but they vary in luxury according to the surrounding neighborhood. Malls can have negative effects on the neighborhood.

Exercise 5

After months of preparation, Christa MacAuliffe, the first teacher-astronaut in NASA, died when the Challenger crashed.

Exercise 6

1. Many people can go white-water rafting in Maine.
2. White-water rafting is done on fast-moving rivers.
3. Rafting is easy and enjoyable.
4. Most rafting trips include an overnight stay with good food.

Summary: Many people can go white-water rafting in Maine. White-water rafting, which is done on fast-moving rivers, is easy and enjoyable. Most trips include an overnight stay and a good dinner.

Exercise 7

1. Fruit flies, newcomers to California, have caused problems for fruit growers, forcing them to use chemicals to kill them.
2. Another newcomer, the zebra mussel, has grown rapidly and caused damage.
3. Loosestrife, an immigrant plant, affects the environment because it quickly takes over an area eliminating other plants.

Summary: New species can cause problems. Fruit flies hurt California farms, the zebra mussel causes damage underwater and loosestrife takes over large areas of land.

Exercise 8

Step 1.
Part 1: Paragraphs 1–3
Part 2: Paragraphs 4–10
Part 3: Paragraphs 11–13
Step 2.
Part I: Picking your own apples in the fall can be fun for the family.
Part 2: Important guidelines for apple picking include planning, picking gently, picking only what you need, and making it a full day outing.
Part 3: You can store apples in the refrigerator or in the freezer.
Step 3.
Summary: Apple-picking in the fall can be an all-day outing for the family. If you pick carefully and pick only the apples you need, you can take them home and keep them for months in the refrigerator or the freezer.

Exercise 9

Step 1.
Part 1: Paragraphs 1
Part 2: Paragraphs 2–3
Part 3: Paragraphs 4–6
Step 2.
1. Two of Hawaii's important traditions are leis and the hula dance.
2. Leis were given to Hawaiians by a goddess as a sign of peace. Handmade of fresh flowers by older women, leis are usually given to welcome guests and to honor someone at a special event. Every island has its own type of lei.
3. Hula dancing, once done by men in religious ceremonies, is now danced mostly by women. Hula dancers tell stories using their hands and bodies, accompanied by special music. Early European settlers in Hawaii discouraged hula, but it still exists today.
Step 3.
Flower necklaces and hula dancing are two of Hawaii's traditions which have survived. Leis are important as a sign of welcome and honor. Hula is a way of telling a story without using words.

Exercise 10

Step 1.
Part 1: Paragraphs 1–2
Part 2: Paragraphs 3–5
Part 3: Paragraphs 6–7
Step 2.
1. Air in tightly closed homes and buildings can contain many dangerous chemicals.
2. Wolverton, a scientist, found that some easy-to-grow houseplants can clean the air.
3. Plants carry pollutants to the soil, where they are broken down by microbes and used by the plant's roots as food. Someday, these air cleaners will be part of every building design.
Step 3.
Although air in tightly closed homes and buildings can be full of dangerous pollutants, house plants can clean the air. Some easy-to-grow houseplants use the pollutants to make food for themselves. Someday, every building will be designed to have plants to clean the air.

Part Three: Thinking Skills

Examples: pages 180–181

b. d   c. a

1. a	2. d	3. b	4. a	5. c
6. c	7. d	8. d	9. b	10. a
11. c	12. c	13. d	14. a	15. d
16. a	17. c	18. b	19. c	20. c
21. c	22. d	23. a	24. b	25. b
26. b	27. d	28. c	29. d	30. c
31. b	32. b	33. d	34. b	35. c
36. d	37. b	38. a	39. a	40. b
41. d	42. c	43. b	44. a	45. c
46. d	47. d	48. b	49. a	50. d
51. b	52. c	53. c	54. d	55. b
56. a	57. a	58. a	59. c	60. c
61. d	62. c	63. a	64. c	65. a
66. c	67. b	68. b	69. c	70. c
71. c	72. a	73. a	74. b	75. d
76. a	77. b	78. d	79. b	80. d
81. a	82. b	83. d	84. b	85. c
86. b	87. d	88. a	89. d	90. b
91. a	92. c	93. a	94. b	95. a
96. c	97. d	98. b	99. d	100. a

Part Four: Reading Faster

Examples: pages 206 and 207

a. 1. He's been busy at work and at home.
   2. He's been fixing something in his house.
   3. They should visit and take a walk on Mt. Grey.
b. 1. She was tall and unusual looking.
   2. When she started to go to modeling school
   3. As a fashion model in Paris

Example: page 210

1. d	5. a
2. c	6. c
3. a	7. c
4. b	8. b

Unit 1: The Hawaiian Islands, page 213

Passages	Questions							
	1	2	3	4	5	6	7	8
1	a	d	d	a	c	c	b	c
2	b	b	a	d	a	c	d	c
3	a	a	b	b	d	d	a	b
4	d	c	b	b	a	b	b	c
5	c	d	b	c	a	c	d	b
6	b	a	a	b	d	b	a	a
7	d	b	b	c	b	a	c	b
8	d	b	a	a	b	b	c	a
9	a	b	c	b	c	d	b	d
10	d	c	c	a	b	c	d	b

Unit 2: Maria Montessori, page 233

Passages	Questions							
	1	2	3	4	5	6	7	8
1	c	d	d	a	b	a	c	b
2	a	c	c	b	b	d	a	c
3	c	d	b	c	a	c	b	d
4	a	d	b	a	c	b	d	b
5	d	a	b	c	a	d	c	c
6	c	d	a	a	c	a	c	c
7	d	b	a	b	c	a	b	d
8	d	c	a	c	c	d	b	a
9	b	d	a	b	c	d	c	a
10	c	a	c	b	a	c	a	c

Unit 3: Global Issues, page 253

Passages	Questions							
	1	2	3	4	5	6	7	8
1	c	a	c	d	c	b	c	d
2	c	a	b	d	c	a	b	d
3	d	a	d	c	a	c	d	b
4	c	d	a	b	c	d	c	d
5	c	d	a	b	d	a	b	d
6	c	a	b	d	c	a	b	c
7	b	d	c	a	a	d	b	c
8	b	a	c	a	d	c	d	c
9	c	c	b	d	a	c	a	c
10	c	b	a	c	b	a	c	b

Teacher's Guide

More Reading Power is unlike most reading textbooks. First, the focus is different. This book directs the students' attention to their own reading processes, while most other books call attention to the subject matter of the material.

Also, **More Reading Power** is organized to be used in a very different way than most textbooks. It contains four separate sections which correspond to four important aspects of the development of proficient reading, and is almost like four books in one. Students should work on materials in all four parts of the book concurrently. They should not proceed through the book in the usual front-to-back fashion.

Introduction

In this Teacher's Guide, you will find general guidelines and specific suggestions for making the most effective use of *More Reading Power*. For a more complete explanation of the theory and methodology used in this book, see *A Short Course in Teaching Reading Skills* by Beatrice S. Mikulecky (Addison-Wesley, 1990).

The purpose of *More Reading Power* is to develop your students' awareness of the reading process so that they will be able to learn to read in ways that are expected in school, college, or business. In order to allow the students to focus on the process of reading, the lexical and syntactical contents of the materials have been kept to a minimum (at the low-intermediate/intermediate) level. No more than about 2,600 different vocabulary items have been used and the sentences do not exceed 18 words in length. The most difficult verb forms are the past continuous, present perfect, present perfect continuous, past perfect, past perfect continuous, infinitives, modals, and passives.

Many students have a conceptualization of reading which interferes with their reading in English. *More Reading Power* aims to help students acquire an accurate understanding of what it means to read in English. To accomplish this, the book addresses the reading process in a direct manner, and the various reading skills involved are presented as part of that process.

Student awareness of reading and thinking processes is further encouraged in many parts of the book by exercises which require them to work in pairs or small groups. In discussions with others, students need to formulate and articulate their ideas more precisely, and so they also acquire new ways of talking and thinking about a text. Students are also asked to write and then read each other's work so they can experience the connections between reading and writing.

Using *More Reading Power* in Your Class

The Role of the Teacher in a Reading Class

The teacher is the most important element in a successful reading class. A good teacher can provide:

- an anxiety-free environment in which students feel comfortable taking risks and trying new ways of reading;
- enough practice so the students can master new strategies;
- friendly pressure in the form of persuasion and timing;
- positive examples of how to approach a text;
- a model for the kind of thinking that good reading requires.
- an inspiring example of an enthusiastic reader.

Planning Your Reading Classes

The materials in this book were designed to take approximately 35 hours of class time. This will vary according to the level of the students in your class and the amount of homework assigned. Classes and individual students also vary in the amount of time they need to complete different kinds of exercises in the book. Students should work at their own pace as often as possible.

Here are some suggestions for using *More Reading Power* in several different types of classes:

- **In an integrated skills class which meets for two to three hours per day, five days a week for one semester:**

  Use *More Reading Power* for a total of about 30–40 minutes, three times a week. For example:

  Monday—Fifteen minutes of Faster Reading
  Twenty minutes of Comprehension Skills

  Wednesday—Fifteen minutes of Thinking Skills
  Twenty minutes of Reading for Pleasure and Book Conferences

  Friday—Fifteen minutes of Faster Reading
  Twenty minutes of Comprehension Skills

Homework assignments can include:
- Reading for Pleasure
- Thinking Skills
- Selected Comprehension Skills exercises
  (Practice on those introduced in class.)

- **In an integrated skills class which meets for three hours per week for one semester:**

  Use *More Reading Power* for about one third of the class time, for a total of about one hour a week, divided approximately as follows:
  - Twenty minutes of Faster Reading
  - Fifteen minutes of Thinking Skills
  - Twenty minutes of Comprehension Skills
  Homework assignments as above.

- **In a reading class which meets two hours per week for one semester:**

  Use the four parts of *More Reading Power* as well as the students' pleasure reading books in every class. Work for about 20–30 minutes on each part of the book.

  Homework assignments can focus on Reading for Pleasure.

- **In a reading lab:**

  As in the classroom, students should work regularly on all four parts of the book, dividing their time about equally among the four parts. It is essential that students be given initial instruction in how to use each part of *More Reading Power* before they begin to work on their own.

  Keep in mind that the Comprehension Skills in Part Two should be introduced by the teacher in class and practiced before any of the exercises are assigned for homework.

Making the Reading Class Exciting and Effective

Here are some general principles for using *More Reading Power:*

- One of your primary aims should be to make reading **enjoyable for the students**. The reading class must always involve them fully and never be allowed to turn into "busy work."
- To this end, make the students aware of the **purpose of their work**. This will increase their sense of involvement and allow them to become more active learners (increasing their metacognitive awareness).
- Always **focus on the thinking process** and not on the "right answers." The answer itself matters far less than how the student arrives at an answer. Encourage students to take this same approach by frequently asking "Why?" or "How can you tell?" or "How do you know?" As the

students are required repeatedly to articulate answers to these questions, they become more conscious of their own thinking processes.

- Ask the students to **work in pairs** whenever possible, especially on the Comprehension Skills exercises in Part Two. **Talking about the exercises** and explaining their reasoning can reinforce the students' awareness of process and purpose. It also facilitates language acquisition (when the conversation is in English).
- Emphasize the importance of trying to **guess the meaning of words** from the context. Students should be discouraged from using dictionaries during the reading class or while doing their reading homework.
- The Answer Key is intended to serve as more than just the repository of "the right answers." Students should **check their own answers** so they can work independently when appropriate. When their answers differ from the Answer Key, they should try to figure out how and why they may have made a mistake. However, they should also be encouraged to question the Answer Key and to defend their answers and their reasoning. Some of the exercises, in fact, have alternative answers.
- When students work individually (especially on Parts Three and Four), allow them to **work at their own pace**. In these exercises, speed should be encouraged, but each student must determine what that speed will be. Faster students should not have to wait for slower classmates, and slower readers should not be pressed too hard or they may become anxious and incapable of comprehending.

Specific Suggestions for Using More Reading Power

Part One: Reading for Pleasure

Many students have never learned to enjoy reading for pleasure (reading extensively) in English. Yet we know that in order to be a good reader, it is necessary to read a lot. But it is not enough for the teacher to just say to students, "Read a book." Students must first come to understand the importance of reading extensively, and then they must be encouraged to develop the habit of reading regularly for pleasure. *More Reading Power* provides several motivating features: a rationale for pleasure reading, guidelines for success, goal-setting, record-keeping, a list of carefully selected books, and suggestions for "Book Conferences" with the teacher.

Extensive Reading

On-going immersion in **extensive reading** is essential for practicing and applying reading skills and for developing all areas of language skills. Research shows that vocabulary acquisition and writing ability, for example, are directly related to the quantity of reading students engage in.

There is a great difference between **extensive reading** and **intensive reading**. Intensive reading is an activity in which students (usually in a class group, led by the teacher) carefully read and examine an essay, short story, or other reading material assigned by the teacher. Many traditional reading classes use this approach almost exclusively. While intensive reading can play an important role in developing an appreciation of English language and literature, it is no substitute for extensive reading. Improvement in general reading ability comes with reading a lot.

Student Selection of Books for Extensive Reading

Extensive reading is included in Part One: Reading for Pleasure. Students are instructed to select books to read for pleasure on an individual basis. These books should be neither too easy nor too difficult. They should not be books that are required in other courses or that students have already read in translation. Most important, students should be encouraged to choose any book they want—fiction or nonfiction, literature or popular culture. What matters most is that the book is of interest to the individual student and that the student actually wants to read it.

In pleasure reading, complete books are recommended, not newspapers, magazines, or "readers," and not books that are made up of extracts of other books (such as *Reader's Digest Selections*) or collections of short stories by many different authors. There are several reasons for this. First of all, many students may never before have read a book in English that they chose for themselves. Thus the selection process will be a new experience for them, one that will help form a new literate identity.

Secondly, while magazines, newspapers, and book selections may provide reading practice, the goal of pleasure reading is for students to develop the habit of **sustained silent reading**, which is only possible with whole books. Reading a whole book by a single author also allows students to become

comfortable with a writer's style and lexicon. This comfort is experienced as success, and actually allows students to read faster and faster as they proceed through their books.

One way to help your students select their books is to bring some favorite books to the reading class and talk about them. These "book talks" serve two purposes. First, students find out about books that they might like to read. Second, students are provided with a model for how to talk about books, so that they will be able to talk about their own books and discuss them with others. When you present a book to the class, you should give a brief summary of the book's content, without too many details about the plot, and give your general reaction (Why did you like it or dislike it? Does it relate to your own experience?) about various aspects of the book: the characters, the setting, the mood, the author's intention, and so on. Discussion about books can be an effective motivating tool.

Students can also find books by participating in a class trip to a bookstore or library where they can browse and ask questions about books. Or, if the classroom has a library of suitable books, students can be guided to ones which they might enjoy. They can also be encouraged to exchange books with classmates or with other students. Since students do not need to and, in fact, should not write notes or vocabulary in their pleasure reading books, there is no reason for them to buy the books (unless they want to be able to keep them afterward).

Motivating students to read for pleasure

Students often tend to regard reading for pleasure as a less important element of the reading class. Since it is, in fact, a key to success in reading development, be sure to encourage your students to take it seriously.

Require your students to bring their pleasure reading books to class and devote some class time regularly to pleasure reading.

Assign reading for pleasure as homework and require your students to keep a record of how many pages they have read. Establish a requirement for the number of pages to be read per week or per semester.

You can check up on the students' pleasure reading by asking about the books they are reading or have read. This can take various forms:

Ask students fill out a Book Response Sheet. (See example in Part One, page 10.) Full written book reports are less useful, since they tend to diminish the student's enjoyment of the book.

Ask students to respond orally to their books, giving their classmates a brief description of the book and their opinion of it.

But the surest way to evaluate students' progress and to promote pleasure reading is through **book conferences**. These conferences can be the key to a successful extensive reading program. Not only do they provide you with feedback on the students' reading, but they also serve several other important purposes.

Your questions about the book often represent a true "knowledge gap" between you and the student: the student knows more about the book than you do, and your questions are authentic, not "school questions." Your questions can serve as a model for the kinds of questions which a literate reader habitually asks herself.

The discussion may also help the student acquire fluency in evaluative and elaborative language which will become the basis for good writing.

The scheduling of book conferences may vary. Some teachers hold conferences during office hours or just before or after class. Others find that they can hold book conferences with one student while the rest of the class is engaged in some other activity.

Part Two: Reading Comprehension Skills

For many students, reading comprehension is a problem, but since they can read in their own language, they tend to attribute their difficulties in comprehension to the English language, or they may feel that the fault lies in their own (alleged) stupidity. In fact, the problem usually lies in their approach to a text. With a better understanding of how information is presented in English texts and a greater awareness of the cognitive processes involved in reading, comprehension will almost certainly improve.

In Part Two of *More Reading Power* each new comprehension skill is introduced with a rationale and practiced in a series of exercises sequenced from simple to more difficult in order to build up the students' mastery of the skill. The skills covered include both "top-down" (concept-driven) and "bottom-up" (text-driven) modes of reasoning and comprehending.

Work on reading comprehension skills can be compared, in some respects, to weight-lifting. The weight-lifter learns how and why he/she must exercise certain muscle groups. Once the muscle group

is targeted, the exercises proceed with gradually increasing weights. This is the same process that students should follow in reading comprehension lessons. As the "coach," you must be sure that the students understand how and why to do the exercises, and then stand by to provide advice, support, and increasing challenges.

How to Use the Comprehension Skills Units in the Classroom

1. Focus on one reading/thinking skill at a time.
2. Explain the purpose for doing the exercises and how this particular skill is important for effective reading.
3. Do an example or a sample exercise with the whole class. Model your thinking aloud as you do the exercise.
4. Put the students into pairs (whenever possible and appropriate) and assign one exercise for practice.
5. When the pairs have completed the exercise, discuss it with the whole class. Ask how the students arrived at their answers. Encourage friendly disagreement among pairs and in the class as a whole. Ask, "What was your thinking as you decided on that answer?" Students are not necessarily "wrong" if they come up with an answer that is different from the Answer Key, as long as they can give a rationale for their choice.
6. That day and in the next few classes, assign additional exercises which focus on the same skill, increasing the complexity of the tasks. Make sure the students work together whenever it is feasible.
7. Assign an exercise to be done by individual students, either in class or as homework, which they will use to check their own ability and confidence in using the skill.
8. Assign further exercises as needed, based on your sense of the students' mastery of the skill.

Note: In working on comprehension exercises, keep these two principles in mind:

- Do not simply judge answers as right or wrong. Instead, always respond to students' answers with questions such as: "Why?" or "How can you tell?" to encourage them to examine their reasoning processes.
- Students should work whenever possible in pairs or small groups since talking about the exercises helps develop awareness of thinking processes and also promotes general language improvement.

Unit 1: Scanning

1. Speed is essential in these exercises. To encourage speed, students may be timed, or they may do the exercises (in pairs) as a kind of race to see who can find all the answers first.

2. Do not spend time correcting or having students correct their answers, which are of very little importance to the exercise. You may want to spend a few minutes, on the other hand, discussing the cultural content of some of the scanning material, with which some student may be unfamiliar.

3. Exercises 4-10 give students an opportunity to practice asking and writing questions. Formulating questions for another student will help students learn to ask themselves questions as they read.

4. Continue to require the students to practice scanning after you have completed this unit by asking them to scan other materials. Continued practice is necessary for students to retain the skill.

5. Notice that though scanning and skimming are often taught as the same thing, they are really two very different skills. Scanning is a fairly simple skill that involves only a visual search for information on a page. Skimming, on the other hand, involves processing text for ideas, which requires far more complex thinking skills. (Skimming is introduced in Unit 8.)

Unit 2: Previewing and Predicting

1. Encourage your students to discuss their answers to these exercises. Additional predictions often come up in the course of these discussions. Point this out to your students when it happens, so they will be aware of the benefits of talking about their work.

2. Exercise 1. For this exercise, make a collection of books available to students, preferably a mixture of types of books (textbooks, fiction, and non-fiction).

3. Ask students to apply the previewing and predicting steps to materials that they are using in their English class or in other classes.

Unit 3: Vocabulary Knowledge for Effective Reading

1. The importance of trying to **guess word meaning** cannot be stressed too much. Students are often bound to their dictionaries. They need to learn that English discourse gives multiple clues to meaning. They also need to realize that there are many advantages to guessing meaning, as pointed out in the introduction to this section.

2. Before you begin to work with students on the exercises on "Using Grammar to Guess Word Meaning," check to be sure that your students know the terminology for the basic parts of speech in English (noun, verb, pronoun, adjective, adverb).

3. Research has shown that **function words** play a fundamental role in reading comprehension because these are the words that give form to the ideas in a text. Thus, it is far more important for readers to understand how the function words work in sentences than to know all the content words in a sentence. Point this out to your students as a further argument for skipping over unknown content words.

4. Writing practice: Lead your students to further awareness of how function words operate in a text and how they can learn to control their use by giving them a chance to analyze the function words in their own writing.

   Use writing done for previous assignments or give your students a new assignment. Then ask your students, in pairs, to exchange papers and analyze the function words as they did in Exercises 15 and 16. If some of the referents are unclear, students should work in pairs to figure out how they might correct the problem.

   Sometimes it is helpful, as well, to take samples from several student papers for a class discussion of how unclear or missing referents can confuse the reader.

Unit 4: Topics

1. Since discourse in English is usually **topic-centered**, finding the topic is an important key to understanding a text. Thus, work on comprehension must begin by teaching your students what a topic is.

2. Encourage your students to work quickly in order to develop efficiency.

3. Working in pairs on these exercises, students will begin to internalize the key questions: "What is this about? How do I know that?"

4. Writing practice: Understanding and being able to work with topics is a fundamental skill in writing as well. Exercise 6 requires students to write out the details for given topics, the first step towards writing coherent paragraphs.

Unit 5: Topics of Paragraphs

1. Point out to your students that the topic of a paragraph is usually mentioned more than once in the paragraph. This is the writer's way of ensuring that the reader understands.

2. Alert students to the fact that the topic sentence of a paragraph is often the first sentence. In English—both oral and written—people expect to find out right away what something is about. With English-language texts, readers expect to find the topic at the beginning, so they can orient their thinking. Thus, writers almost always provide the topic early on.

3. In a class that combines work on reading and writing, the introductory section of this unit can also be used to discuss the concepts of unity (the idea that a paragraph has a single topic) and coherence (the idea that all the sentences in the paragraph relate to that one topic). These terms can be introduced here and applied in later units as well.

4. Writing practice: Ask your students to write a unified paragraph, based on one of these topic sentences:

   - Life in the country is better than life in a big city. (Or life in a big city is better than life in the country.)
   - Shopping is an enjoyable pastime.
   - Television, movies, and computers have made the world a different place in the past 35 years.
   - Families are not the same all around the world.
   - Everyone needs to know how to drive these days.

Unit 6 : Main Ideas

1. In this unit, students may have difficulty with the fact that the main idea is always a complete sentence which states both the topic and what the writer wishes to express about that topic. In other words, the main idea includes a topic and a comment. This might also be seen as a subject and a predicate. Students often think a topic by itself is the main idea.

2. Give students practice in producing a main idea in a complete sentence that accurately reflects the author's intended meaning by doing the following:

   a. Assign students an exercise on main ideas as homework.

   b. In the next class, divide students into groups of three or four.

   c. Ask the students in each group to compare the main ideas they wrote individually. They should then combine their efforts and write the best main ideas they can come up with.

   d. Have a representative of each group write that group's main ideas on the chalkboard.

   e. Elicit suggestions from the class about problems

and possible improvements of the sentences. This exercise offers an opportunity for a review of sentence definition and structure.

3. Writing practice: After your students have mastered writing main ideas, you can have them do the following exercise.

   a. Ask your students to write main idea statements about these three topics:
      - Winter sports
      - Getting married
      - How colors can influence you

   b. Working in pairs, have the students check each other's work to make sure that they have written complete sentences.

   c. Ask students to choose one main idea statement and write a unified paragraph supporting the main idea statement.

   d. Tell the students to form small groups and compare paragraphs. Within the group, students can help each other improve the paragraphs.

   e. Collect the paragraphs and copy a few of them to use as a basis for discussion in the next class.

Unit 7: Patterns of Organization

1. Research has shown that readers comprehend and remember best those materials which are organizationally clear to them. However, many students are not familiar with the patterns of textual organization used in English and so have a more difficult time comprehending and remembering.

   The explanation given here for why recognizing patterns can help comprehension is similar to the explanation given for the advantages to reading faster in the introduction to Part Four. In both cases, the same basic factors are at work: the brain does not work well with random pieces of information that must be stored in the memory as so many separate items. It much prefers and works more efficiently with information that has a recognizable order. Thus, to allow the brain to work well while reading, the reader must constantly look for order in the text, by grouping words according to meaning and by following the patterns of discourse that writers normally use to express certain kinds of ideas in English.

2. In this unit, students will work with four of the most common patterns: Listing, Sequence, Comparison/Contrast, and Cause-Effect. There are other patterns of organization in English, of

course, including problem-solution, argument, and classification. You may wish to introduce one or more of these other patterns to your students, depending on their interests. Suitable examples may be found in books and magazines, and presented to your students in a sequence of exercises similar to those presented in this unit.

3. Note that in almost every exercise, students are asked not just to identify, but also to write out the signal words and the details they signal. Although this may seem time-consuming and repetitious, it gives the students important practice that will help them gain confidence in their ability to recognize patterns and read for important points.

4. In an appropriate class context, you may want to point out to your students (and do additional work on) the connection between the patterns presented here and the patterns used in outlining for note-taking or as preparation for writing.

5. Several of the exercises in this unit include some review of Units 5 and 6 (Topics of Paragraphs and Main Ideas).

6. In a writing/reading class, point out that the "signal words" for patterns can also be referred to as transitional words. They are the signposts that writers use to mark the shifts and turns in their thinking, and that readers should use to follow the writer from one idea to the next.

7. Writing practice: To give students further practice with patterns and with the use of signal words, find topics that fit clearly into each of the patterns and ask students to write paragraphs about each one, using at least three signal words per paragraph.

In Exercises 4 and 12, students are asked to write paragraphs according to certain patterns. The same kind of assignment can be given after Exercise 8 (Sequence pattern) and Exercise 18 (Cause-Effect pattern).

Unit 8: Skimming

1. Skimming is not (as it is sometimes thought) a simple matter of reading very fast; it is selective reading, in which only certain parts of the text are actually read. In order to know what to select, students must call upon all the reading skills previously practiced in this book. In this way, skimming practice naturally involves review of concepts included in previous units.

2. These exercises must be timed in order to force students to work quickly through a text. Without the pressure of time, they will be tempted to read

unnecessary parts and may be distracted from the purpose of the exercises.

3. As in the previous units, students should work in pairs to compare and explain their answers. This also helps students realize that there is no absolute right way to skim a text. What readers actually read while skimming depends on what they already know and on their interpretation of the text—in other words it depends on what they are thinking, and, of course, no two people ever think exactly alike. Teachers should point this out to students and should allow for different responses to the exercises.

4. Students can be given additional skimming practice in the classroom by using several copies of a daily newspaper in English. The teacher may then divide the class into small groups and give each group a newspaper. They should skim the newspaper for articles of interest and then discuss them.

5. Writing practice: A short research paper.

Have students choose one of the topics in this unit: AIDS, Eleanor Roosevelt, or the population problem. Students should read and summarize the article(s) in the unit. Then they should find two or more articles about the same topic (from books, encyclopedias, newspapers, etc.) and skim them to see if they include any additional information. When they have found enough new information, they should write a short paper about their topic, taking care to cite the sources of their ideas.

Unit 9: Making Inferences

1. All reading is, of course, inferential by nature; the purpose of this chapter is to make students aware of what it means to infer and how it is an essential part of reading. In these exercises, an answer which is different from the Answer Key is often possible. A "correct answer" is an answer which can be supported by the student with an argument based on the passage.

2. Writing practice: Most of the inference exercises have questions requiring short answers. Stress the importance of clear and complete sentences in answering those questions.

In Exercises 9-12, the students are asked to tell what they think will happen next in the story or play. These questions can be the basis of additional writing assignments.

After students have completed Exercise 16, ask them to write a review of a movie, play, or book in which the reader would have to infer their point of view. Then select some of the reviews to use in small groups or with the whole class. First, students should try to guess the writer's opinion about the movie, play, or book. Then they may discuss any differences of opinion on the subject.

Unit 10: Summarizing

1. Summarizing is usually viewed as a writing skill, but it is also a very useful reading skill, since it requires the reader to monitor comprehension. (Comprehension monitoring is a cognitive process which enhances comprehension.) In order to summarize, in fact, the reader must arrive at a thorough understanding of the main idea and the main points of a text.

2. Note that work on summarizing necessarily involves review of the concepts of topics, main ideas, and patterns. Teachers should point this fact out to students.

3. Writing practice: Most of the exercises in this unit involve the students in actively writing summaries. In summarizing, they must try to condense and paraphrase the ideas in the text. These skills often do not come easily to students, but they are essential for many kinds of writing.

Part Three: Thinking Skills

Learning to read well in English means learning to think in English. However, many students are used to translating as they read and have great difficulty thinking in another language. The exercises in this part of the book are designed to help students make a transition from translating to thinking in English.

In order to complete the Thinking Skills exercises successfully, students will need to follow the way the ideas are presented in English. Correct completion could involve understanding English syntactic, semantic and/or logical connections. The exercises gradually increase in length and complexity.

1. In order to ensure that students get the most out of this part of the book, be sure to go through the introduction very carefully with the whole class. In fact, you will come to a better understanding of the thinking process involved in these exercises if you actually work on at least ten of them before introducing this part of the book to your students.

2. Keeping track of progress is an important aspect of this part of the book. As described in the section called "Guidelines for Success" on page 181, students should always write the date in the margin when they finish working so that they know how they are progressing. This also makes it possible for you to monitor your students' work.

3. Students should complete these exercises at their own speed. However, they should be encouraged to work as quickly as possible. If they work slowly, they may continue to translate as they read, and they will not develop efficient reading habits.

4. Students may look back at the paragraph if they wish, but they should not study it for long. Their first response is very often the correct one.

5. Some students may have trouble at first in following the logic of these exercises. If so, assign several exercises in class to pairs or small groups of students. They should discuss and decide on the answers and on the thinking processes involved. Afterward, those logical processes can be further clarified in a whole class discussion.

6. Students should not use dictionaries or ask anyone about word meanings while they are working on these exercises. They should be encouraged to try use the context of the paragraph to guess the meaning on their own.

Part Four: Reading Faster

Learning to read faster must be a key part of any reading improvement program. There are two basic reasons for this. First, students in most academic settings are faced with an enormous quantity of reading in English. Many ESL/EFL students take three to four times longer than native-language students to complete reading assignments, which means that they have little time left to assimilate what they have read.

The other reason for learning to read faster is that it leads to better comprehension. When reading faster, the eyes cannot focus on every word; they must focus on groups of words together. This makes it much easier for the brain to reconstruct meaning. Furthermore, since reading faster forces the reader to skip unknown or nonessential words, the brain can concentrate better on the general meaning of the text.

Be prepared to meet some resistance on the part of your students! Breaking them of the habit of word-by-word reading is not always easy. The habit may be of long standing and it may be connected with the student's insecurities about understanding English. If this is the case, do not push too hard for immediate change, but try to build up the student's confidence and willingness to take risks. Other students may be reluctant to read faster because of different attitudes to reading in their native culture that lead them to feel that reading word by word is the only "real" way to read. With these students, you may need to spend extra time discussing the nature and diverse purposes of reading in English.

Why read faster?

1. It is important to have a thorough grasp of the rationale behind reading rate improvement so that you can explain it in terms the students will understand. For this reason, you should go through the students' introduction carefully first and, if necessary, consult other reference books for clarification.

2. Notice that the reasons given here for improved comprehension with faster reading are similar to those given in the rationale to Part Two, Unit 7: Patterns of Organization. Both explanations are based on a fundamental understanding of how the brain works in receiving and storing information; that is, that it works most efficiently when the information can be grouped into some kind of order. This is the basic reason for reading faster. When you read faster, your eyes sweep over larger pieces of text. That provides you with more data to use in grasping the author's meaning, which makes it easier to build up comprehension and to retain the information.

3. Along with a discussion of the rationale for reading faster, it is important for you to discuss with your students the diverse ways of reading. Students may, in fact, need to be reassured at this point that not all reading must be fast. There are times when slow reading is appropriate, as in reading poetry, complex technical material, instructions or other material very dense with essential information. More often than not, however, slow reading is the only kind of reading students do. They need to understand that learning to read faster will give them more flexibility.

How to read faster

1. Skip over unknown words.

   You may be familiar with the use of cloze passages to determine reading ability, or to teach grammar and vocabulary. The cloze passages here, however, serve a very different purpose: to convince students that they can understand the main points of a passage without reading every word. Furthermore, this kind of work with cloze passages encourages students to infer general meaning from partial information—a fundamental skill.

As always, students should know the rationale for these exercises before they begin. Do not ask students to fill in the blank spaces, because this would completely alter the purpose of the exercise in the students eyes.

Stress the idea that unknown words can usually be ignored. Occasionally, it may be necessary to understand some words in order to comprehend the general meaning. In that case, the reader should continue reading and try to guess the meaning from the context. This skill is developed in Part Two, Unit 3.

If you wish to provide students with additional practice with cloze passages, choose a suitable text and blank out every seven or five words (the more frequent the blanks, the more difficult). The text should not contain difficult vocabulary or complex ideas that will be hard to grasp.

2. Do reading sprints regularly.

   Be sure to study the procedure for reading sprints before using them with your students. Explain the procedure thoroughly to avoid confusion in the middle of the exercises. Students should use their pleasure reading books for doing the sprints. Later, they can do some more in the same book to measure gains in reading rate.

   After the first session of sprints, students should be asked to repeat the sprints at regular intervals in class (once a week, once a month, etc., according to the frequency of class meetings) and at home.

   Given the concentration required for doing these exercises, you should follow them with some relatively relaxing activity.

3. Check your reading habits.

   Some of your students may have a habit of moving their lips while they are reading or of following the text with their fingers. If so, these students should be alerted, as often they are unaware of this habit, which slows them down as they read.

   While working on faster reading passages students should never write down meanings of words. This only reinforces the habit of translation and drastically slows down reading. Students may need to be reassured that it is useful to write down new vocabulary, but not during faster reading sessions.

4. Do timed readings.

   The Example introduces the students to the procedures they will follow for all the Reading Faster passages. They will have more success with the passages if they learn to **time themselves**. This allows them to work independently at their own pace.

Before reading any passage for timed reading, including the Example, students should be instructed to **preview** before they read. (If they have not yet started Unit 2: Previewing and Predicting in Part Two, you may need to introduce the concept of previewing.)

Note that the students should time themselves only while reading the passage, **not while answering the questions!** Students should correct their own work after they complete each passage, using the Answer Key on page 289.

Timing procedure

1. When the class is ready to begin the Example, the students should write the starting time on the line at the top of the passage. They should then start reading and read as quickly as possible with understanding. If there is a large clock visible in the classroom, the students can use it to read the time. If not, you can write the starting time on the chalkboard. (Many students prefer to use their own watches, which often have timing devices on them.)

2. As soon as they have finished reading, students should write the finishing time on the line at the end of the passage. If there is no clock, the students should signal when they finish and you can write the time on the chalkboard.

3. Students should then turn the page and circle the best answers to the questions (according to the text) without referring back to the passage.

4. After they have finished, they can check their answers in the Answer Key on page 289. They should write down the number of correct answers. This is their comprehension score.

5. Students can then calculate their reading time by subtracting the starting time from the finishing time. Using this reading time, they can find their reading rate on page 273.

The Example usually raises some questions about timing procedures. Review the procedures again. Make sure that the timing procedures are clearly understood before you start your students on the first unit of Reading Faster. The reading rate for the Example is the student's initial reading rate.

Reading Faster Passages

1. After students have gone through the introduction and before they start the Reading Faster passages, re-examine with your students their answers to the Questionnaires in the introduction to the book. By now, students may have gained some insight into the reading process and have changed some of their views of what makes for good reading habits. In reviewing the Questionnaires, students will, in effect, be reviewing some of the important aspects of reading covered so far.

2. Students are more likely to improve their reading rate if they set goals for themselves after they have established their initial rates. Many students find that they can double their rate by the end of a semester. A class discussion may help each student decide on a realistic goal. Students should then be reminded of that goal and pushed to try to achieve it.

3. Remind students regularly about previewing. Students may also need to be assured that previewing will not slow down their reading. The few seconds they spend on previewing (it should only take a few seconds) will save them reading time afterward.

4. These timed reading passages should not be used for other purposes (discussion, comprehension skills, or grammar) during faster reading sessions. If students think that they may be held accountable to the teacher for what they are reading, they will not feel free to take risks and experiment with rate-building strategies. However, after all the students have completed a passage, it may be used in another context of the reading class. Many of the passages provide interesting material for general class discussion.

5. As they chart their progress in reading rate improvement, students may notice a drop in their rate when they start a new unit. This is a natural reaction to the change in subject matter and most likely the rate will increase again as they become more familiar with the new subject. They may also notice that there is a correlation between their interest and knowledge in a subject and their reading rate and comprehension level. That is, the more interesting the passage and the more familiar the subject, the easier it is to read—and the better the reading rate and comprehension will be.

6. For a more complete explanation of the rationale and methodology for teaching faster reading and for additional practice materials for timed reading, see *A Short Course in Teaching Reading Skills* by Beatrice S. Mikulecky (Addison-Wesley, 1990).

Credits

Text Credits

Page 15, Museum of Fine Arts, Boston, MA. **Page 29**, *Honolulu Advertiser*, Jan. 2, 1992. **Page 31**, From "Curie," by Caleb W. Davis, *Collier's Encyclopedia*, Vol. 7, p. 571. Copyright © 1994 by P.F. Collier, L.P. Reprinted by permission. **Page 33**, From "Communications Satellite," by Joseph V. Charyk, *Collier's Encyclopedia*, Vol. 7, pp. 81–83. Copyright © 1994 by P.F. Collier, L.P. Reprinted by permission. **Page 36**, From *The Autobiography of Malcolm X* by Malcolm X with Alex Haley. Copyright © 1965 by Alex Haley and Betty Shabazz. Reprinted by permission of Random House, Inc. **Pages 45–48**, From *Timed Readings* by Edward Spargo and Glenn Williston. Copyright © 1989 by Jamestown Publishers, Providence, RI. Reprinted by permission. **Page 135**, Reprinted with permission from *Science News*. Copyright 1993 by Science Service, Inc. **Page 138**, Audrey Foote. **Pages 143–144**, Copyright 1992 Time Inc. Reprinted by permission. **Page 145**, From "Anna Eleanor Roosevelt," by Alfred Steinberg, *Collier's Encyclopedia*, Vol. 20, pp. 204–205. Copyright © 1994 by P.F. Collier, L.P. Reprinted by permission. **Page 146**, Joseph P. Lash. From the *Encyclopedia Americana*, 1993 Edition. Copyright © 1993 by Grolier Inc. Reprinted by permission. **Page 148**, William Haseltine. From the *Encyclopedia Americana*, 1993 Edition. Copyright 1993 by Grolier Inc. Reprinted by permission. **Page 149**, From "Acquired Immune Deficiency Syndrome (AIDS)," by Frederick P. Siegal and Marta Siegal, *Collier's Encyclopedia*, Vol. 1, pp. 87–88. Copyright © 1994 by P.F. Collier, L.P. Reprinted by permission. **Page 157**, An excerpt from "A Domestic Dilemma," *The Ballad of the Sad Cafe and Collected Stories* by Carson McCullers. Copyright © 1936, 1941, 1942, 1950, © 1955 by Carson McCullers, renewed 1979 by Floria V. Lasky. Reprinted by permission of Houghton-Mifflin Co. and The Lantz Office, (U.K.) All rights reserved. **Pages 158–159**, Excerpt from "The Day Mr. Prescott Died," from *Johnny Panic and the Bible of Dreams* by Sylvia Plath. Copyright © 1977, 1979. by Ted Hughes. Reprinted by permission of Harper-Collins Publishers, Inc. and Faber & Faber Ltd., (U.K.) **Pages 159–160**, An excerpt from *A Streetcar Named Desire*. Copyright © 1947 by Tennessee Williams. Reprinted by permission of New Directions Publishing Corp. and Casarotto Ramsay Ltd., (U.K.) **Pages 161–162**, Copyright © 1954 by Edith Sommer Soderberg as an unpublished dramatic composition. Revised Edition, Copyright © 1956. Copyright, Renewed, 1984, by Edith Sommer Soderberg. Reprinted by permission of Dramatists Play Service, Inc. **Page 177**, Reprinted with permission from the Jan/Feb 1993 issue of *Sierra* magazine.

Photo Credits

Page 14, Mark Morelli. **Page 22**, Hazel Hankin, Stock Boston. **Page 27**, Sissie Brimberg, Woodfin Camp & Assoc. **Page 31**, BBC Hulton, Woodfin Camp & Assoc. **Page 32**, NASA. **Page 34**, Mark Morelli. **Page 39**, Paula Lerner, Woodfin Camp & Assoc. **Page 42**, J.D. Levine, Northeastern University. **Page 43**, C/Z Harris. **Page 91**, Ralph P. Turcotte. **Page 142**, G. Hall, Woodfin Camp & Assoc. **Page 145**, National Lawyers Guild. **Page 146**, Franklin D. Roosevelt Library. **Page 211**, J.D. Levine, Northeastern University.